Offshore Financial Centers and Regulatory Competition

Offshore Financial Centers and Regulatory Competition

Andrew P. Morriss, Editor

The AEI Press

Publisher for the American Enterprise Institute
WASHINGTON, D.C.

Distributed by arrangement with the Rowman & Littlefield Publishing Group, 4501 Forbes Boulevard, Suite 200, Lanham, Maryland 20706. To order call toll free 1-800-462-6420 or 1-717-794-3800. For all other inquiries please contact AEI Press, 1150 Seventeenth Street, N.W. Washington, D.C. 20036 or call 1-800-862-5801.

NRI NATIONAL RESEARCH INITIATIVE

This publication is a project of the National Research Initiative, a program of the American Enterprise Institute that is designed to support, publish, and disseminate research by university-based scholars and other independent researchers who are engaged in the exploration of important public policy issues.

Library of Congress Cataloging-in-Publication Data

Offshore financial centers and regulatory competition / Andrew P. Morriss, editor.
   p. cm.
  Includes bibliographical references and index.
  ISBN-13: 978-0-8447-4324-0
  ISBN-10: 0-8447-4324-0
  1. Banks and banking, International. 2. Banks and banking, International—Law and legislation. 3. Investments, Foreign. I. Morriss, Andrew P., 1960-
  HG3881.O335 2010
  332.1'5—dc22

2010001641

14 13 12 11 10   1 2 3 4 5 6 7

© 2010 by the American Enterprise Institute for Public Policy Research, Washington, D.C. All rights reserved. No part of this publication may be used or reproduced in any manner whatsoever without permission in writing from the American Enterprise Institute except in the case of brief quotations embodied in news articles, critical articles, or reviews. The views expressed in the publications of the American Enterprise Institute are those of the authors and do not necessarily reflect the views of the staff, advisory panels, officers, or trustees of AEI.

Printed in the United States of America

Contents

INTRODUCTION, *Andrew P. Morriss*   1

1. OFFSHORE FINANCE AND ONSHORE MARKETS: RACING TO THE BOTTOM, OR MOVING TOWARD EFFICIENT? *Anna Manasco Dionne and Jonathan R. Macey*   8
   The Critics and the Supporters of Offshore Competition   10
   Modern Offshore Finance   13
   A Review of the Controversy   17
   Offshore Finance Benefits Onshore Regulatory Regimes and Investors   18
   Public Choice: Sources of Opposition to Regulatory Competition   26
   Conclusion   27

2. THE LEGITIMACY OF THE OFFSHORE FINANCIAL SECTOR: A LEGAL PERSPECTIVE, *Rose-Marie Belle Antoine*   30
   The Context of Offshore Legal Rules   31
   Tax Issues   33
   Confidentiality   35
   Offshore Trusts   39
   Conflict of Laws   45
   Copycat Support   47
   Conclusion   48

3. REGULATING TAX COMPETITION IN OFFSHORE FINANCIAL CENTERS *Craig M. Boise*   50
   International Income Taxation   51
   Defining Tax Competition   53
   Arguments for Regulating OFC Tax Competition   57

Arguments against Regulating OFC Tax Competition 61
Regulating International Tax Competition 66
Directions for the Future 69

4. **The International Monetary Fund and the Regulation of Offshore Centers,** *Richard K. Gordon* 74
   The International Monetary Fund and Harmful Tax Practices 74
   The IMF and Prudential Supervision 76
   The IMF and Money Laundering and Terrorism Financing 88
   Recent Developments 99
   Some Conclusions 100

5. **The Role of Offshore Financial Centers in Regulatory Competition,** *Andrew P. Morriss* 102
   For What Do Jurisdictions Compete? 105
   Competition among Jurisdictions 112
   The Rise of Competition and the Role of Offshore Jurisdictions 123
   The Impact of Regulatory Competition 139
   Conclusion 144

Notes 147

Index 185

About the Authors 197

Introduction

Andrew P. Morriss

Since World War II, offshore financial centers (OFCs) have played an increasingly significant role in the world economy. For the United States, the benefits of that role have been substantial. Bermuda-based captive insurance companies have dramatically lowered insurance costs for thousands of U.S. businesses, permitting them to reduce product costs and thereby benefit their customers. Health-care captives, largely domiciled in the Cayman Islands, have allowed U.S. health-care providers, including many nonprofit hospitals, to devote a greater proportion of their resources to providing health care to those in need. Particularly since the 1990s, hedge funds predominantly domiciled in the Cayman Islands have funneled billions in foreign investment into the U.S. economy. Structured finance arrangements in OFCs have given U.S. companies, in industries from aircraft manufacturing to television sales, increased access to global capital markets while permitting them to monetize noncore assets. From the mid-1960s to the mid-1980s, when tax law changes rendered them unnecessary, finance subsidiaries domiciled in the Netherlands Antilles reduced the global cost of capital for thousands of U.S. parent companies.

Nor have benefits been limited to the U.S. economy. Because of a network of tax treaties there, entities formed in Barbados play a key role in the international competitiveness of Canadian multinationals by preventing double taxation of income earned outside Canada. European countries have found captive insurance solutions in Guernsey, one of the Channel Islands. Investors in the People's Republic of China have sought security and access to commercially sophisticated courts through Hong Kong entities, bringing substantial foreign investment into China that otherwise might not have been available. OFCs, too, have benefited, as offshore financial intermediation has created legitimate business and employment opportunities in jurisdictions having limited natural resources. Moreover, for companies in countries with weak financial systems and few financial services professionals, the clustering in OFCs of corporate, accounting, and legal services, together with strong legal systems committed to the rule of law, has offered a low-cost means of creating the business structures necessary to participate in the global economy.

OFCs have been a mixed blessing, however. While the most developed ones have institutional expertise equivalent to or better than many onshore governments, not all OFCs share this characteristic. A few examples reveal the legitimate concerns of onshore governments about certain aspects of the OFC world. In 1985, several ministers from the Turks and Caicos Islands were convicted of narcotics charges in the United States; more recently, a commission of inquiry found "general administrative incompetence" and "serious dishonesty" in the islands' government.[1] Aruba earned the title of "the world's first independent mafia state" from terrorism expert Claire Sterling.[2] American financier R. Allen Stanford used the island nation of Antigua as the base for what appears to be a vast Ponzi scheme involving his Antigua-domiciled Stanford International Bank.[3] Some bankers in Switzerland and Liechtenstein went well beyond giving traditional tax planning advice to private banking clients and encouraged European Union and U.S. citizens to commit tax fraud.[4]

Combined with the regular portrayal of OFCs in popular fiction (for example, John Grisham's *The Firm*) and film (*National Treasure*) as the locations of unsavory financial dealings, these scandals have left many people dubious about the role of OFCs in the world economy. Even where OFCs provide onshore economic benefits, onshore regulators dislike competing for business with more nimble jurisdictions, and certain elements within onshore governments may be inconvenienced or threatened by the competition OFCs provide. Tax authorities in high-tax jurisdictions insist that low- and zero-tax OFC regimes are "unfair tax competition." Law enforcement authorities worry that strong financial confidentiality principles offshore prevent investigators from tracking down illegal funds. National security authorities fret that OFCs will serve as conduits for operations that finance terrorism.

As a result of these concerns, OFCs today face serious threats from onshore governments determined to limit OFC competition. Channeling popular distaste for, and ignorance of, OFCs, the United States and various European countries are once again attempting to restrict their use. In the United States, the Stop Tax Haven Abuse Act is progressing through Congress and, in some form, appears likely to become law by the end of 2010.[5] In Europe, Germany and France are leading efforts to restrict the ability of individuals and firms to make use of offshore business structures. The April 2, 2009, G-20 communiqué promised "action against noncooperative jurisdictions, including tax havens."[6] The secretary general of the Organisation for Economic Co-operation and Development (OECD) announced that same day that he was "confident that we can turn these commitments into concrete actions to strengthen the integrity and transparency of the financial system."[7] Efforts by politicians, from British prime minister Gordon Brown to New York district attorney Robert Morgenthau, to blame offshore financial centers for at least some of the current global financial crisis also pose a serious threat to their continued viability.[8] Unless they are preceded by more thoughtful consideration of the overall effects of international regulatory competition, efforts like these present a serious risk of destabilizing the global financial system.

Before embarking on such efforts, we need to examine carefully the role OFCs play in the global economic system. This volume begins that task by addressing five neglected and misunderstood aspects of that role. In the first chapter, attorney Anna Manasco Dionne and corporate law expert and Yale Law School professor Jonathan R. Macey examine the role of OFCs through the lens of jurisdictional competition, a framework often employed in assessing competition within the United States, but rarely applied to competition from offshore jurisdictions. After evaluating OFC critics' complaints, Dionne and Macey argue that jurisdictional competition from OFCs has led to improvements in offshore regulation, which in turn has fostered onshore innovation and further regulatory competition. Because some financial market regulation is value-increasing, the authors find a race taking place to optimal regulation rather than one to the bottom.

Two issues that dominate the discussion of OFCs are tax competition and confidentiality, the subjects of the next two chapters. University of West Indies professor Rose-Marie Belle Antoine examines the legal principles underlying OFCs' efforts to resist pressure from onshore governments.

Antoine, a leading authority on both confidentiality and trust law issues, argues that well-established legal principles spawned in onshore jurisdictions underlie confidentiality and trust law in OFCs. Drawing on Commonwealth court decisions in both areas as well as OFCs' statutes, Antoine shows how offshore legal systems have evolved and explains why these legal developments deserve respect by other nations' courts under widely accepted conflict of laws principles.

International tax expert and DePaul University professor Craig M. Boise explores the efforts of onshore jurisdictions to regulate international tax competition through the transnational organizations they influence—specifically, the OECD and the European Union (EU). He begins by outlining the architecture of international taxation and describing the tax benefits that individuals and corporations seek in OFCs. Boise assesses how onshore jurisdictions have defined "tax competition" and "harmful tax competition" in ways that frame the tax competition debate and pave the way for regulation of such competition. He provides the first complete taxonomy of the arguments for and against regulation and summarizes the efforts undertaken by the OECD and the EU to regulate tax competition by OFCs. Finally, Boise looks ahead at the future of the tax competition debate, contrasting the approaches of the OECD and the EU to suggest how onshore jurisdictions and OFCs might move beyond heated rhetorical exchanges to find ways of resolving at least some of their differences.

Much of the debate over the role of offshore jurisdictions takes place within transnational organizations like the International Monetary Fund (IMF), the OECD, and the Financial Action Task Force (FATF). Case Western Reserve University law professor Richard K. Gordon, a former IMF official, describes how these organizations became involved in offshore issues. Gordon finds evidence that transnational organizations have played two significant roles. On the one hand, their efforts helped the race to optimal regulation described by Dionne and Macey by pushing some jurisdictions to improve their regulatory mechanisms. On the other hand, onshore governments sometimes have been able to use transnational organizations as a quasi-cartel to limit competition from OFCs.

Finally, University of Illinois law and business professor Andrew P. Morriss asks how OFCs change the game when they are added to the jurisdictional competition among larger states. Morriss concludes that OFCs alter the shape of competition because they face different incentives than onshore jurisdictions do. As a result, they provide a check on their onshore competitors that is qualitatively different from that which Britain provides for the United States. Further, he concludes that the impact of offshore jurisdictional competition is most significant for autocratic states, creating market pressures that discipline at least some autocracies.

Three themes recur throughout the book: the role of jurisdictional competition in promoting legal innovation; the need to engage with the legal principles involved rather than rely on slogans; and the efforts of onshore jurisdictions to limit competition. With respect to the first theme, Dionne and Macey, Antoine, and Morriss all supply examples of legal innovations introduced by offshore jurisdictions in their efforts to gain a competitive edge. Each of these innovations has positive value, not just for OFCs, but for onshore jurisdictions, as well.

All five chapters highlight the second theme: the importance of the underlying legal principles for understanding the stakes in the policy debate. Dionne and Macey highlight how the market for law promotes efficiency-enhancing evolution of regulatory law. Boise uncovers the policy concerns underlying the conflicts between OFC and onshore tax regimes, offering the possibility for compromise rather than conflict. Antoine shows the connection between offshore legal regimes and widely accepted international legal principles, shifting the debate from ad hoc policy disputes into the arena of international law, where well-settled conflict of law rules can guide the crafting of a satisfactory resolution. Gordon notes that onshore jurisdictions' efforts to use transnational organizations to limit competition were hindered by those organizations' insistence on the formulation of neutral standards. This insistence exposed the hypocrisy of onshore jurisdictions' failures to meet their own standards. Morriss focuses on the impact of competition on different kinds of states, arguing that jurisdictional competition over economic regulation serves as an effective limit on autocrats.

Turning to the third theme, the restriction of competition, we know that incumbent firms generally dislike competition from new competitors, and onshore governments have a similar reaction to competition from OFCs. Both Boise and Gordon describe efforts by onshore governments to limit competition, while Antoine describes the legal arguments that underlie

OFCs' rights to compete. Finally, Morriss suggests why autocratic onshore governments in particular dislike competition from OFCs.

These five chapters offer fresh perspectives for an increasingly heated debate over the role of OFCs, raising issues not currently under discussion. Most OFCs have evolved far beyond the shady locales portrayed in popular film and fiction, and onshore policy toward them should reflect that reality. The debate would be more constructive if it were shaped by consideration of the issues addressed in this book:

- *Is international regulatory competition a race to the bottom or a race to optimal regulation?* Dionne and Macey make the case that regulatory competition among jurisdictions will help efficient regulatory measures emerge. If this is true, the correct response to regulatory failings at the national level is to increase rather than restrict competition.

- *What policies are in conflict in tax competition?* Boise argues that tax competition is not a question of rates alone, but implicates a wide range of policy interests. Falling back on charges of "unfair" competition or demands for a "level playing field" is unlikely to lead policymakers to discover ways to enable the coexistence of tax systems built on different assumptions. Rather than asking if a particular tax regime is "unfair," we should instead seek to identify both the conflicting policies and the points of friction caused by conceptual differences.

- *Do "reform" proposals respect established international legal principles?* Antoine establishes that offshore financial centers are not modern-day pirates to be reined in by a squadron of marines but jurisdictions with the same legitimacy under international law as that possessed by onshore nations. International conflict of law principles require recognition of offshore jurisdictions' laws, many of which are different expressions of shared principles rather than ideas alien to the common heritage of Western legal systems.

- *What are the impacts of multilateral international institutions, and how can they foster rather than restrict competition?* Gordon shows how institutions like the IMF have played a constructive role by channeling onshore pressures into the creation of neutral principles, which both help foster efficiency-enhancing competition as described by Dionne and Macey and expose onshore jurisdictions' hypocrisy when they fail to comply with the principles themselves. At the same time, however, international organizations can also serve as an enforcement device for onshore jurisdictions' efforts to cartelize the law market, enabling them to coordinate efforts against OFCs. Which role will prove more important will depend on the relative successes of onshore and offshore governments in influencing the debate within these organizations.

- *How do offshore jurisdictions change the nature of the regulatory competition?* Morriss suggests how offshore jurisdictions' differences from onshore jurisdictions change the nature of the competition when they are added to the mix, pushing onshore regimes toward improvements in their legal systems. In addition, offshore jurisdictions' impact is greatest on autocratic regimes, giving offshore jurisdictions an important role in providing discipline for some of the world's less savory governments.

Focusing on these questions has the potential to improve the debate over the role of offshore financial centers and, perhaps, to help keep the welfare-enhancing baby from being thrown out with the money-laundering bathwater as the ongoing financial crisis produces new regulatory regimes within countries and internationally. Competition among jurisdictions can produce important benefits for both onshore and offshore governments.

1

Offshore Finance and Onshore Markets: Racing to the Bottom, or Moving toward Efficient?

Anna Manasco Dionne and Jonathan R. Macey

A strange theoretical anomaly exists in the academic literature regarding the public policy implications of robust competition among competing jurisdictions to attract business, jobs, and tax revenues. Generally speaking, such competition is viewed as highly beneficial for consumers, as it transforms largely moribund and sclerotic regulators into energetic and responsive policy entrepreneurs. Another widely recognized advantage of meaningful jurisdictional competition is that it stymies the destructive and welfare-reducing efforts of special-interest groups to influence the content of regulation in ways that transfer wealth to themselves from relatively less powerful and well-organized groups.

Thus, for example, most experts understand that the jurisdictional competition existing among the states to provide corporate law rules for U.S. corporations has led to generally efficient rules (or, at least, rules that are more efficient than they would be in the absence of such competition).[1] Strangely, however, the jurisdictional competition provided by offshore financial centers (OFCs) has not been embraced with the same enthusiasm as that for corporate charters, despite there being no qualitative difference between the two.

In this chapter, we argue that offshore jurisdictional venues do, in fact, provide salutary and beneficial regulatory competition and create an environment for promoting the development of innovative regulatory regimes that offer improved asset and risk management and financial planning. By offering an efficient alternative for some firms to opt into the market for these services, offshore markets produce direct benefits to onshore regimes. Most important, offshore regimes guard against excessive regulatory burdens and support innovation in financial products and services and flexible regulatory regimes. Furthermore, concerns about criminal activity do not diminish these benefits; recent international developments suggest that OFCs have made important strides in strengthening anticrime laws, and onshore firms may actually benefit from the ability to do business across jurisdictional lines without worrying about negative stigmas or vulnerabilities. Consequently, rather than precipitating a collective regulatory collapse, offshore jurisdictions support growth, both in their own regimes and in onshore markets. For these reasons, OFCs do not present an intractable or even substantial problem for onshore jurisdictions. In fact, in many important ways they are beneficial.

This is an important conclusion, not only because it offers a new view of OFCs' role in the global economy, but also because it counters the negative stigma that often attaches to OFCs and may, if it gains enough steam, become a self-fulfilling prophecy. Hilton McCann, a former finance official in Mauritius, has explained this risk:

> Perceptions . . . in respect of financial matters . . . have a nasty habit of becoming reality. For example, if, in error, customers perceive their bank to be in financial difficulties, they might anticipate a run on the bank. As one nervous depositor reveals his anxiety to another, the probability of the actual collapse of the bank increases—to the extent that it might even become a reality. . . . In respect of "offshore," the perception is likely to gain momentum if there is no contrary action and message that are coherently presented to demonstrate otherwise.[2]

Indeed, to the extent that OFCs have grown in number and wealth, and that financial system instability offshore would have far-reaching effects, it is especially important to explore and appreciate OFCs' positive contributions to other jurisdictions and the larger global economy. Our effort is only a start, but it suggests new reasons that objections to OFCs are exaggerated and overblown and serve more to protect the narrow self-interests of incumbent regulators and entrenched interest groups than the interests of the public.

We proceed first by summarizing the principal arguments of the critics and the supporters of jurisdictional competition in the offshore context. Along with an overview of offshoring and a review of the related legal literature concerning its costs and benefits, we then present the argument that OFCs benefit onshore markets and governance and ought not to be treated as a threat. We next argue that the offshore jurisdictions are an important part of jurisdictional competition generally because they counteract the efforts of special-interest groups to undermine more localized jurisdictional competition by diverting the gains generated by such competition to themselves. This analysis, in our view, explains the strong and visceral backlash against offshore regulatory competition: Such competition threatens the advantages of incumbent special-interest groups that benefit from the regulatory status quo in place prior to the emergence of offshore competition.

The Critics and the Supporters of Offshore Competition

Offshore financial centers have sparked great controversy since their rise to prominence forty years ago. The root of the dispute is the confidentiality such jurisdictions promise to provide to individual and corporate investors; typically, OFCs shield from disclosure information about offshore structures, the beneficial ownership of corporations, and bank account information in the absence of a request from law enforcement authorities supported by specific evidence of criminal activity. Coupled with low rates of taxation and less oppressive regulatory burdens,[3] the confidentiality associated with doing business in offshore jurisdictions makes them highly attractive for wealthy individuals and firms attempting to manage regulatory risk, lower transaction costs of doing business, and minimize the bureaucratic red tape associated with doing business in highly regulated venues such as France and the United States, as well as markets such as China and Russia that may be viewed as presenting problems of risk and regulatory uncertainty.

Wealthy individuals often utilize OFCs to protect their assets against expropriation by local governments, avoid mandatory provisions regarding heirship, and trade derivatives, while corporations typically form asset-holding structures, joint ventures, hedge funds, and special purpose vehicles for financing.

The sharpest critics have accused OFCs of serving as "crime havens,"[4] with U.S. lawmakers traditionally ascribing to this view. In the 1970s, the United States launched an anti-secrecy initiative against OFCs in an effort to control the flow of illegal drugs into the country; Congress sought to limit dealers' ability to launder their profits.[5] In 1985, the Senate described offshore secrecy laws as "the glue that holds many U.S. criminal organizations together."[6] More recently, congressional staffers have lamented that "too often these jurisdictions have . . . become havens for tax evasion, financial fraud, and money laundering."[7]

Other, more tempered critics complain that OFCs significantly reduce onshore tax revenue[8]—a criticism amplified by the rapid growth in offshore financing. Twenty-five years ago, OFCs were estimated to enable the concealment of between $150 billion and $600 billion in unreported income.[9] That figure grew to nearly $5 trillion by 2000[10] and $11.5 trillion in 2005.[11] According to the U.S. Internal Revenue Service, this translates to a loss of approximately $70 billion in taxes.[12]

Finally, the increase in corporate governance scandals and the heightened awareness of terrorism have given rise to two new worries. Critics allege that fraudsters have exploited OFCs to hide losses as well as revenues,[13] and opponents protest that terrorists may use OFCs to conceal funds, particularly in light of stronger anti-secrecy laws onshore.[14]

Proponents of OFCs contend that these objections are exaggerated, particularly the concerns about criminal activity. Increased international attention to the issue of criminal behavior and OFCs, they argue, provides strong incentives for OFCs to engage and attempt to ameliorate these concerns.[15] Furthermore, tax avoidance is not the same thing as tax evasion, and OFCs provide an important and entirely legitimate[16] tax-reducing mechanism for corporations and for individuals of high net worth.[17] Proponents argue that at least in theory, because all financial centers find reductions in tax burdens to be an important economic stimulus, all countries are more or less tax havens.[18] For example, in his instruction book on how to use OFCs, attorney Marshall Langer has argued that the United States' policy of not collecting income tax on interest paid to foreigners on U.S. bank accounts positions the country as a tax haven of sorts.[19] He posits that "billions of dollars would leave the United States if this exemption were eliminated," which "might effectively destroy New York as a major capital market."[20] According to this reasoning, OFCs share many important characteristics with onshore markets that routinely engage in jurisdictional competition.

Indeed, some commentators have argued that some OFCs are at least as well regulated as, if not better regulated than, prominent onshore markets such as the United States and the United Kingdom, particularly following a recent international effort to improve transparency and combat money laundering.[21] The *Financial Times* has pointed out that

> many US states, including Delaware and Nevada, do not require companies to provide beneficial ownership information. Many industrialised countries permit the use of bearer shares, which reduce transparency. Switzerland limits exchange of tax information to cases of fraud; Hong Kong and Singapore limit information ex-change [sic] to cases where they have a domestic interest.[22]

Even if OFCs are taken to be qualitatively unlike onshore markets, however, proponents claim they have other advantages. At the micro level, they argue, OFCs provide legitimate alternative markets for law-abiding individuals and corporations[23] and protect corporations' ability to take risks in an increasingly global economy. OFCs are also said to have more generalized benefits for onshore governments, particularly to the extent that they give companies access to tax-free or low-tax capital, improving the free flow of capital and contributing to onshore markets.[24]

In light of the growth in resources parked at OFCs and the relatively new concerns about corporate fraud and terrorism, how should we assess the costs and benefits of OFCs for onshore markets and governments? There are remarkably few academic engagements of this question. Scholarship typically presents it as one of interjurisdictional competition, and disagreement persists regarding the results of the contest. Some argue that regulatory competition results in a race to the bottom for the lowest tax rates, lightest regulation, and least information disclosure,[25] while others proclaim the benefits of OFCs for individuals, firms, and the global economy.[26]

We accept the interjurisdictional competition lens, but suggest a new refraction. OFCs provide healthy regulatory competition by offering legitimate, innovative tools for improved asset and risk management and financial planning. Because offshore finance represents an efficient choice on the part of some firms to opt into the market for these services, and out of onshore regulatory regimes, offshore markets produce direct benefits to onshore regimes—most important, they guard against excessive regulatory burdens and support innovation in financial products and services and flexible regulatory regimes. Furthermore, concerns about criminal activity do not diminish these benefits; recent international developments suggest that OFCs have made important strides in strengthening anticrime laws, and onshore firms may actually benefit from the ability to do business across jurisdictional lines without worrying about negative stigmas or vulnerabilities. Consequently, rather than precipitating a collective regulatory collapse, offshore jurisdictions support growth both in their own regimes and in onshore markets. For these reasons, OFCs do not present an intractable, or even substantial, problem for onshore jurisdictions. In fact, in many important ways, they are beneficial.

This is an important conclusion, not only because it offers a new view of OFCs' role in the global economy, but also because it counters the negative stigma that often attaches to OFCs and may, if it gains enough steam, become a self-fulfilling prophecy.

Indeed, to the extent that OFCs have grown in number and wealth, and that financial system instability offshore would have far-reaching effects, it is especially important to explore and appreciate OFCs' positive contributions to other jurisdictions and the larger global economy. Our effort is only a start, but it suggests new reasons that objections to OFCs are exaggerated and overblown and serve more to protect the narrow self-interests of incumbent regulators and entrenched interest groups than the interests of the public.

Modern Offshore Finance

Offshore finance first rose to prominence in the 1970s.[27] In the early years, OFCs were primarily cash repositories for wealthy individuals and large corporations, and they served a limited tax haven purpose.[28] R. A. Johns identified four "primary regions of activity" that emerged during this time:

1) The Caribbean area and Central America for servicing North and South America; 2) European enclave states and independent islands for servicing European business interests; 3) the Gulf area for servicing the Middle Eastern oil surplus countries; and 4) Hong Kong and Singapore with the sub-region of Oceania for servicing the Asian-Pacific area.[29]

As tax havens proliferated, onshore jurisdictions hoping to minimize lost revenues launched a regulatory offensive to limit the confidentiality that enables tax avoidance.[30] For proponents of tax havens, this offensive is better understood as an effort to eliminate tax competition among jurisdictions.[31] Offshore courts and other authorities have, however, hesitated to accede to disclosure requests where they are proffered exclusively for tax purposes, invoking principles of comity to remain faithful to their own public policy preference for confidentiality protections.[32] As a result, the anti-secrecy initiative has gained much of its momentum from its efforts to combat money laundering.[33]

Recently, there has been enormous international pressure—not only from the United States, but also from other large countries and organizations like the Organisation for Economic Co-operation and Development (OECD) and the Financial Action Task Force (FATF)[34]—for OFCs to limit or eliminate confidentiality protections and participate in efforts to reduce tax evasion and criminal activity.[35] The OECD launched its initiatives in 1998 with a report on "harmful" tax competition,[36] and it continues to press for transparency and information exchange for tax collection purposes, even in light of substantial progress toward that end in many jurisdictions.[37] Moreover, starting in 2000, the FATF issued a "blacklist" of countries perceived to be uncooperative with international efforts to combat terrorist financing and money laundering; that year, the list included the Bahamas, the Caymans, Cook Island, Dominica, Israel, Lebanon, Liechtenstein, the Marshall Islands, Nauru, Panama, the Philippines, Russia, St. Kitts and Nevis, and St. Vincent Grenadines.[38] The FATF updated this report annually until 2006, when the last country (Myanmar) was delisted.[39]

Some have objected to these efforts on the grounds that OFCs have no international obligation to be any more transparent than they are, and that the efforts sound more like self-serving strong-arming from a few powerful countries than broad international consensus with objective standards for compliance.[40] Not surprisingly, OFC governments are in this group. Aside from expressing concerns about being excluded from the international dialogue,[41] OFCs objected in 2002 to the imposition of "disproportionate and excessive regulation applied selectively to particular market participants [which] burdens those participants with a competitive disadvantage" and could be expected to shift demand away from their jurisdictions.[42] Timothy Ridley, then chairman of the Cayman Islands Monetary Authority, echoed the concerns about damage to offshore economies: Markets, he said, "that implement the various international initiatives are lead [sic] to believe they will not be discriminated against, will be allowed to participate and thus will benefit economically. But the reality-to-date is rather different."[43]

Nevertheless, the pressure has generally worked. Concerned that blacklisting by the OECD and the FATF would deter legitimate investors and damage their capital markets, many OFCs have responded positively to pressure for more transparency and less confidentiality.[44] The FATF blacklist is now empty. Furthermore, the OECD surveyed eighty-two countries in 2006 and reported extensive cooperation:

> Many of the economies reviewed have enhanced transparency by introducing rules on customer due diligence, information gathering powers and the immobilisation of bearer shares. Most have entered into double taxation conventions and/or tax information exchange agreements, and many are engaged in negotiations for such agreements. No OECD countries and few non-OECD economies now make domestic tax interests a condition for responding to a treaty partner's request for information on a specific taxpayer.[45]

Of course, because confidentiality is a primary—if not *the* primary—offshore commodity, OFCs have aimed to walk a thin line between too much and too little of it. Efforts to maintain a balance between providing more confidentiality than onshore jurisdictions but not so much as to risk blacklisting have swung "in favor of disclosure where criminal, but not civil matters are involved."[46] Modern OFCs are thus typically more transparent than their tax haven predecessors, but not completely so.[47]

Indeed, offshore jurisdictions have evolved significantly since tax havens first became prominent.[48] At the same time that international pressure has prompted increased transparency, globalization has made capital increasingly mobile, and more wealth has become available for offshore management. As a result, necessity has forced OFCs to compete on grounds other than confidentiality offerings and rates of taxation. Stiffer competition for bigger business has resulted in more sophisticated offshore regimes,[49] and the modern OFC tends to offer not only low taxation rates and company registry services, but also regulatory advantages and financial products competition. As one observer wrote just five years ago,

> Offshore tax havens as we know them are heading the way of the dodo. Under intense pressure from global watchdogs, regional authorities and individual countries, notably the United States, they are falling into line with international standards of reporting and disclosure, hoping against the odds to refashion themselves as successful financial centers.[50]

Successful OFCs are now complete alternative markets.[51] Rose-Marie Belle Antoine describes the main offshore financial services as "international banking services; dynamic investment functions and funds; tax planning services and other financial services associated with transnational business; and employment savings to avoid costly employment protection, social security or pension requirements."[52] Related financial products usually include "succession and asset protection vehicles like offshore trusts, mere incorporation facilities or . . . 'paper companies,' active companies, captive insurance, offshore shipping registers, fund flotations, offshore pensions . . . investment bonds or unit trusts, and the international business company."[53] Modern OFCs also boast accounting, legal, and insurance services. Offshore insurers "paid more than 60% of the World Trade Center insurance claims and 50% of the claims from Katrina."[54] In particular, Bermuda is a major world player in insurance and reinsurance.[55] Finally, OFCs are active in hedge fund offerings—as of 2005, 70 percent of the hedge fund market was offshore.[56] In 2006, the British Virgin Islands were the second largest hedge fund domicile in the world, with 9 percent of the global market, nearly 2,500 funds, and funds larger than €100 billion.[57] Bermuda ranked third, with 7 percent.[58]

A Review of the Controversy

The current literature assessing OFCs is relatively scant, even though it emerges both from the academic and governmental communities.[59] The offshoring controversy is usually conceptualized as a question of regulatory competition, and the dispute is whether and to what degree the presence of viable offshore markets precipitates an interjurisdictional race to lower tax rates, transactions costs, and costs arising from environmental and labor standards—a "race to the bottom." This label refers to competition among jurisdictions that is thought to result in a common effort to deregulate as much as possible, in hopes of winning the lion's share of business. The race to the bottom is alternatively known as a "competition in laxity."[60] Interestingly, this label originated in a Supreme Court opinion authored by Justice Louis D. Brandeis, concerning interjurisdictional competition among states regarding the size and powers of corporate structures.[61] Both terms are often applied to Delaware, to the extent that its favorable law of corporations has attracted firms from other states.[62]

International organizations first made the "race to the bottom" claim. Their principal original complaint was that OFCs "poached" capital and labor that were essential to onshore tax bases by offering secrecy and preferential tax treatment, and that this forced onshore jurisdictions to lower tax rates and regulatory burdens only to keep what was rightfully theirs.[63] Based on this logic, the "competition" was "harmful" because the onshore jurisdiction could never win, and instead could only hope to contain its losses; furthermore, it could not lower tax burdens for honest taxpayers. This type of objection has endured in the international community,[64] and extant scholarship voices similar concerns.[65] It endures even among those who protest the international community's current response to the problem.[66]

Other scholarship has discussed countervailing benefits. Much of this reiterates that OFCs benefit individuals and firms by providing legitimate, legal tools for financial management, and that the recent international offensive is damaging to thriving offshore economies.[67] A core part of this argument is that these tools and economies are available at decreasing cost to onshore markets, thanks to improved anti–money laundering measures.[68] Another small body of literature emphasizes OFCs' ability to self-regulate as sovereigns,[69] and a final literature focuses on the benefits of offshore finance to regulatory competition at the global level.[70] These have been thorough efforts, and we do not rehash here these costs and benefits. Rather, we focus on exploring a point that has thus far generally been ignored: the benefit to onshore regulatory regimes.

Like other scholarship on this issue, we use the lens of interjurisdictional competition to evaluate the significance to onshore regimes of the modern, sophisticated OFC. We break with other scholarship, however, in separating the prediction of a race to the bottom from the acceptance of a competition in laxity, positing that these labels have been mistakenly treated as synonymous. To this end, we reconceptualize the individual's or firm's decision to "go offshore" as an efficient decision to opt out of an onshore regulatory regime. This is premised on an appreciation of modern OFCs as allowing firms to make efficient—not just cheap—choices about financial markets. According to this logic, the availability of a well-regulated offshore market forces domestic markets to guard against excessive regulation, lest they lose valuable business. Furthermore, we argue, OFCs' financial and regulatory innovativeness support innovation onshore. As a result, fierce interjurisdictional competition enables a race to optimal regulatory laxity, not complete regulatory laxity.

Offshore Finance Benefits Onshore Regulatory Regimes and Investors

OFCs are serious competitors in the market for financial products. Here we provide a basic economic argument about how this benefits onshore jurisdictions. Although the idea that some competition in laxity may not necessarily precipitate a race to the bottom is new to the legal literature, it is not new to those closest to the OFC controversy—regulatory officials. As one observed recently,

> The UK and US are not keen to see SIFCs ["Small International Financial Services Centers," which are essentially OFCs] thrive too much, but they recognize that, for their own financial services industries to be competitive, they must allow their service providers to use SIFC domiciled structures, otherwise they risk their service providers migrating to SIFCs.[71]

The benefits to onshore jurisdictions are primarily in the areas of regulatory efficiency and legal and financial innovativeness, and concerns about criminal activity ought not to diminish these benefits.

To begin with, there are basic indications that the race to the bottom argument cannot be entirely correct. Some rules and regulations are essential to robust capital markets. Markets do not function well without investor protections, on both the shareholder and creditor sides. Rather, finance research suggests, debt and equity markets are likely to be bigger where legal rules and law enforcement engender confidence from investors.[72] Markets also tend to be more robust where rules and regulations protect investments from expropriation by managers.[73] And, as a matter of practicality, onshore investors in domestic firms that make use of offshore subsidiaries, joint ventures, or other structures profit from that use while at the same time enjoying the strong legal protections available onshore, which would diminish in a race to the bottom or regulatory collapse. They have the best of both worlds, and it seems unrealistic to expect this type of ability to go away. In the simplest terms, a race to the bottom cannot be possible because we know that some regulations are essential to vibrant capital markets and that investors profit from dual use of onshore and offshore investment. If this is so, what is the result of interjurisdictional competition?

Efficiency Benefits. Domestic jurisdictions complain that OFCs have too little regulation—or at least too little regulation to prevent tax evasion and money laundering—but the debate ought not to be so one-sided. What about the possibility that onshore jurisdictions have *too much* regulation— or at least regulations too stringent and burdensome, such that investors and firms find it easier, more attractive, and more profitable to do their business offshore? Perhaps predictably, the optimal balance is somewhere in the middle:

> Regulation is merely an imprecise tool that is used to assist supervisory authorities to monitor financial services providers. Regulation is used to identify and to manage the risks to which the providers of financial services are exposed. Regulation has another part to play—in protecting consumers and the financial services environment from those who would try to abuse it.

> Regulation will not eradicate risk—it is only a tool used to manage risk, not a panacea. . . . *Having little or no rules is just as ineffective as having too many. . . . Over-regulation . . . is just as dysfunctional as inadequate regulation.*[74]

Evidence that OFCs contribute to movement toward this middle ground, either in domestic jurisdictions, or globally, or both, would be a powerful indictment of the idea that they precipitate a race to the bottom.

Indeed, this seems to be the case. OFCs force onshore governments to compete for business. They compel domestic jurisdictions to be sensitive to the regulatory and tax burdens that their investors face, and to be aware of and concerned about markets that offer lower transactions costs. Judge Frank Easterbrook has explained the value of this competition in the context of competition within the United States:

> When entrepreneurs want to raise capital for a corporate venture, they must decide where to incorporate. The choice of where to incorporate in turn affects the price investors are willing to pay for shares. . . . States that enact laws that are harmful to investors will cause entrepreneurs to incorporate elsewhere.[75]

Judge Easterbrook's argument applies with equal force to competition among national jurisdictions. When investors and firms find that onshore regulations are, relative to their offshore counterparts, excessively cumbersome, expensive, harmful to confidence, or inhibiting to the free flow of capital, corporations have a strong incentive to relocate at least some of their business, if not their entire structures.

This argument offers an immediate rebuttal to the "race to the bottom" view of OFCs. To the extent that competition forces onshore jurisdictions to offer only as much (or as little) regulation as is necessary to attract business away from offshore markets, and offshore jurisdictions to offer only as much (or as little) regulation as is necessary to attract business away from onshore jurisdictions, competition does not necessarily precipitate a race among jurisdictions to offer *no* regulation. Rather, it precipitates movement from both jurisdictions toward an ideal middle ground. The result of healthy competition should be that each jurisdiction will offer the most efficient amount of regulation and taxation to attract and keep business—the optimal laxity.[76] In this way, offshore jurisdictions keep onshore governments from overregulating and harming their markets.

The international community's recent efforts to improve anti–money laundering rules and contain tax evasion in OFCs lend support to this view of the relationship between offshore and onshore markets. Prior to OECD and FATF action, OFCs frequently were accused of being too lax in their regulation of criminal activities within their jurisdictions. This, in turn, resulted in OFCs receiving a stigma, attracted the ire of international organizations, and threatened to compromise the competitive position of such OFCs. As a result of concerted efforts by interested groups both inside and outside of the onshore jurisdictions, these jurisdictions enhanced their controls, which, in turn, improved the legitimacy of their financial products and services and, at least to some extent, leveled the playing field among offshore and onshore markets. The OECD and the FATF were somewhat less concerned with regulating in the public interest than they were with stymieing the competition that offshore venues posed for the high-tax jurisdictions that constitute their core constituency. Once the actions of the OECD and the FATF are understood in this context, it becomes easier to see how the situation could be reversed and the push–pull dynamics could work the other way around, so that offshore jurisdictions could keep high-tax, onshore jurisdictions from implementing too many and too burdensome and anticompetitive rules.

The Securities and Exchange Commission's (SEC's) recent efforts to increase its oversight of hedge funds also illustrate the cross-jurisdictional impact of regulation.[77] In 2004, the SEC changed its interpretation of the Investment Advisers Act of 1940 such that more hedge fund advisers would be required to register with the commission. This requirement increased the cost of doing business as a hedge fund by imposing reporting requirements and levying an associated annual fee. The change strengthened the extant incentives for domestic funds to relocate offshore,[78] suggesting that it exceeded the optimal amount of regulation for the onshore economy. Although oversight is important to the extent that hedge fund investors do not want to be ripped off, too much regulation actually elevates the risk as more funds move offshore and off the domestic radar. As a result, the regulation should have been fashioned so as to avoid overburdening onshore funds relative to offshore ones. The efficiency argument would predict that strong offshore hedge fund offerings will eventually trigger such regulation.

Finally, global shifts in initial public offerings following the passage of the Sarbanes-Oxley Act in 2002 illustrate the more general regulatory competition point. When the statute imposed additional reporting and registration requirements, the cost of the investment banking and legal advice needed to go public soared to $1.5 million, sending some companies to Toronto and London to be listed.[79] In response, some on Wall Street have called for a reduction in requirements,[80] agitating to push the United States' regulatory regime away from overregulation and toward the optimal laxity that companies are finding elsewhere. In this way, interjurisdictional competition creates a strong dynamic that opposes excessive regulation in domestic markets.

In sum, the presence of viable OFCs presents a serious competitive threat to onshore markets. This forces onshore governments to be sensitive to the transactions costs that their regulations impose on investors and firms, and to make some concerted effort to contain those burdens so as not to lose economic activity to OFCs. More generally, it results in a cross-jurisdictional regulatory relationship, as illustrated by onshore jurisdictions' concern with improving crime controls offshore and the SEC's recent efforts to improve regulation of hedge funds. This connection has the direct benefits to onshore investors of guarding against too much regulation and preserving the optimal amount of laxity, undermining the idea that OFCs are damaging to onshore markets by precipitating a race to the bottom.

Innovation Benefits. OFCs also benefit onshore markets by pushing them to innovate in the areas of law and finance. Offshore markets are offering increasingly sophisticated financial services and products in an effort to compete—both among themselves and with onshore jurisdictions—for economic activities. OFCs may be inherently likely to be more innovative than onshore markets because they lack alternatives for national prosperity.[81] Typically developing nations and/or small islands without stores of natural resources,[82] OFCs are often unable to maintain self-sufficient economies, and they look to the market for financial services and products as their only means of establishing a vibrant, profitable economy. Crucially, the argument here is not only that OFCs are financially more innovative or sophisticated, but that they also have incentives to be legally more innovative than onshore jurisdictions, and that these incentives are entrenched by their small size:

> Offshore jurisdictions' limited alternatives motivate them to be more aggressive in innovating in law. Their small size makes their governments more flexible and responsive in adopting legislation and regulations to facilitate transactions by reducing the transactions costs of government action.[83]

As offshore markets progress, onshore jurisdictions must be more innovative to compete. When OFCs were essentially simply tax havens, the only grounds for regulatory competition were tax rates; now, the whole range of fiscal policymaking is fair game, and onshore jurisdictions must be more creative and comprehensive in their responses to competition from OFCs. As one influential scholar has observed,

> When a government has a monopoly with respect to the organization of economic transactions within its borders, it has little reason to . . . devote resources to innovating in its product offerings (e.g. by providing new legal vehicles for the organization of transactions), or offer efficient services (e.g. by reducing the transactions costs of organizing a transaction by providing speedy responses).[84]

Reality suggests that these expectations are not off-base. As business professor Ravi Aron has observed,

> If necessity is the mother of invention then competition is the mother of innovation. And competition has unleashed innovations in the financial services industry in mature markets such as the United States and EU.[85]

Professor Aron studied the onshore benefits of offshore innovation in 2006 by surveying senior executives at Fortune 1000 companies; the question was whether the executives were willing to source innovations in financial services and products from offshore providers, regardless of whether they owned the offshore providers.[86] For 68 percent of respondents, the answer was yes, depending on the executives' ability to manage the risk involved (by wholly owning the firm as a subsidiary, establishing a joint venture with a foreign firm, or exerting control over the firm and making it a strategic partner).[87] Although this is just one study, it suggests that, at least under some conditions, onshore firms profit from innovation offshore.

Like the efficiency benefits, the innovation benefits from OFCs are ongoing in nature. Because innovativeness results from OFCs' own demographics, together with their need for prosperity, it is not temporary, nor merely the result of evolution from single-minded tax havens to sophisticated markets. Rather, OFCs are likely to continue to innovate and to push onshore jurisdictions to compete for cutting-edge financial products and low-cost legal vehicles. Either way—whether one accepts the milder version of the argument, that offshore innovation prompts onshore innovation, or the stronger claim, that offshore innovation will always prompt onshore innovation—regulatory and economic competition from vibrant offshore economies forces onshore markets to be creative in their offerings and progressive in their legal structures.

In sum, the presence of innovative offshore markets as strong competitive threats has the direct benefit of forcing onshore regulators to be forward-thinking and creative. To the extent that OFCs are becoming increasingly sophisticated, and that they remain dependent on their financial markets for prosperity given their small size, this benefit is likely to continue to accrue for some years. Finally, the innovation benefit is illustrated at the firm level by recent research suggesting that executives are willing to work across borders when they expect to profit and when they can manage the risk of interjurisdictional collaboration. This suggests that, far from racing to the bottom, OFCs help to propel onshore jurisdictions forward.

Concerns about Criminal Activity Do Not Diminish These Benefits. Faced with important efficiency and innovation benefits of fierce interjurisdictional competition, opponents of strong offshore markets might emphasize concerns about criminal activity and terrorist financing as the hard core of their objections. Offshore jurisdictions have a strong reputational interest in repudiating crime, however,[88] and recent improvements in offshore markets' self-regulation and the growth in multilateral treaties and agreements regarding information disclosure suggest that these concerns are outdated, or at least that they have diminished. The international community has been forced to acknowledge this reality, as is clearly demonstrated by the now-empty FATF blacklist.

Improved criminal accountability yields benefits greater than merely deterring crime, however; onshore markets will benefit from these improvements in offshore jurisdictions. Aside from the obvious benefit of less money laundering, or drug running, or terrorist financing, improved criminal accountability offshore helps investors onshore by reducing the legal disparities between the jurisdictions. The argument is that weak anti–money laundering measures offshore force domestic jurisdictions to be especially aggressive in targeting offshore activity, while stronger criminal accountability offshore reduces the interjurisdictional competition for law (or enforcement of it) as a product,[89] refocusing the competition on financial products and economic activity. In this way, onshore jurisdictions' law enforcement costs are lowered, the playing field becomes more level than it was before, and individuals and firms may feel more secure and find it easier to do business across jurisdictional lines. Onshore investors, business, and governments benefit.

At first glance, stronger laws offshore may seem to diminish a key advantage of onshore markets—well-established justice systems—but this reduction in disparity is better understood as an improvement in onshore individuals' and firms' ability to make efficient business choices on the basis of traditional indicators such as price, financial risk, and expected returns, and not worries about stigmas. In this way, stronger protections offshore benefit investors onshore—at least the legitimate ones.

Opponents of offshoring who do not believe that offshore jurisdictions have materially improved their anti–money laundering measures may argue that onshore jurisdictions remain vulnerable to criminal behavior conducted in OFCs. Even if this is true, however, it does not necessarily mean a net loss for the onshore market. To the extent that concerns about criminal behavior will mean that some firms will refuse to do business offshore, onshore markets still have a competitive edge over OFCs. Indeed, onshore jurisdictions will always have the upper hand as far as legal regimes are concerned, and rights-based protections for shareholders and creditors are essential to maintaining investor confidence and retaining economic activity. Finance literature has presented strong positive correlations between investor protections and capital markets[90] and between investor protections and good corporate governance,[91] and a negative correlation between investor protections and the use of earnings management to conceal poor firm performance from outsiders.[92] This literature suggests that onshore jurisdictions are highly unlikely to lose the competitive edge their legal systems provide even if OFCs strengthen their criminal controls and cooperate in global anticrime efforts.

The bottom line is that, *regardless of whether criminal accountability in offshore jurisdictions has improved or remained the same, there are strong arguments that onshore jurisdictions benefit from the regulatory competition OFCs provide.* In light of recent international developments and onshore jurisdictions' strong investor protections, concerns about money laundering and terrorist financing cannot be the basis of a strong case against robust offshore economies. Rather, recent improvements in OFCs' criminal laws suggest that onshore firms may find it easier to do business across jurisdictional lines and to make business decisions on the basis of economic rather than reputational factors.

Public Choice: Sources of Opposition to Regulatory Competition

By now it is not just well settled but universally acknowledged that powerful special-interest groups play an important role in policy development.[93] Consistent with this general observation, it is also the case that powerful special-interest groups play an important role in influencing the regulation of offshore entities.

Regulation is a high-stakes game. In particular, the emergence of offshore entities as an important source of regulation for companies doing business in developed nations is a significant threat to powerful entrenched interest groups, especially the lawyers, regulators, and politicians whose power and influence are threatened by the rise of offshore rivals. Offshore competition is particularly threatening for entrenched local interests because of the inability of onshore interest groups to influence offshore regulators. Indeed, the relative isolation of offshore regulators from onshore interest groups is likely one of the primary reasons for their success.

In our view, the sequence of events is likely to follow the following pattern. First, in time period 1, healthy and robust jurisdictional competition onshore generates efficient legal rules that reduce capital costs and promote low prices and high-quality production. Gradually, interest-group machinations press for federal preemption of efficient local rules. In cases where a particular locality such as Delaware has amassed market power, interest groups use their influence to divert the rents associated with such market power to obtain for themselves some of the benefits generated by these regimes. In other words, as interest-group pressures threaten the long-term value of onshore jurisdictional competition, they lead to inefficient rules in dominant jurisdictions such as Delaware and to the outright preemption of local legal rules by the federal government; we saw this in the case of Sarbanes-Oxley's wholesale preemption of large swatches of issues that heretofore had been the exclusive domain of state corporate law. Thus, once the efficient local regulation enacted in time period 1 is displaced by federal regulation or by interest-group activities at the local level in time period 2, an opportunity for offshore regulatory entrepreneurs emerges in time period 3. Relatively unaffected by powerful onshore interest groups, these can attract revenue to their own jurisdictions by offering more regulations that benefit both local consumers and producers at the expense of onshore special-interest groups.

Conclusion

In this chapter, we have used the lens of interjurisdictional competition to evaluate the significance to onshore regimes of the modern, sophisticated OFC. We have argued that current OFCs are important competitors with onshore jurisdictions. They offer complete alternative markets, which provide individuals and firms with an opportunity to opt out of domestic markets and regulatory regimes in search of flexible, innovative, and less costly alternatives.

We have further argued that this competition does not result in the predicted interjurisdictional "race to the bottom" to lower rates of taxation, regulatory burdens, and transactions costs. An acknowledgment of the practical reality that some regulations are essential and profitable indicts the "race to the bottom" argument and flags the need for a new view. We thus propose that regulatory competition precipitates an interjurisdictional competition in laxity, which should result in optimally burdensome regulation onshore. Efficiency benefits accrue because OFCs force onshore governments to be sensitive to the transactions costs that their regulations impose, and to make concerted efforts to contain those so as not to lose economic activity to OFCs. This relationship is illustrated by onshore jurisdictions' concern with improving crime controls offshore and the SEC's efforts to improve regulation of hedge funds, and, more generally, by the United States' loss of initial public offering (IPO) activity to London and Toronto following Sarbanes-Oxley. This efficiency benefit is crucial for domestic jurisdictions, which might otherwise overregulate their markets, discouraging investment and inhibiting the free flow of capital; and it undermines the idea that OFCs damage onshore markets by precipitating a race to the bottom.

Competition from strong OFCs also provides other benefits to onshore markets. To the extent that OFCs are becoming increasingly sophisticated, and that they remain dependent on their financial markets for prosperity given their small size, they have become increasingly innovative in their financial and legal offerings. To compete, onshore markets will have to step up their own products and services, and onshore regulators will have to be more creative in their work. This benefit is illustrated at the firm level by recent research suggesting that executives are willing to work across borders when they expect to profit and when they can manage the risk of interjurisdictional collaboration. Increased innovativeness suggests that, far from racing to the bottom, OFCs help to propel onshore jurisdictions upward.

We have also argued that these benefits are not vulnerable to diminution because of concerns or stigma resulting from criminal activity offshore. OFCs have improved their criminal controls substantially, as the international community has acknowledged. As a result, firms should enjoy greater flexibility to do business across jurisdictional lines and to develop strategies on the basis of economic rather than reputational factors. Even if this is not entirely true, onshore jurisdictions' strong investor protections suggest they will retain an edge over OFCs in the competition for law as a product, and finance literature has linked this edge with bigger capital markets. So, however the criminal concerns cut, they ought not to reduce the benefits that onshore jurisdictions reap from fierce regulatory competition.

In short, OFCs promote efficiency and nurture innovation. They provide important regulatory competition that should result in a regime just lax enough to retain these benefits—not a regime that is completely lax, and that might be vulnerable to concerns about criminal accountability (or might, at the least, lose the legal protections that support the capital market). At best, this argument offers a new but commonsense view of OFCs' role in the global economy; at the very least, it suggests that objections to OFCs and regulatory competition may be exaggerated and overblown.

2

The Legitimacy of the Offshore Financial Sector: A Legal Perspective

Rose-Marie Belle Antoine

While the offshore financial sector confronts many challenges to its credibility and existence, strong arguments remain that underscore its legitimacy, in particular with respect to the legal precepts and policies underpinning it. What is remarkable is that the well-established legal principles that support offshore jurisdictions are often presupposed to be legitimate in one context but unacceptable and even unlawful in another. This has often been forgotten in the onshore jurisdictions' zeal to "blacklist" their competitors among the offshore financial centers (OFCs). Ironically, offshore legal paradigms are being emulated by the same onshore jurisdictions that challenge them. Moreover, the offshore sector makes significant contributions to the development of the law, both introducing important new legal concepts and clarifying and correcting gaps in the legal framework.

Because of the rampant hypocrisy in the stance taken by onshore countries, it is important for those in the offshore sector not to just lobby in an apologetic way, begging for lifelines by promising to toe the line, but to engage seriously in the debate about legal principle. The assumptions and deliberate attempts to illegalize and denigrate the perfectly legitimate principles of law and policies based on these legal concepts must be challenged.[1] This chapter sets out to delineate these legal rationales in an attempt to examine and support the offshore legal infrastructure.

The Context of Offshore Legal Rules

First, let us be clear about what we mean by offshore financial law. My own definition is this: Offshore financial law is a body of law

> concerned with investment, financial arrangements and entities, created by non-residents of a particular jurisdiction but structured within that jurisdiction. Such investments or arrangements are typically focused on some business advantage, tax avoidance, protection from creditors and judgment debtors or privacy.[2]

Offshore financial law may be seen as a subset of the entire legal system, or, put another way, an alternative legal system that has been created primarily, or even exclusively, for foreign investors. The subject includes company law, banking and finance law, trust law, tax law, and constitutional law. Private international law also has a heavy impact on offshore financial law. Offshore financial law may borrow from, define, or clarify traditional areas of law, or it may create innovative forms in a particular subject area, such as trust, banking, or insurance. Offshore financial law always operates, however, within a legal framework designed for the needs of offshore investment.

The offshore legal infrastructure is one created purely for commercial and developmental reasons. And herein lies the dilemma: It is the success of the offshore sector in attracting business and income from foreign, wealthier shores that has made it a magnet for controversy. Yet the commercial rationales of offshore financial law should not be an element in the indictment of the offshore financial sector. The raison d'être of many laws similarly speaks to business and commercial enterprise, and offshore financial laws are no less worthy in this regard. Indeed, even traditional trust law as developed in the United Kingdom was intended to assist wealthy persons in saving their property, during war and later, in particular, to protect them from taxes owed to a greedy state.[3] Similarly, the evolution of current legal entities and principles, or the creation of radically new ones by the offshore sector, speaks to real commercial needs. The creation of the limited liability company, which was first thought to be unethical and unconscionable (once described as company law's "race to the bottom"), is now credited with advancing company law. Indeed, the principle of limited liability can be viewed as a foundation of free enterprise, making company law more relevant to today's commercial environment. Offshore financial laws, in seeking to uphold the principles and needs of commerce and international business, are thus in sync with other areas of commercial law and should be judged in the same way.

Of course, some financial impropriety occurs offshore. Financial impropriety exists everywhere; most of the money laundering, financial transactions that benefit terrorism, and other illegitimate transactions occur in large, metropolitan financial centers of the world (New York, London, and Russia).[4] Furthermore, the onshore financial sector has been rocked regularly by financial scandals (Enron, BCCI, and Madoff). Yet, rather than set its own house in order, the onshore sector has launched a barrage of financial regulations and attacks requiring OFCs to do much more self-regulation than onshore financial centers. For example, despite the absence of any known significant abuse of the offshore financial sector by money launderers, all offshore jurisdictions in the Caribbean have drastically upgraded their anti–money laundering legislation[5] and created special regulatory bodies to address this issue, such as the Financial Intelligence Unit in the Bahamas.[6] Further, some features protecting confidentiality in offshore financial jurisdictions have been abolished in favor of enforcement options friendlier to onshore jurisdictions. For example, the Bahamas abolished bearer shares for this reason.

The attack on offshore financial centers has been fueled by international organizations such as the Organisation for Economic Co-operation and Development (OECD) and powerful nations such as the United States and France through "blacklisting," and especially through accusations of money laundering. Questioning legal concepts such as confidentiality and trusts utilized by the offshore financial sector, as the OECD and like-minded governments have done, rather than addressing possible abuses is not the way forward. Detractors have engaged in a concerted effort to criticize such well-established legal principles and concepts, and offshore financial jurisdictions should be careful not to accept blindly the erroneous precepts upon which many of these attacks upon them have been based.

The entire dialogue (or is it a monologue?) on the offshore sector and money laundering has been something of a legal farce—an attempt to cloak the real issue, which is the loss of monies being filtered off from developed countries to relatively poor, politically less influential developing jurisdictions. Particularly significant is the loss of potential tax revenue through legal maneuvers, suggesting that the blacklisting initiatives were not primarily about money laundering. By not contesting the terms of the debate, we have allowed those who wish to destroy the offshore sector for reasons of self-interest to define and label it.

Tax Issues

Much of what may be said about other areas of offshore financial law stems from the basic principles which attach to the tax function of offshore jurisdictions. An appreciation of the appropriateness of the legal principles that ground the offshore legal sphere significantly informs other aspects of offshore financial law, such as rules on the trust, confidentiality, and international business companies (IBCs), as many of these concepts have been constructed with tax issues in mind.

But offshore centers have not been legally vulnerable on tax grounds, since legal principles in relation to both domestic revenue law and international law actually favor the position that an investor is free to invest his or her money offshore for tax mitigation purposes. Offshore trusts have clear, well-grounded justifications for their tax functions in two well-established rules of law: the rule on the nonenforcement of foreign fiscal law,[7] and the *Westminster* rule embodying the form-over-substance approach in tax arrangements,[8] which makes a distinction between lawful tax avoidance and unlawful tax evasion. While these rules are being constantly eroded, they are by no means dead. Onshore countries themselves rely on these same legal principles and concepts. Moreover, no clear rules of international law address who should have the jurisdiction to tax what is, in essence, transnational investment. Indeed, the international community should be lobbying for such principles so as to ensure fairness and transparency in international taxation. As a result, onshore jurisdictions have relied on the introduction of a red herring—the accusation of financial impropriety, such as money laundering—to overcome their poor legal position on tax issues.

Forced to accept these incontestably legitimate tax law principles, onshore jurisdictions have taken aggressive, sometimes unilateral, measures to counter the capacity of offshore financial products to serve as efficient tax-planning vehicles, resulting in considerable erosion to such products.[9] These countermeasures apply hitherto unknown tax liabilities to nonresident entities, such as trusts and those connected with trusts. Through them, for example, the fundamental trust principles of "ownership" and consequent allocation of tax liabilities have been challenged. Previously, it was the trustees and the beneficiaries of trusts who were the prime targets of the tax authorities and even then, with respect to beneficiaries, only when they actually received trust benefits. Now, in many onshore countries, as a direct result of the revenue lost by offshore trusts employing nonresident trustees to man the trusts and siting the trust out of the onshore jurisdiction, tax laws place tax liability on the settlor, the co-trustees, and the beneficiaries even before a benefit is received.[10] In many cases, tax liabilities go hand in hand with tax reporting. Tax may be sought at disposition, transfer, and migration. Legislation may declare that settlors or beneficiaries have the right to be reimbursed from the trust fund and by the trustee.

These mutations of tax liability for trusts introduce important questions which have yet to be resolved, however. Indeed, these countermeasures themselves may be challenged as illegitimate based on legal principle. What, for example, are the duties of trustees with respect to trust assets where a request is made by a settlor to be reimbursed for taxes that he has paid in relation to the trust? In traditional trust law, the trustee owes no such duty to the settlor, and, indeed, it may be a breach of the trustee's duty; but onshore legislation makes allowance for this. Yet the onshore country typically has no jurisdiction over the offshore trustee who is resident elsewhere. Further, the established rule against enforcing the tax laws of a foreign state comes into play. Case law is already beginning to address this issue, but it is an area fraught with contradiction.[11]

Even where the trust instrument pronounces on this question and expressly provides for the payment of such taxes, a court may override the provision because of conflicting rules on nonenforcement of foreign tax law. This was the case, for example, in the Barbadian decision of *Bank of Nova Scotia v. Tremblay*.[12] Where the power to pay taxes is unexpressed, there is considerably more difficulty. Recent case law suggests that the best interests of the beneficiaries (but not necessarily the settlor) will be an important consideration, but this is an important emerging area of trust litigation.[13]

Trust law principles militate against these unilateral, foreign demands on the offshore trust and in favor of the sanctity of the offshore trust. Additional new areas of trust jurisprudence "piggyback" on these developments, such as strict duties placed on the trustee not to incur new tax liabilities.[14]

Confidentiality

Confidentiality is an important precept in offshore legal paradigms. The offshore legal concept of confidentiality is somewhat different from its common-law neighbor. It is what I call a hybrid concept, as are other offshore financial legal concepts. It encompasses strict and extremely broad-based statutory duties of confidentiality, sometimes with criminal penalties attached, in all aspects of business. Indeed, it is a good example of the efficiency and dynamism of offshore financial law.[15] Confidentiality in offshore jurisdictions is valuable, and since many investors choose offshore jurisdictions specifically for the added confidentiality norms, confidentiality is appropriately described as a financial or legal product in the offshore sector. Confidentiality as an offshore financial law product has been responsible for creating significant and sustaining opportunities in the offshore sector. On the other hand, it is the concept which has perhaps most antagonized onshore actors.

In my view, confidentiality has been used largely as a scapegoat, blamed for encouraging money laundering and tax evaders. The result of linking it so intimately to such criminal activity has been that confidentiality in the offshore sector has acquired a negative image. On examination of the jurisprudence, however, confidentiality remains a viable and much respected principle in areas of commercial endeavor not associated with offshore investment. For example, the United States and Canada have fought hard and long to protect the principle of financial confidentiality in terms of trade secrets, arguing precisely that it is essential for business. Several cases outside of the offshore arena may be identified in which the United States, the archenemy of offshore confidentiality, has argued vociferously against disclosure in commercial endeavors, asserting a "strong and vital interest" in protecting confidentiality.[16] Yet, as seen below, that same vital interest for protecting confidentiality in offshore jurisdictions dependent on the offshore sector for their lifeblood has not been acknowledged.

In employment and commercial law, duties of trust and confidence are well established. More broadly, we accept without question the notion of confidentiality in fiduciary relationships. This is considered a foundational principle of the common law, recognized as essential in tort law, contract law, company law, and employment law. For example, the banking sector has long operated on the understanding of the value of the confidentiality ethic. This is supported by the common law, as embodied in the landmark 1924 United Kingdom decision *Tournier v. National Provincial Bank*,[17] and other common-law norms. Thus, confidentiality in other quarters is treated as a legitimate principle precisely because of its value to business and wealth creation. In the case of trusts, trustees have a well-established duty under orthodox trust law to keep the affairs of the trust confidential. Amazingly, the OECD even sought to attack this duty, although it applies equally to every single onshore trust.

We also need to address the supposition that confidentiality must be eliminated simply because it can be abused. That confidentiality can sometimes be abused does not make it an abusive or illegitimate concept. Rather, we have accepted that in every financial endeavor and structure there will be weaknesses, and what we need to do is to have checks and balances and avenues for redress. Yet once there is the mere suggestion (and it is often simply a suggestion) that confidentiality leads to some type of abuse, we begin to question its very legitimacy as a legal principle.

The effective campaign onshore to whittle away the confidentiality norms in offshore states has resulted in stricter anti–money laundering laws, increased tax reporting, and other information requirements, including information treaty principles. These have undermined the strong confidentiality laws in place in offshore jurisdictions. Yet confidentiality is still a valuable, legitimate legal principle and product. Investors whose hands are clean have nothing to fear, as reasonable suspicion underlines the several laws put into place that can thwart confidentiality. To such investors, confidentiality and the legal principles now attached to it will in no way hinder investment.

Limits to Confidentiality. The issue of confidentiality in considering the legitimacy of the offshore sector is also significant. We should distinguish the different kinds of pressures for disclosure. For example, where there is prima facie evidence of fraud or money laundering, confidentiality must succumb to the greater interest in disclosure and law enforcement. In contrast, offshore jurisdictions have resisted attempts to defeat confidentiality automatically where routine reporting or disclosure relating to fiscal matters is involved. This approach is supported by the well-established rule of international law that no country enforces the fiscal laws of another. Such resistance is enhanced because of offshore structures and arrangements that seek to ensure that onshore states do not have jurisdiction over offshore entities and actors. Consequently, for confidentiality to be effective and aid in wealth creation, it must work in tandem with jurisdictional strategies. For example, offshore trustees fall outside onshore jurisdictions' reach and cannot be forced to disclose matters relating to offshore investment, whatever laws exist onshore for such disclosure.

While some offshore states have succumbed to onshore pressures and signed tax information agreements, the status quo with respect to confidentiality in such matters largely remains intact. This ensures that the opportunities that exist with respect to confidentiality endure. Further, while offshore legislatures eroded confidentiality because they feared concealment of tax evasion, money laundering, or even terrorist activity, in other areas of offshore financial law confidentiality has been enhanced judicially, as in the case of the trust, discussed below.[18]

Constitutional Protections. Fundamental norms on confidentiality may exist outside of the common law under human rights law, under the rubric of the right to privacy or the privilege against self-incrimination. Such constitutional underpinnings enhance the value of confidentiality as an offshore financial product. While constitutional privacy protections were not successfully upheld by the court in the Bahamas in one case which challenged the financial reporting requirements in that jurisdiction, *In re Financial Clearing Corporation*,[19] this was not because confidentiality failed to be identified, but rather because it succumbed to greater interests of law enforcement. Other successes have been scored for confidentiality, however. The European Court on Human Rights has found that documents and financial records, even those wanted for tax purposes, are protected by privacy, and that governments must act in accordance with the principle of proportionality, taking the route least invasive of individual human rights.

Furthermore, as echoed in our courts, governments must act reasonably, and only as is necessary in a free and democratic society.[20]

Automatic demands for information unrelated to some reasonable cause—in other words, fishing expeditions—are, therefore, unacceptable. In most offshore jurisdictions the issue has not been tested directly in the courts. In the Caribbean, Australia, and other parts of the Commonwealth, however, progressive courts sensitive to commercial concerns have located privacy interests in financial confidentiality.[21] The clothing of financial confidentiality with a human rights ethos gives the concept added legitimacy, as well as better security in practice. This supplements financial objectives, such as investment and wealth protection.

Comity and Confidentiality. In an infamous line of bank cases fought on confidentiality issues, offshore banks were threatened with contempt actions by U.S. courts for refusing to disclose information on offshore clients, in accordance with offshore financial law. It is telling that these cases were framed within the context of comity—that is, the context of which state had the "greater interest" in protecting confidentiality or dismantling it.[22] The political and economic dimensions of this legal battle contextualized within principles of private international law were evident to, and even commented upon by, other onshore states, such as Canada and the United Kingdom. They saw it as a question of might over right. In one such case, the United Kingdom court protested that such an approach merely resulted in a win going to the "highest bidder."[23] The U.S. courts made no apologies, stating that this confidentiality debate was about revenue, especially tax revenue, "the lifeblood of their economy."[24] In every case going before the U.S. courts, although they claimed to balance conflicting interests between offshore and onshore in the name of comity, the interests of the United States prevailed. The U.S. courts reached this conclusion despite the offshore sector's being the sole or most important revenue earner in the offshore jurisdictions concerned, while tax was but one aspect of the U.S. economy.

At the end of the day, the key issue is balance. We can respect the requests of onshore jurisdictions for more disclosure where activities such as money laundering are suspected, as this is a morally accepted, neutral rationale for disclosure. Where disclosure has as its aim only the facilitation of revenue creation in onshore jurisdictions at the expense of offshore jurisdictions, however, then it is ethically suspect. This is all the more so when we consider that the mores, practices, and legal principles created and developed by offshore jurisdictions have now been adopted in certain onshore jurisdictions, which make no apology for this phenomenon.[25]

Offshore Trusts

The trust can be described as the most interesting and important offshore vehicle, as well as the one with greatest potential for investors. Like offshore confidentiality, the offshore trust is a statutory creature, related to, but different from, its well-known common-law cousin. It deviates significantly from the orthodox common-law trust, allowing certain features, such as self-settling and spendthrift provisions, historically forbidden by the common law. The offshore trust is versatile, providing opportunities in probate, facilitating tax mitigation, allowing protection from creditors, making company matters more efficient, and protecting trustees against negligence suits.[26]

The evolutionary, sometimes revolutionary, character of offshore trust law is manifested both in the type of trusts offered and in the functions permitted under offshore financial law. Offshore financial law allows trusts to do a host of things that a traditional trust cannot do at all or cannot do effectively. Most importantly, given the commercial objectives of offshore financial law, offshore trusts are more closely aligned to business than their onshore counterparts. The latest offshore trust creation, the VISTA trust,[27] demonstrates the symbiotic relationship between the offshore trust and the company in offshore financial centers against the broader backdrop of commercial efficiency. The VISTA trust allows traditional obligations of trustees with respect to the use of shares in investment to be exercised by directors of underlying companies. By recognizing the limitations of professional trustees, it insulates the trustees from bludgeoning common-law liabilities that may accrue from risky commercial ventures.[28]

The offshore sector has been responsible for significant developments in trust law. Some of these innovations remain insular, peculiar to offshore business; but many others have filtered through to the onshore sector, or, at least, acted as catalysts for onshore trust law reform, as offshore modifications of traditional onshore law enter the mainstream of trust jurisprudence.

Recognition is growing that offshore trust law and its accompanying *grundnorms*, such as confidentiality, can improve onshore law.[29]

In general, the offshore sector makes a significant contribution to our legal system, introducing many important new legal concepts and clarifying and correcting several gaps in our legal framework.[30] Of the many creative jurisprudential changes brought about by the offshore sector, however, none are more dynamic than those of trust law. The simple reason is the attractiveness of the trust as a tool for offshore investment and the relative flexibility of the trust concept, an ingenious tool of equity created to introduce flexibility into rigid legal systems and to enable accommodation of important business and societal goals. Although grounded in statute, the offshore trust borrows heavily from the familiar principles of equity while also introducing radical changes to the traditional trust. As mentioned earlier, I coined the term "hybrid trust" to describe this new entity.[31] Indeed, the offshore sector can be applauded for creating the first indigenous and well-regulated trust concept of modern times. In so doing, it has compelled jurisprudential rethinking about the nature and functions of the traditional trust.

One of the reasons the offshore trust is such an attractive vehicle for wealth creation and business is because of its three-tiered structure of trustee, settlor, and beneficiary, in which the trustee holds the assets provided by the settlor on behalf of a beneficiary. This dual nature of trust ownership is crucial for the success of the trust in investment, as it allows the manipulation of the elements of ownership and control. With the establishment of a trust, an offshore settlor is no longer considered the owner of the assets under trust law, although the settlor is able initially to determine the pattern of investment.[32] The potential escape route with respect to tax and other liabilities is significant, although, as we will see later, onshore jurisdictions have countered with legislative changes of their own to prevent the logical applications of trust law. Where, as is often the case, the offshore trust is created with an underlying company or utilizes a confidential bank account, a triple level of security is created for investors. The evolutionary and adventurous nature of offshore trust law is manifested both in the type of trusts offered and in the functions permitted under offshore financial law. Even new officers have been created, such as the protector and the enforcer, which, in turn, conjure up new jurisprudential questions to resolve.[33]

Just as company law was liberated by limited liability, so, too, these developments have freed the trust objective from traditional limitations. The trust is now a more viable commercial entity, granting wider control to settlors and business interests associated with the trust, and attempting to insulate investment from restrictive principles. In doing this, it has championed the cause of the freedom of disposition of property, including the prioritization of the interests of named beneficiaries over future, unidentifiable creditors.

Importantly, offshore financial law and practice give settlors more leeway than does traditional trust law. Offshore settlors are typically allowed a greater degree of self-settling than those under onshore trusts. Commonly, the settlor will be one of the discretionary beneficiaries and will have a life interest or another limited or reserved interest. Under more aggressive legislation, the settlor may also be a trustee, a beneficiary, or a protector.[34] In addition to the more generous interests that may be reserved to the offshore settlor, more channels of potential influence are open to him or her. For example, the settlor's wishes may be communicated through a memorandum of agreement to the trustee, or the settlor may retain powers of appointment and revocation. Further, the existence of the protector to liaise between the beneficiaries and trustees creates an additional route to settlor influence, albeit, in many cases, indirectly. (This perhaps surprising legislative maneuver does nothing to allay fears of excessive settlor influence, a significant factor in those U.S. cases that questioned the integrity of trusts.)[35]

Another remarkable advancement of the offshore trust is its ability to cater to the needs of investors from civil law jurisdictions unfamiliar with the trust. It allows civil law settlors to do specific things, impossible or difficult to achieve under their own law and legal vehicles, such as avoiding forced heirship or mandatory succession regimes. Offshore legislation permits such investors to establish trusts, granting them capacity and making provision for the recognition of the offshore trust. This last feature is, in fact, compatible with the Hague Convention on Trusts,[36] further underlining the legitimacy of offshore products. Most important for such investors, they are able to avoid onerous forced heirship succession rules. This would be difficult under ordinary trust law, which does not specifically contemplate such usage. Other examples of changes to trust law wrought by offshore jurisdictions for direct commercial advantage include providing the ability to abolish perpetuity and accumulation rules or extend the life of trusts, allowing the creation of trusts that can continue for periods longer than allowed by the common law, fulfilling longer-term investment objectives, and defeating the *Saunders v. Vautier* rule, whereby beneficiaries can come together to conclude the trust and thereby frustrate trust objectives.[37]

Offshore trust provisions that allow greater roles for settlors have sometimes run afoul of the law under the sham rule, despite offshore legislation which sought to prevent sham attacks.[38] The sham rule seeks to invalidate trusts which demonstrate that the settlor retains control over the trust, thereby violating the fundamental rule of trust that it is the trustee who retains discretion and control over the trust. More recent developments, however, illustrate that the sham doctrine is not as great a danger as previously thought. These important decisions have revised the harsh *Rahman* interpretation of the sham concept, which was threatening to overwhelm offshore trusts.[39] The correct interpretation, as demonstrated in *Re Abacus*,[40] is that for a trust to be declared a sham, mere evidence of settlor influence is insufficient. Rather, both the trustees and the settlor must have had a common intention to create a sham. Further, the court found nothing odd about trustees succumbing easily to settlor demands for benefits under the trust, since the trustee should be seeking to preserve a harmonious relationship. Thus, the notion of the unilateral sham is now severely undermined, if not totally discredited. It is unclear, however, to what extent U.S. courts, as opposed to United Kingdom and other courts in the common-law world, will accept the *Re Abacus* analysis, since U.S. courts have been aggressive in declaring offshore trusts to be shams, even treating offshore confidentiality rules as evidence of a sham.[41]

Particular types of offshore trusts are considered below. These special trusts sometimes present unique problems for trust creation.

The Purpose Trust. The flexibility and dynamism of offshore trust law are very evident in the offshore sector's creation of the purpose trust. Such a trust seeks to abolish the rule under orthodox trusts law that a trust must have an identifiable beneficiary. The revolutionary purpose trust holds the trust assets only for a specific purpose, such as to hold shares in a particular company.[42] In fulfilling its commercial objectives, the purpose trust also clarifies problematic issues of equity relating to who are legitimate, identifiable beneficiaries and the nature of the "beneficial purpose" exception. This rule against the absence of identifiable beneficiaries is without real justification in a modern commercial environment.

Purpose trusts are established under special legislation which, along with permitting trusts without identifiable beneficiaries as valid trusts in defiance of the traditional rule, endeavor to solve the accompanying problem of regulating the trust. In an orthodox trust created by equity, it is to the beneficiaries that the trustees must account. Without identifiable beneficiaries, a mechanism must be found to ensure the accountability of the trust generally. Purpose trust legislation overcomes this obstacle by creating a special officer to regulate the trust. In many offshore jurisdictions, this officer is known as the enforcer.[43] The enforcer is regulated by a governmental authority and/or directions from the court. Permitting purpose trusts has had a wide impact internationally. For example, Hayton has recommended such a change for the United Kingdom,[44] and in Canada, law committees are now considering appropriate law reform.[45] This is but one example of the new legal ideas emanating from offshore jurisdictions and being transplanted from offshore to onshore.

Asset Protection Trusts. Offshore trust law has coined the term "asset protection trust" or "creditor protection trust" for trusts that seek to offer more comprehensive protection against potential creditors for assets placed into the trust. While all trusts are set up to preserve assets on some level, it is the degree of preservation that is important here. Such a trust may be viewed as a type of insurance. It seeks to relax or clarify areas of trust law concerning creditors who are not already in existence. Such new legislative norms, however, combined with the greater levels of control typically afforded offshore settlors and the existence of flight and duress clauses,[46] have brought some offshore trusts into contention, particularly with respect to the laws on shams and on fraudulent conveyances, discussed below. Such trusts are approached with caution by many practitioners and some offshore jurisdictions.

Trust Information. The offshore trust, like its other offshore financial law counterparts, is protected by the confidentiality laws of the offshore jurisdiction. One important question is how much information beneficiaries should have where a trust is essentially a commercial enterprise and the beneficiary is unschooled in business, or where the trust is set up to prevent a spendthrift heir from wasting away the assets. Beneficiaries often do not even know of the existence of the trust, given offshore confidentiality laws. Further, confidentiality militates against the thrust toward a generous attitude to information. Offshore legislation attempts to balance these competing needs of accountability, confidentiality, and business efficacy. The traditional view was that the law merely required beneficiaries to have information about accounts or to be informed about the existence of the trust, since the trustee is ultimately accountable to the beneficiaries. In a landmark Privy Council judgment, *Schmidt v. Rosewood Trust Ltd.*,[47] the court found that there was no legal principle which required beneficiaries or any other party to have information on the trust, and that this was a question to be left to the discretion of the court. Thus, beneficiaries who are mere objects of a discretionary trust cannot be automatically excluded from such rights to information, but neither do they have an inherent right or entitlement to such information. The parameters of the court's discretion have yet to be determined, however, and this is an area ripe for juristic clarification. The judgment is a success not only for offshore confidentiality, but for the purposes and functions of offshore trusts.

Fraudulent Conveyances. The reach of offshore financial law to encompass fraudulent conveyancing issues is a good example of how offshore financial law took the uncertainties surrounding traditional trust law with respect to future unidentifiable creditors and trust creation and clarified or modified the law for the benefit of investors.[48] Consequently, under offshore trust law, whether by legislation or precedent, a creditor who was not in existence at the time of the establishment of the trust is not easily harnessed by the law. Many jurisdictions have enacted time limits for the bringing of a claim. The law may also require intent before the claim is proved[49] and may even allow for the survivability of the trust in a successful fraudulent conveyances claim by permitting the settlement of creditors' claims, provided that the trust itself is not voided.[50] The essential principle of fraudulent conveyances remains, however.

Even in the absence of specific fraudulent conveyancing legislation, offshore courts have been clarifying the key questions of who is a legitimate creditor for the purposes of fraudulent conveyancing law. For example, this was seen in the case of *In re Higginbotham's Petition*, which answered in favor of a restrictive interpretation, thereby facilitating the viability of offshore trust creation.[51] Similarly, other cases, even in onshore courts, have placed checks on the boundaries of the concept.[52] There are still, however, important questions to be answered, such as whether and in what circumstances a tax authority can be considered a legitimate creditor under fraudulent conveyancing law. Such a question may well need to be considered under conflict of laws rules, such as the rule against the enforcement of foreign fiscal law, considered further below.

Issues related to frauds and potential frauds, particularly in view of the prevalence of flight and duress clauses in offshore trusts, have served as catalysts for new and more restrictive directions in the principles on restraint orders and the enforcement of judgments. Some courts, even offshore courts, have found a greater risk of the removal of assets or fraud where offshore trusts are involved and, consequently, a greater need for a generous approach to restraint orders, such as worldwide Mareva injunctions and regulation generally.[53] The typical configuration of offshore trusts as self-settled, spendthrift trusts, already vulnerable to sham challenges (discussed earlier), only exacerbates presumptions of fraud.

This discussion has demonstrated that the significant mutations of the traditional trust created by the offshore trust have addressed deficiencies in traditional trust law. While these may raise questions about the appropriate limits and principles of trust law, clearly the offshore trust provides the mechanism to meet the needs of a modern commercial environment. Importantly, such questions provide further opportunities for expanding trust jurisprudence generally and arriving at appropriate balances for trust law.

Conflict of Laws

The offshore sector has sought to clarify existing, and even to create new, conflict of laws rules. This is especially important in relation to trusts, where traditionally few such rules existed, since for innovative trust law principles to survive, the offshore trust must fall under the jurisdiction of the offshore financial law regime rather than the onshore jurisdiction. Further insulation for the trust thus comes from the conflict of laws rules found under offshore financial laws, which preclude enforcement of hostile onshore judgments, provide for exclusive jurisdiction over offshore entities, and facilitate offshore financial law as the proper law. These laws clarify and define considerably the somewhat undeveloped and vague conflict of laws rules for trusts under the common law.[54] Some of these laws have already been tested successfully in the courts, even by onshore courts. For example, in *Green v. Jernigan*,[55] a Canadian court upheld an exclusive jurisdiction law clause used in the formation of an offshore trust in Nevis, where the trust designated Nevis as the exclusive forum. The court found that there must be a "strong cause" to displace such exclusive jurisdiction clauses. Thus, even onshore courts are beginning to respect offshore financial law and practice. In the area of the recognition of trusts, offshore trusts have made a significant impact. The offshore legislative approach of stating clearly that the offshore trust is to be recognized, and to be governed by offshore financial law, should now be regarded as an accepted one.

In particular, offshore trusts are to be recognized under offshore financial law, whether or not the settlor originates from a civil law jurisdiction. Again, this is a difficult issue under onshore law. The difficulty arises because, under traditional trust law, the question of capacity is determined by personal characteristics, such as insanity or residence. Often, trusts created by civil law settlors were not recognized or were transformed into some other similar entity, such as the foundation or a type of contract—a defect that the Hague Convention on the recognition of trusts sought to cure. Offshore legislation clarifies the position and grants or deems capacity to such persons, then declaring that the question of capacity is to be determined by the offshore financial law.[56] Such provisions are further insulated by a holistic legislative regime, which dictates that the capacity question is also to be addressed in conjunction with provisions on the nonenforcement of judgments that may challenge offshore structures.[57] Thus, the offshore approach facilitates the goals of the Hague Convention on Trusts.

These positive outcomes have occurred despite the absence of ratification of the Hague Convention on Trusts in some cases. For example, in the important case of *Casani v. Mattei*,[58] the trust was recognized by an Italian court and, thereby, in the civil law system of Italy. This recognition came even though the trust sought to defeat forced heirship rights in Italy, thereby answering a question which had long been asked in relation to the survivability of anti–forced heirship provisions such as are found in offshore trusts when addressed by civil law courts. The Italian court found that such a trust did not violate public policy and so was not invalid on that ground, particularly where other means could be found to satisfy disappointed heirs. These are significant contributions to trust jurisprudence.[59]

These innovations mean that these legislative solutions to gaps in the law are credible legal solutions for onshore trusts as well, particularly since the offshore sector has sought to be in line with the Hague Convention on Trusts as far as possible. Indeed, I would argue that the offshore trust sector has considerably advanced the existing meager jurisprudence, particularly with regard to the recognition of the trust, capacity, and choice of law. For example, offshore jurisdictions promote the settlor's choice of law as the proper law of the trust, in keeping with the modern position as gleaned from the Hague Convention on Trusts, and gives priority to the autonomy of the settlor and the owner of property. Few courts have pronounced on this emerging issue, but the decisions thus far suggest that this is an appropriate approach.[60] Such judgments are certainly helpful for the viability of offshore financial law, which depends on jurisdiction and proper law issues as initial questions before substantive questions such as the recognition of the trust, capacity, and trust law content can be addressed.

Copycat Support

Perhaps the greatest tribute to be paid to offshore jurisdictions is the fact that they are being copied wholesale by onshore jurisdictions, even by their archenemies. Indeed, the attractiveness of the offshore legal solution and its developmental approach have proved so effective that today even states in the United States have sought to emulate offshore jurisdictions. The legislation enacted by states such as Alabama, Colorado, Delaware, Nevada, and Vermont have introduced trust, banking, insurance, and tax laws that borrow heavily from offshore legal paradigms. They offer similar products to those created by offshore jurisdictions to persons and companies not resident in their states.

The rationale of what I have termed "offshore–onshore regimes" is competition: "If we can't beat them, we will join them." This copycat approach should be welcomed, as it supports the credibility, legitimacy, and viability of the offshore legal approach. Surely, offshore financial law cannot be effectively challenged if onshore states are now redefining their own legal systems so as to incorporate legal concepts previously frowned upon. For example, self-settled, protective trusts are now allowed in such states for nonresident trusts, despite long-standing rules in U.S. courts that such trusts are against U.S. public policy.[61]

And so, while offshore jurisdictions have begun to doubt both themselves and the financial products they have created for economic sustainability, based on sound business and legal principles, those who criticize offshore centers are busy emulating them, putting into place the very financial products they have criticized, including the principles of confidentiality. What better argument do we need for accepting not only that confidentiality, offshore trusts, and IBCs are legitimate and lawful, but that they are great for business and wealth creation? These "onshore–offshore" sectors should be welcomed, for while they are the business competitors' forestablished offshore jurisdictions, they help to legitimize the offshore sector and encourage the movement of its more innovative concepts and products into the mainstream of commerce. This can only aid in wealth creation, as it creates a certain comfort level. In the final analysis, there is no greater testimony to the legitimacy, efficiency, and viability of offshore precepts than their "borrowing" by hostile neighbors.

Conclusion

Offshore modifications of traditional onshore law are gradually entering the mainstream. Slowly, recognition is dawning that offshore financial law, including trust law, captive insurance, and confidentiality, can elevate traditional areas of law found onshore. Offshore legal precepts help to inform, expand, and clarify legal principles that are essential for efficient international commerce. They build upon well-established, traditional principles and cannot easily be challenged for either irrelevancy or inappropriateness. In some cases, as we have seen, legal principles that are noncontentious in

THE LEGITIMACY OF THE OFFSHORE FINANCIAL SECTOR

onshore jurisdictions are treated as controversial and inappropriate and even unlawful by those same jurisdictions when the concepts are used in offshore jurisdictions, with no apparent rationale other than that they challenge the economic superiority of onshore jurisdictions. Such arguments are not sufficient to contest the legitimacy of the offshore financial sector.

3

Regulating Tax Competition in Offshore Financial Centers

Craig M. Boise

One of the more entrenched issues in international taxation over the past thirty years has been the question of how to address tax competition among nations, especially where that competition has benefited offshore financial centers (OFCs), or tax havens, at the perceived expense of onshore jurisdictions.[1] As early as the mid-1950s, onshore jurisdictions began to observe a significant migration of capital from their shores to OFCs, where investment income was lightly taxed or not taxed at all, and where bank confidentiality laws made it difficult for onshore jurisdictions to locate and collect tax on that income.[2] Over the intervening decades, capital flight from onshore jurisdictions to OFCs has increased dramatically, hastened both by the reduction or outright elimination of exchange controls by many countries[3] and by advances in banking and technology that have facilitated the movement of funds around the globe.[4]

Onshore jurisdictions have been particularly concerned about two features of OFCs to which they have attributed their offshore tax evasion problems: low or no income taxation and bank confidentiality. The first has given rise to the accusation by onshore jurisdictions that OFCs are engaged in "tax competition." The second underlies the claim by onshore jurisdictions that such tax competition is "harmful" because it enables (and thus encourages) onshore residents to evade taxes. Based on these concerns, onshore jurisdictions have mounted aggressive efforts to regulate tax competition through both the Organisation for Economic Co-operation and

Development (OECD)[5] and the European Union (EU).[6] Although these efforts have had a tremendous influence on OFCs and their internal policies, they have not had any discernible impact on the migration of onshore capital to offshore jurisdictions.[7]

This chapter explores onshore efforts to regulate international tax competition first by discussing the nature of international taxation and the policy issues it raises. It then examines the definitions of "tax competition" and "harmful tax competition" articulated by the OECD and the EU, respectively, and describes the various arguments asserted both in support of and against regulating international tax competition. This is followed by a summary of the efforts undertaken by the OECD and EU to eliminate tax competition, as they define it. Finally, the chapter draws on the ways the OECD and EU have dealt specifically with the twin touchstones of virtually all definitions of OFCs—low or no income taxation and bank confidentiality—to suggest the direction that attempts to regulate international tax competition should take in the future.

International Income Taxation

The right to impose taxation is a core element of sovereignty that jurisdictions historically have exercised unilaterally. That is, states impose taxes based on their revenue needs and the tolerance of their residents for governmental exactions without regard to the extent of such needs and tolerances in other states.[8] Two principal normative bases for the imposition of income taxes, however, have emerged in international law—residence and source.[9] Residence-based taxation is rooted in a state's sovereignty over its residents. It is a state's assertion of a tax claim on income based on the owner's residence within that state's borders.[10] Source-based taxation derives from a state's sovereignty over its territory and the activities taking place within that territory. It is a state's assertion of a tax claim on income based on the fact that the income putatively arose within that state's borders.[11]

States generally exercise sufficient control over their residents and the income arising within their territorial boundaries to be able to collect both residence- and source-based income taxes. When imposed by an onshore jurisdiction, however, such taxes may be avoided (or evaded) by shifting either the residence of the income recipient or the source of the income to an OFC that imposes no or low income tax.[12] The following sections describe how this is accomplished, first for individuals, then for corporations.

Individuals' Tax Use of OFCs. The prospect of shifting one's residence from an onshore jurisdiction to an OFC to avoid residence-based taxes may be appealing, but doing so is not necessarily easy. First, employment opportunities generally are limited in OFCs.[13] Coupled with social and cultural considerations, this makes physically moving to an OFC out of the question for most individuals.[14] Even for wealthy individuals who do not rely on employment for their income, expatriation to an OFC with fewer amenities and conveniences than are available onshore requires a level of personal sacrifice that may outweigh potential tax advantages. Moreover, many OFCs make it difficult to obtain citizenship or permanent resident status even for those not seeking employment. Thus, individuals are rarely induced to relocate physically to an OFC to avoid onshore residence-based taxation.

Much more common are schemes by individuals in onshore jurisdictions to shift assets that produce passive income (such as cash and securities) to bank accounts or trusts organized in OFCs, which typically do not tax such income. Although countries (like the United States) that impose "worldwide" taxation[15] (as well as many countries that impose "territorial" taxation) still generally require the beneficial owner of passive income earned in an OFC to report and pay tax on it,[16] many individuals choose instead to illegally evade taxation, relying on complex layering structures and the bank confidentiality laws of the OFC to prevent onshore jurisdictions from discovering their offshore income.

So whether the onshore jurisdiction in which an individual resides imposes worldwide or territorial taxation, an OFC's no- or low-tax regime generally is beneficial only in those cases of actual expatriation to an OFC, or when an individual illegally evades onshore taxation by failing to report offshore sources of income.

Corporate Tax Use of OFCs. By contrast to individuals, corporations may make beneficial tax use of an OFC without physically relocating to the OFC or committing tax evasion. This is because most onshore jurisdictions consider a corporation resident, for tax purposes, in the jurisdiction in which it was organized, or from which it is managed and controlled, regardless of whether the corporation's assets or activities are located there.[17] The practical effect of this nearly universal onshore approach to defining corporate residence is to make both residence- and source-based taxation largely elective for most corporations.

To avoid *residence-based* taxation, a new business venture may simply be operated through a newly organized corporation in an OFC from the outset.[18] An established onshore corporation may be able to accomplish the same objective by reincorporating in, or moving its management and control functions to, an OFC.[19] To avoid *source-based* taxation of income earned in an onshore jurisdiction, a foreign corporation might conduct its branch activities, such as sales and the provision of services, through a subsidiary organized, and thus resident, in an OFC.[20] Similarly, where onshore assets (such as cash, trademarks, and copyrights) generate income subject to source-based taxation, that tax may be avoided by transferring the assets to a subsidiary organized in an OFC.[21] A related and even more serious tax avoidance strategy involves shifting profits from intangible assets out of onshore jurisdictions and into OFCs through manipulation of transfer pricing,[22] a practice that has increased dramatically in recent years, particularly among pharmaceutical and technology companies.[23]

Opportunities like these for tax avoidance or evasion (along with streamlined regulatory structures)[24] have created tremendous demand for OFCs and made them quite successful in attracting investment capital at the expense of the tax revenues of onshore jurisdictions. Through their proxies, the OECD and the EU, onshore jurisdictions have responded aggressively to stanch the offshore flow of capital by attempting to regulate "tax competition" that they deem "harmful." We next explore how the OECD and the EU have defined these critical terms.

Defining Tax Competition

Competition can be defined as "the effort of two or more parties acting independently to secure the business of a third party by offering the most favorable terms."[25] This suggests that tax competition, properly defined, would involve OFCs' reducing their income tax rates to secure the migration of onshore capital to their shores. The definitions employed by the OECD and the EU, however, are more complicated.

The OECD's Definition of Tax Competition. The most widely publicized recent effort to define and regulate international tax competition was undertaken in 1996 by the OECD.[26] The OECD's involvement with OFC issues began in the 1970s with its drafting of a model agreement on exchange of taxpayer information. Based on that experience, in 1977 the OECD issued a mandate to its Committee on Fiscal Affairs to strengthen detection and prevention of international tax avoidance and evasion.[27] A discussion followed over the next several years about the scope of this mandate and the precise definitions of tax avoidance and tax evasion. Ten years later, at the urging of Group of Seven (G-7) country representatives, the OECD published a key study on the subject.[28]

The first part of the four-part 1987 study addressed the problem of international tax avoidance and evasion through "tax havens." It first defined "classical tax havens" as jurisdictions actively making themselves available for the avoidance of tax that otherwise would be paid in high-tax countries.[29] Then, borrowing heavily from an earlier U.S. report,[30] the 1987 study identified as tax havens those jurisdictions having relatively low rates of tax; high levels of bank or commercial secrecy; disproportionately large financial sectors; modern communications facilities; the absence of currency controls on foreign deposits of foreign currencies; and self-promotion as offshore financial centers.[31]

In 1996, a communiqué issued by its ministers called upon the OECD to expand its investigation of the tax haven issue and, in particular, to develop measures to "counter the distorting effects of harmful tax competition on investment and financing decisions and the consequences for national tax bases."[32] This request was endorsed by the heads of state of the G-7 countries,[33] who stated, in their own communiqué to the OECD, "Tax schemes aimed at attracting financial and other geographically mobile activities can create harmful tax competition between States, carrying risks of distorting trade and investment and could lead to the erosion of national tax bases."[34]

Two years later, in 1998, the OECD responded with a report which, surprisingly, contained minimal empirical analysis of its member countries' claims regarding either the existence or extent of international tax competition.[35] Instead, the report summarily asserted that certain countries had exploited the globalization phenomenon by "developing tax policies aimed primarily at diverting *financial and other geographically mobile capital.*"[36] In thus describing the problem, the 1998 report simply ignored tax competition for *nongeographically mobile capital*—the sort of tax competition that onshore jurisdictions engage in—choosing instead to address only tax competition from jurisdictions having significant financial and other service activities. The OECD's definition of tax competition, then, successfully shifted the principal focus of its inquiry to the activities of nonmember countries, and specifically OFCs.

The 1998 report described three types of regimes under which lower taxes might be levied on geographically mobile income than the tax levied by another country, and then identified two of those regimes as embodying the harmful tax competition problem. The first type of regime, termed a "tax haven," was described as a jurisdiction in which no or only nominal tax is imposed on geographically mobile income, and which "offers itself, or is perceived to offer itself, as a place to be used by non-residents to escape tax in their country of residence."[37] In addition, the report concluded that tax havens generally have bank or other secrecy rules, lack legislative, legal, or administrative transparency, and impose no requirement that substantial activities be carried out in the jurisdiction in connection with the investment of mobile capital.[38]

The second type of regime identified by the OECD, a "harmful preferential tax regime," is one that imposes a general income tax but qualifies the application of that tax with preferential features that result in geographically mobile income being effectively subjected to low or no taxation.[39] The report stated that a harmful preferential tax regime is also characterized by the existence of "ring-fencing,"[40] along with a lack of transparency and of effective exchange of information. The OECD acknowledged that harmful preferential tax regimes could exist in OECD member countries, but, as discussed below, it treated member countries with harmful preferential tax regimes more favorably than nonmember "tax haven" jurisdictions.

In short, the 1998 report made clear that the OECD was principally concerned with the use of low tax rates to attract geographically mobile capital.[41] The OECD's close identification of nonmember OFCs with harmful tax competition ultimately presented credibility problems for the organization, because many member countries were engaged in the same sort of activity that was deemed harmful when it involved nonmember OFCs.

The EU's Definition of Harmful Tax Competition. While the globalization of the world economy highlighted the issue of tax competition for the OECD, the problem was brought into focus in the case of the EU by its efforts to provide for the free movement of goods, persons, services, and capital among its member states.[42] In a communiqué issued in 1974, the European Commission observed a problem of "international tax evasion and avoidance." In a follow-up to the communiqué, in 1975 the Council of the European Union adopted a resolution that noted that tax evasion and tax avoidance practices "reaching beyond national borders of member states lead to budget losses, violations of the principle of fiscal Justice and distortions of capital movements and conditions of competition."[43] The council resolution went on to recommend adoption of various measures for combating international tax evasion and avoidance, including mutual information exchange between member states in cases "where transactions are carried out between undertakings in two Member States through a third country in order to obtain tax advantages."[44]

A number of factors, including a country's stability, infrastructure, markets, workforce, financial capabilities, and rates of taxation, drive decisions about where to invest. As the development of the EU harmonized many of these factors among member states, however, taxation—and, in particular, direct taxation (that is, taxes on income and corporations)—became an increasingly important point of differentiation. The European Community treaty requires that member states harmonize their national legislation relating to "indirect taxes" (for example, value-added taxes and excise duties), but it contains no such requirement with respect to direct taxes.[45] Thus, EU member states began to compete for relatively mobile economic activity (for example, financial services, capital, insurance, and the provision of intangibles) by reducing taxes applicable to such activity.

In 1997, the European Council responded by adopting a "code of conduct" for business taxation designed to curb "harmful" tax measures.[46] The code is directed solely at business taxation and applies to tax "laws or regulations and administrative practices" that "provide for a significantly lower effective level of taxation, including zero taxation, than those levels which generally apply in the Member State in question."[47] The European Council also asked the European Commission to propose a directive on the taxation of interest income within the EU to "prevent undesirable distortion of competition."[48] The result was a June 2003 directive that highlighted the EU's concern with bank confidentiality in OFCs. The directive required member states, as of July 2005, either to breach their bank confidentiality rules and provide information on interest payments made from their jurisdictions to individuals in other member states, or to levy a withholding tax on interest payments made to individuals resident in other member states and transfer 75 percent of the revenue from the tax to the investor's state of residence.[49]

The EU's definition of harmful tax competition, which is implicit in the terms of the code of conduct and the savings tax directive, is similar to the OECD's definition. Like the OECD, the EU has focused on jurisdictions having no or low income taxation of geographically mobile capital—in particular, interest from savings—and, through the savings tax directive, on bank confidentiality. By defining "harmful tax competition" in essentially the same terms as did the OECD, the EU also effectively limited its regulation of tax competition to the tax regimes of OFCs.

Arguments for Regulating OFC Tax Competition

Having defined tax competition in a manner that targeted OFCs, onshore jurisdictions have sought to regulate such competition through the OECD and EU based on a number of arguments, some of which follow.

Tax Competition Is Economically Inefficient. Onshore jurisdictions argue that, from a global welfare standpoint, tax competition is economically inefficient. Consider hypothetical states X and Y, each of which imposes tax on capital income at a rate of 30 percent. State X, an onshore jurisdiction, has a large, well-developed economy that produces $1,000 of taxable income each year, resulting in annual tax revenue of $300. By contrast, State Y, an OFC, is small and poorly developed and produces only $100 of income per year, resulting in annual tax collections of $30. If State Y reduces its income tax rate to 10 percent to attract capital from State X and is successful in siphoning off half of that state's annual income ($500),

State Y's tax revenues will increase by 100 percent to $60. State X, however, will lose half its tax revenue, collecting only $150 per year. More importantly, states X and Y together will lose tax revenue of $120 (collecting a combined $210 instead of $330), making State Y's tax competition scheme inefficient from a global welfare perspective. In this exaggerated example, a $30 direct transfer payment from State X to State Y would achieve the same result for State Y with an overall tax revenue loss of only $30.

Of course, the inefficiency argument is persuasive only if one accepts the premise that efficiency should be viewed from the perspective of global welfare. In a world of sovereign states having divergent national interests, efficiency is not always so viewed. State Y acts rationally in setting its tax policy to promote its interest in collecting more tax revenue, as opposed to promoting some nebulous concept of global economic efficiency. After all, State Y politicians are evaluated and either reelected or voted out of office based on the benefits they have conferred on State Y citizens; they are unlikely to be particularly responsive to concerns about maximizing global welfare. Similarly, while State X might elect to reduce the impact of State Y's tax competition by making a voluntary transfer payment to State Y, it is easier to respond to the latter's actions by imposing sanctions or other punitive measures on it.

Diversion of Capital and Investment. A key assumption underlying the economic efficiency argument is that State Y's lower income tax rates attract net capital investment away from State X. If an OFC provides a location for holding passive investments or for booking "paper" profits but serves no other substantive purpose, we can presume that the diverted investment was made to take advantage of the OFC's low- or no-tax regime. Indeed, in the taxonomy of the OECD and the EU, an identifying factor for "tax havens" is the lack of any requirement that substantial activities be carried out in the jurisdiction in connection with the investment of mobile capital.[50] Although this conclusion seems intuitively correct, some economists have argued that the presence of an OFC within the same region as an onshore jurisdiction may actually facilitate, and thus increase, net capital investment in the onshore jurisdiction.[51]

Moreover, an OFC may attract capital offshore for other reasons. It might seek to attract more substantive investment from other countries by offering, in addition to low tax rates, a cheaper workforce or less governmental regulation than in onshore jurisdictions, perhaps even requiring that some quantum of activity be performed in the jurisdiction. Here the argument against tax competition is more difficult to make, as the OECD's 1998 report acknowledges:

> The determination of when and whether an activity is substantial can be difficult. For example, financial and management services may in certain circumstances involve substantial activities. However, certain services provided by "paper companies" may be readily found to lack substance.[52]

In other words, the diversion of capital and investment is apparently permissible so long as some vague quantum of "substantive" activity is present.

And yet this concession seems fatal to the diversion of capital argument itself. Why "substantial activity" in an OFC—even if that concept could be objectively defined—should make diversion of capital and investment permissible is not clear. The difficulty with the diversion argument is that it is not normatively compelling in and of itself. To justify regulation, tax competition arguably must be harmful for some reason other than that it simply diverts investment from one location to another. The following arguments begin to get at the substantive objections to tax competition.

Tax Base Erosion. The OECD and the EU both assert that diversion of capital offshore erodes the tax bases of onshore jurisdictions. Thus, an OFC arguably has harmed an onshore jurisdiction to the extent that competition-induced offshore migration of capital has reduced the onshore jurisdiction's welfare. As the OECD's 1998 report puts it, the tax revenue associated with mobile capital that "rightly" belongs to one country is effectively hijacked or "poached" by another.[53] In the United States, it is estimated that taxpayers utilize offshore tax havens to hold more than $1 trillion in assets and annually evade between $40 billion and $70 billion in U.S. tax liability.[54]

Tax base erosion by OFCs has potentially damaging secondary effects on onshore fiscal policy. When an onshore jurisdiction must forgo tax revenue as a result of capital and investment diverted to an OFC, that revenue must be replaced from other sources. The onshore jurisdiction may choose to impose higher rates of tax either on the capital that remains in its tax base or on other, less mobile factors, such as labor and consumption. In all probability, the latter option will be chosen, since the former likely will only exacerbate the offshore flight of capital. At some point, however, it becomes politically infeasible to continue to raise payroll tax rates and taxes on consumption. At that point, the onshore jurisdiction will either increase government borrowing to finance outlays for public goods, including social programs, or it will eliminate those programs. Reuven Avi-Yonah has termed this dilemma the "fiscal crisis of the welfare state."[55] Thus, tax competition has the potential to require onshore jurisdictions to recalibrate their fiscal policies in an environment where there may be few acceptable alternatives for raising revenue.[56]

The "Free Rider" Problem. Another argument for eliminating tax competition is that it may result in a "free rider" problem within onshore jurisdictions competing with OFCs. Put simply, the free rider problem reflects the basic tendency of individuals in a group to let others take (or pay for) actions that will benefit the entire group.[57] Where the affected group is small, members generally are more accountable to one another, and securing cooperation from each member in sharing the cost of group benefits is less problematic.[58] As group size increases, however, each member has relatively greater anonymity and less accountability to others. If a member allows others to incur the costs of actions beneficial to the group, he or she may obtain a benefit without a corresponding contribution.

This phenomenon is magnified in the context of governments' provision of societal goods.[59] Governments impose taxes to finance public goods like national defense, education, social security, and transportation infrastructure. Tax competition from OFCs may encourage some residents of onshore jurisdictions (generally those members with the greatest resources) to move their wealth to OFCs to minimize or avoid taxation, and hence shift their share of the cost of the public good to others. To the extent that such residents remain in the onshore jurisdiction, they unfairly benefit from the societal goods underwritten by tax dollars without making adequate contribution to the cost of those goods.[60]

Reduction in Income Tax Progressivity. Closely related to the free rider problem is the potential for tax competition to reduce progressivity within the tax systems of onshore jurisdictions, a feature of those systems that generally is considered desirable.[61] The base of an income tax typically includes income from capital. Because the wealthy possess more capital than the poor, an income tax is more progressive than a tax that excludes income from capital (such as a consumption or payroll tax). If corporations and wealthy residents of onshore jurisdictions are able to shift their capital income to OFCs, however, a greater portion of the onshore tax burden is borne by labor and other immobile factors, and progressivity is reduced.[62]

One historic justification for progressive taxation is that the wealthy within a society have a disproportionately greater interest in preserving the public goods financed by taxation, since the absence of those goods would result in greater loss to the wealthy than to the poor.[63] This argument is distinguishable from the argument in the previous section that the wealthy should merely bear the same share of the cost of public goods as other members of society. Perversely, however, the nature of offshore tax competition is such that only the wealthiest members of society are able to benefit from it. To the extent that tax competition reduces progressivity, it *disproportionately* reduces the tax burden on the wealthy.[64]

Increases in Tax Administration Costs. A reduction in the progressivity of income taxation within a high-tax jurisdiction has secondary effects, as well. As taxpayers within the society perceive that some members are able, by virtue of their greater wealth, to avoid or significantly reduce their tax burdens, overall compliance with tax laws is likely to be undermined.[65] As tax competition reduces voluntary tax compliance, onshore jurisdictions are forced to bear greater administrative costs to collect the same amount of tax revenue. Moreover, as additional base-preserving safeguards are put in place, the costs of compliance with the onshore jurisdiction's tax system become ever greater.

Arguments against Regulating OFC Tax Competition

For each of the arguments marshaled by the OECD and EU in support of regulating tax competition, an equally persuasive countervailing argument is asserted by OFCs accused of engaging in harmful tax competition. The following are some of these arguments.

Infringement of National Tax Sovereignty. The setting of tax rates and the establishing of tax policy in general have long been viewed as essential prerogatives of national governments. Intrusion upon a state's tax sovereignty is therefore viewed as intolerable.[66] It is not surprising, then, that OFCs objected strenuously to the OECD's 1998 report and to the recommendations and subsequent actions undertaken by the OECD to regulate tax competition.[67] Jurisdictions singled out as tax havens by the report objected that the onshore jurisdictions that comprised the OECD were wielding their substantial economic clout to bully OFCs into compliance with a set of norms they had no part in formulating. OFCs viewed this as an infringement of their rights to develop and implement their own economic and tax policies.

Arguably, a sovereign nation has the right to set its own tax policy, even if that tax policy is predatory with respect to another jurisdiction. A common misperception, however, is that in exercising their sovereignty in the tax arena, OFCs purposely set out to undermine the income tax regimes of onshore jurisdictions by abandoning income taxation themselves.[68]

Most OFCs possess two distinctive features that informed the historical development of their tax policies. First, they tend to be relatively small in terms of geography, population, and economic activity. The OECD initially identified forty-one countries that met its criteria as tax havens.[69] The combined landmass of those forty-one countries is less than that of New Zealand, as is their combined gross domestic product (GDP).[70] The combined population of the forty-one tax havens is less than the population of the state of Illinois.[71] Second, most OFCs are located on islands or are otherwise geographically isolated in ways that onshore jurisdictions are not.

Taken together, OFCs' small size and relative isolation make the imposition of an income tax typical of those employed in onshore jurisdictions a highly inefficient means of extracting fiscal resources. Government services in an OFC are relatively inexpensive to provide and do not require the vast outlays typical in onshore jurisdictions. An OFC government generally is able to meet its financial needs with the revenue generated by levying duties on imported goods.[72] Moreover, as most OFCs are islands, it is relatively simple to minimize tax leakage—tax officials need only monitor the offloading of vessels delivering goods to the jurisdiction. Enterprising smugglers occasionally may manage to avoid customs duties by landing goods in remote island harbors at night, but the system generally works well and is much more efficient than an income tax system with its extensive printing, reporting, auditing, and recordkeeping requirements.

Another consequence of the system of customs duties relied upon by many OFCs for revenue is that the government collects very little financial and related information about its citizens. Without the returns required by a system of income taxation, the government will not possess records of the amount, type, and source of an individual's income, his deductible expenditures, bank account information, and so on. It is not surprising that those accustomed to such a system would object to being involved in the collection of this kind of information about foreign taxpayers conducting activities within the OFC.

In short, OFCs object strongly to onshore jurisdictions' attempts to regulate the rates and types of tax they impose. The decision not to tax income has been taken on the basis of a thoughtful balancing of the OFC's revenue needs against the costs of administering various systems of taxation. OFCs view regulation of such decisions as a gross imposition on internal tax sovereignty and onshore jurisdictions' insistence on such regulation as bullying.

Resistance to Assisting Onshore Jurisdictions to Collect Taxes. A related and keen point of contention between onshore jurisdictions and OFCs is the issue of bank confidentiality. In most OFCs, banks are legally prohibited from disclosing any information about bank account holders and their banking transactions to third parties, including the tax enforcement authorities of other countries, except in certain limited circumstances. Failure to comply with the bank confidentiality laws generally subjects the party disclosing the information to criminal penalties in the tax haven jurisdiction.[73] Ironically, bank confidentiality in most OFCs has its origins in the common law of Commonwealth countries.[74] Statutory bank confidentiality in the Cayman Islands,[75] for example, rests on the landmark case *Tournier v. National Provincial and Union Bank of England*,[76] in which a British court of appeals held that the relationship of banker and customer gave rise to a duty of confidentiality.

Although bank confidentiality did not evolve as a tax policy issue, it has become closely entwined with tax policy because of its use by taxpayers to screen evasion transactions from tax authorities in onshore jurisdictions.[77]

OFCs generally resent attempts by onshore jurisdictions to dilute their bank confidentiality laws and argue that the use of bank confidentiality by tax evaders is an issue to be dealt with by the jurisdiction attempting to enforce its income tax rules. Nonetheless, bank confidentiality in most OFCs is not absolute; it is subject to statutory or common-law exceptions,[78] as well as to the provisions of mutual legal assistance treaties (MLATs) and tax information exchange agreements (TIEAs). OFCs supply information to onshore jurisdictions about bank customers whenever a request is made under an MLAT or TIEA, notwithstanding that compliance with these requests requires the expenditure of significant (and often scarce) OFC resources.

Objections to "Ownership" Claims on the Capital Income Tax Base. OFCs also object to arguments that, to the extent they attract capital from onshore jurisdictions, they are "poaching" a tax base that "rightly" belongs to the onshore jurisdictions.[79] Tax havens view themselves as developing countries competing with the rest of the world for capital investment. They see no rational basis for an onshore jurisdiction's a priori tax claims on capital that its owners elect to employ elsewhere.[80]

Competition Fosters Efficient Government Taxation and Spending Policies. In the 1950s, the influential and well-known economist Charles Tiebout developed a theory of local public goods provision. Tiebout asserted that governmental jurisdictions offer varying packages of public goods, whether those jurisdictions be nations or national subdivisions such as states, cities, and counties. He argued that as consumers select from among those jurisdictions the ones that offer public goods most closely matching their own preferences, competition among jurisdictions emerges, thus creating a market that leads to near-optimal outcomes.[81]

A number of economists have expanded Tiebout's theory to apply to tax competition.[82] They argue that consumers (or their mobile capital) will migrate from onshore jurisdictions with high rates of tax on income to jurisdictions like OFCs having lower tax rates. This migration will continue until either the level of public goods provided by OFCs fails to satisfy consumer needs or the cost of the public goods provided by onshore jurisdictions (reflected in their tax rates) is reduced to a level closer to that of OFCs, thus producing efficient outcomes. The Tiebout hypothesis is intuitively appealing, but economic models applying it to tax competition have been questioned, particularly where competition produces so-called fiscal externalities—situations in which the public policies of one jurisdiction affect the budget of another.[83]

Tax Competition and the "Level Playing Field." OFCs frequently seek to attract mobile capital because economically they are not on an equal footing with most onshore jurisdictions. In many cases, the only strategic advantage OFCs possess in the global competition for capital is their tax sovereignty. Exercising that sovereignty by preserving a regime with low taxes or no taxes at all potentially helps OFCs level the playing field by increasing the revenues they receive from the fixed fees and customs duties paid by offshore investors, creating greater employment opportunities for their residents and expanding tourism and other related industries. Regulating tax competition strips OFCs of an important means of overcoming their inherent geographic, resource, and size limitations.

OFCs also believe that the playing field is not level with respect to the regulation of tax competition itself. The OECD's 1998 report recommended that member countries identify and remove their own harmful preferential tax regimes by April 2003. Nonmember OFCs, however, were required to commit to eliminating their harmful tax practices by July 2001, nearly two years before member countries, to avoid imposition of sanctions.[84] Moreover, the 1998 report principally targeted geographically mobile activities, which disproportionately affected OFCs and did not take into account the sort of "tax incentives designed to attract investment in plant, building and equipment" employed by onshore jurisdictions.[85] Further, the report did not address the tax treatment of interest on cross-border savings instruments, an exclusion that benefited onshore jurisdictions like the United States that compete for foreign debt investment by exempting outbound portfolio interest flows from withholding or other income taxation.[86] Similarly, the EU's regulation of tax competition applied only to tax on interest payments, which comprise a tiny fraction of all types of income, but which disproportionately affect OFCs.

In response to the inequities of the OECD's approach to regulating tax competition, OFCs called for a process in which "uniform rules, developed in an inclusive process are implemented by all states, on the same time frame, with the same consequences for [all] states," and for rejection of the "imposition of more onerous 'compliance requirements' exclusively on non-OECD Member countries."[87]

Regulating International Tax Competition

Having purported to define tax havens and the "harmful tax competition" in which they were engaged, both the OECD and the EU undertook to regulate such tax competition, albeit in different ways.

The OECD. The OECD's regulatory efforts began with recommendations set forth in the 1998 report and continued through a series of progress reports released over the following six years. Initially, the 1998 report encouraged countries whose tax bases had been eroded by harmful preferential tax regimes or tax havens to unilaterally implement defensive measures against OFCs.[88] The 1998 report also noted, however, that "coordinated defensive measures" applied "by a wide number of countries in a similar manner" would be more effective, and the OECD ultimately adopted this approach in its 2000 progress report.[89] Coordinated defensive measures against uncooperative OFCs included enhancing audit and enforcement activities, disallowing deductions, exemptions, credits, or other allowances related to transactions with them, requiring comprehensive information reporting rules for such transactions, and imposing withholding taxes on payments to their residents.

The OECD's 2000 progress report listed thirty-five OFCs that were found to satisfy the tax haven criteria described in the 1998 report, but it specified that a list to be used as the basis for coordinated defensive measures would not be published until July 2001.[90] The list ultimately was issued in November 2001 as part of a progress report, which, by contrast to earlier reports, stressed cooperation between the OECD and nonmember countries in eliminating harmful tax practices.[91] The report's recommendations seemed almost conciliatory—no doubt influenced by two events occurring after the release of the earlier reports.

First, in mid-2001, U.S. support for the OECD's anti-OFC initiative was rather abruptly withdrawn under the new administration of President George W. Bush. Second, following the release of the tax haven list that was part of the 2000 progress report, the OECD committee entered a busy period of negotiations with countries that anticipated being designated as tax havens but wished to avoid the "uncooperative tax haven" label.[92] The ensuing dialogue between the OECD members and the tax haven jurisdictions resulted in the OECD's "having a better understanding of the concerns of the jurisdictions regarding the commitment process and participation in the harmful tax practices work."[93] Accordingly, the OECD decided that the coordinated defensive measures against tax havens promised in the 2000 progress report would not apply to uncooperative tax havens any earlier than such measures would apply to OECD member countries with harmful preferential tax regimes.[94]

The next development, a 2001 progress report, committed the OECD to the creation of a framework for applying the coordinated defensive measures against uncooperative tax havens that had been threatened since the 1998 report. The framework would provide, first, that defensive measures be proportionate and targeted at neutralizing the deleterious effects of harmful tax practices. Second, defensive measures would be adopted only at the discretion of each country. Third, each country would be free to choose to enforce the defensive measures in a manner that would be proportionate and prioritized according to the degree of harm potentially inflicted by the harmful tax practices.[95]

The 2001 progress report also extended, until the end of February 2002, the deadline for OFCs to commit to eliminating harmful tax practices and be excluded from the uncooperative tax havens list.[96] To be removed from the list, an OFC was required to commit to *transparency* and the *effective exchange of information*.[97] The commitment to transparency meant that, first, the jurisdiction's tax system would not have nontransparent features like "secret" tax rulings or negotiated tax rates; second, the jurisdiction would require entities to keep financial accounts in accordance with generally accepted accounting principles; and, third, the jurisdiction would have access to ownership information for all types of entities and to bank information that might be relevant to civil and criminal tax matters.[98]

The effective exchange of information commitment required that, first, the jurisdiction have a legal mechanism in place to allow information to be given to a tax authority of another country in response to a request for information that might be relevant to a specific tax inquiry; second, the jurisdiction have in place appropriate safeguards within the process to ensure that such sensitive information would be used only for the purposes for which it was sought; third, the jurisdiction exchange the information regardless of whether the conduct being investigated would be a crime under its laws; and fourth, the jurisdiction have administrative practices in place to ensure that the exchange of information mechanism would function effectively.[99]

When the OECD's uncooperative tax haven list was finally completed in April 2002, only seven jurisdictions were left of the thirty-five included on the original list. The uncooperative tax havens on the 2002 list were Andorra, Liechtenstein, Liberia, Monaco, the Marshall Islands, Nauru, and Vanuatu.[100] The list was followed by the release of yet another progress report in 2004,[101] which disclosed that the list of uncooperative tax havens had been whittled down to just five jurisdictions, after Vanuatu and Nauru made commitments in 2003 to transparency and information exchange.[102] At this point, the OECD had made remarkable progress in getting OFC jurisdictions (now fondly referred to as "participating partners"),[103] to agree to abolish harmful tax practices.

Given that so many OFCs had made commitments, the OECD began work on a process to assist committed jurisdictions to comply with its transparency and effective exchange of information requirements. The OECD created an Informal Contact Group to encourage dialogue between the committed countries and the OECD Forum on these requirements.[104] In addition to facilitating dialogue, the OECD published a model agreement for the effective exchange of information to promote international cooperation and provide a structure for such cooperation.[105] The OECD Forum also chartered the Joint Ad Hoc Group on Accounts to develop common standards of transparency.[106]

The 2004 progress report effectively marked the end of the OECD's efforts to regulate international tax competition. What began as an aggressive attempt to force OFCs to conform to a set of standards established by the onshore jurisdictions of the OECD without consultation with the OFCs themselves ended as a largely conciliatory effort to obtain OFCs' agreement to a relatively modest program of transparency and information exchange.[107]

The EU. The EU's regulation of tax competition has been far less comprehensive than that undertaken by the OECD. The European Council has directed its efforts specifically toward taxation of interest payments[108] in an effort to ensure "a minimum of effective taxation of savings [interest] income within the Community."[109] To this end, it requested in 1997 that the European Commission propose a directive on the taxation of interest income. The result was a proposed directive under which a member state would disclose any interest payments made to a resident of another member state to ensure that the interest was declared in the recipient's country of residence.[110] The directive also anticipated that non-EU countries would agree to disclose information about interest earned by EU residents.[111]

Under this approach, State X (whether or not an EU member state) would be required to disclose to State Y any interest paid by a State X payor to a State Y resident so that State Y could tax the payment. Information reporting would not, of course, resolve the potential for tax evasion that would arise if the State Y resident were to arrange for the interest payment to be made to a bank account he controlled in an OFC. If the OFC had bank confidentiality laws, they would preclude State X from discovering that the State Y resident was the beneficial owner of the account and the interest payment. Indeed, Austria, Belgium, and Luxembourg all objected to the proposed directive on the grounds that their bank confidentiality laws prohibited disclosure of interest payment recipients.[112]

Although this presented a real dilemma for the EU, the final savings tax directive dealt with the problem by requiring most member states to provide information on interest payments made by paying agents established in their jurisdictions to individual residents of other member states.[113] Austria, Belgium, and Luxembourg, however, were permitted to comply with the information-sharing provision at a later date. In the interim they were required to withhold tax on interest payments made to individual residents of other member states and transfer 75 percent of the revenue from the withholding tax to the investor's state of residence (as non-EU states were permitted to do).[114]

Directions for the Future

As noted earlier in this chapter, onshore jurisdictions are concerned that OFCs attract capital offshore by not taxing income, or by taxing income at very low rates. Onshore jurisdictions characterize this phenomenon as a form of "tax competition" which, when combined with OFCs' bank confidentiality laws, becomes "harmful." Hence, the two recurring elements in onshore (OECD and EU) definitions of "tax havens" or "harmful tax competition" are low or no income taxation and bank confidentiality. The above examination of the ways in which the OECD and EU have attempted to address these two characteristics of OFCs leads to a couple of conclusions about the direction that regulation of international tax competition is likely to take next.

First, onshore jurisdictions are not likely to be successful either in eliminating low rates of income taxation in OFCs or in requiring a minimum level of income taxation in an OFC that has none. Indeed, both the OECD and the EU have made clear on numerous occasions that individual states should have the prerogative to determine their own tax policies,[115] and the Gordon report, on which the OECD relied in formulating the definition of tax haven contained in its 1987 study,[116] conceded that tax policies of OFCs frequently are established for legitimate reasons having nothing to do with tax competition.[117]

Nonetheless, the OECD and EU have persistently made low or no income taxation the sine qua non of their definitions of both "tax haven" and jurisdictions engaged in "harmful tax competition."[118] The OECD's 1987 study defined as a tax haven any jurisdiction "actively making itself available as a tax haven for avoidance of tax which would otherwise be paid in relatively high tax countries."[119] It is not clear what an OFC does to "actively make itself available" or how doing so converts a legitimate tax regime to one that essentially aids and abets tax avoidance by residents of high-tax countries, but the implication is that regimes with no income tax are bad.[120]

As noted earlier in this chapter, to dictate to a country what forms or rates of taxation to impose is an attack on sovereignty at a fundamental level, and is not likely to foster cooperation by OFCs. OFCs will continue to resist attempts to regulate international tax competition and the tax evasion it may engender so long as onshore jurisdictions' first response to domestic tax evasion problems is to undermine the sovereignty of OFCs by attacking their decisions about the forms and rates of taxation they deem appropriate. This sort of imperialist response is uncomfortably similar to the way that onshore jurisdictions have often dealt with other domestic problems that are affected by the developing world.[121] OFCs are correct in demanding that onshore jurisdictions pay more than lip service to their right to set their own tax policies.

Second, whether their efforts are successful or not, onshore jurisdictions likely will continue periodically to attempt to regulate international tax competition so long as OFCs retain bank confidentiality laws. OFCs zealously guard their right to require confidentiality in financial matters, and, for some, bank confidentiality is a core value. Just as OFCs insist that onshore jurisdictions recognize their right to set appropriate domestic tax policy, however, they also must acknowledge that principles of sovereignty permit onshore jurisdictions to act cooperatively to protect their income tax bases. Onshore jurisdictions perceive OFC bank confidentiality as the principal threat to the integrity of residence-based taxation.[122] They see OFCs effectively functioning as "black boxes" that shield from view the real beneficial owners of mobile capital, and thwart attempts by onshore jurisdictions to impose residence- and source-based tax on the income such mobile capital produces. Consequently, onshore jurisdictions likely will continue to use the leverage of coordinated sanctions—or the threat of such sanctions—to chip away at confidentiality laws in OFC jurisdictions.

The manner in which the OECD has addressed the issue of confidentiality is likely to be unsatisfactory to both onshore jurisdictions and OFCs. As discussed above, the organization has secured "commitments" from most OFCs it identified as "tax havens" to adopt effective exchange of information policies.[123] These commitments were obtained, however, by presenting OFCs with an ultimatum to comply with a set of demands formulated by OECD member countries without OFC input or participation. There was no consensus between OFCs and the OECD regarding whether tax competition was even a problem, and certainly no confluence of objectives in addressing it. OFCs that did not comply with the OECD's tax competition mandate were threatened with a range of sanctions to be applied in a coordinated manner by OECD member countries. This created ill will that likely will have a significant half-life. Only after OFCs objected strongly and the United States withdrew its support did the OECD seek input from OFCs, limit its demands, and begin working cooperatively to address the harmful tax competition problem.

Securing information exchange commitments from virtually all OFCs appears to have been a successful denouement to the OECD anti–tax haven initiative. There is scant substance in the commitments made by OFCs, however. The essence of an information exchange commitment is an OFC's agreement to respond to requests for information relevant to specific tax inquiries from onshore jurisdictions.[124] An onshore jurisdiction must first discover that one of its residents has engaged in tax evasion and then determine which OFC jurisdiction was used to facilitate that evasion before it may make a request for information from the OFC and expect a response. This backward-looking arrangement does little to ensure the integrity of residence-based taxation on a prospective basis.

In contrast to the OECD, the EU has been more successful in eliminating confidentiality through its savings tax directive. As described above, the directive requires most EU member states to provide information to one another regarding the identity of persons receiving interest payments. This type of forward-looking information exchange permits residence countries to appropriately tax interest payments made through OFCs. Moreover, to the extent all member states agree to such information sharing, the all-important "level playing field" is created among competing jurisdictions.

Of course, a critical difference between the OECD and the EU is that the former lacks the authority to compel even member countries to comply with its policies.[125] Without such authority (and in the absence of consensus), OECD member countries are free to pursue their individual agendas, as did the United States when it withdrew its support for the OECD's tax competition initiative following the election of a new administration in 2000.[126] Non–OECD member countries are even less likely to cooperate with OECD initiatives, particularly in the absence of consensus about the problem being addressed, and where the OECD has failed to solicit the input of those countries.

The EU has the advantage of being able, within limits, to require member states to comply with its directives.[127] But even where there is disagreement within the EU, its member states are inclined to seek a cooperative solution because of their shared economic destiny and need to operate from a position of policy unity vis-à-vis the rest of the world. Thus, when EU member states Austria, Belgium, and Luxembourg objected to the EU's proposed information exchange requirement because it violated domestic bank confidentiality laws, the EU adopted its savings tax directive, permitting them to impose withholding tax on interest payments instead. This approach mitigates the most damaging consequence of bank confidentiality—namely, lost tax revenue to onshore jurisdictions—by insuring that a tax in lieu of residence-based tax is collected and remitted to the appropriate country of residence.

In summary, regulation of international tax competition is likely to remain high on the agendas of onshore jurisdictions and organizations, like the OECD and the EU, that represent their interests. Success in mitigating the deleterious effects of tax competition on onshore jurisdictions, however, will only come as they work cooperatively with OFCs in the manner exemplified by the EU and evident in the concessions the OECD ultimately made in its harmful tax competition initiative. Such cooperation will be more difficult where the divergence of economic interests between onshore jurisdictions and OFCs is not subject to supranational or intergovernmental resolution, as it is in the EU. The desire of OFCs to participate meaningfully in the global economy must be given the same consideration as onshore jurisdictions' desire to prevent the erosion of revenues through income tax evasion.

4

The International Monetary Fund and the Regulation of Offshore Centers

Richard K. Gordon

Onshore jurisdictions have long complained that offshore financial centers (OFCs) provide a willing sanctuary for tax evasion, poor financial regulation, and money laundering by onshore residents. Onshore centers have couched these complaints in terms of both domestic damage (the onshore centers themselves have suffered, though not the OFCs) and universal damage (all jurisdictions have suffered, including the OFCs).

As a general matter, onshore centers have claimed that by allowing some residents to escape from their regulatory grasp, offshore financial centers have handed out tickets for a free ride in exchange for the financial benefits of handling the onshore residents' business. More specifically, onshore jurisdictions have claimed, by allowing onshore residents to circumvent prudential regulations, offshore financial centers have threatened the safety and soundness of all financial systems. And by allowing onshore residents to circumvent anti–money laundering (AML) (and later terrorism financing) policies, OFCs have allegedly been enablers of both serious and often violent crime and terrorism, both at home and abroad.[1]

The International Monetary Fund and Harmful Tax Practices

There is little question that, at least early on, most offshore centers (as well as some onshore centers) offered onshore residents an opportunity to evade taxes on income from capital by neither levying tax on income from nonresident capital investments nor reporting such income to resident countries, an issue that is discussed at length by Craig Boise in this volume. In effect, these offshore tax havens invited onshore taxpayers to shift their capital investments from onshore financial intermediaries to tax haven–based intermediaries. Because offshore financial center tax havens had no significant domestic economic activity beyond basic financial intermediation, and therefore little need for local investment, the capital was then on-lent somewhere else, typically back into the resident's country or some other onshore country. In other words, according to the onshore jurisdictions, the tax haven–based financial intermediary played no real economic role other than to permit tax evasion.

Beginning in the mid-1980s (and continuing through the 1990s), the larger onshore jurisdictions attempted to involve the International Monetary Fund (IMF) in analyzing and criticizing offshore center income tax policies. Under the IMF's Articles of Agreement, members are obligated to direct their "economic and financial policies" toward the objective of fostering orderly economic growth and underlying economic and financial conditions; the articles also give the IMF the jurisdiction to exercise surveillance over these policies, which it does by writing and discussing a (usually) annual report on each member's economy. The articles also allow the fund to provide financial assistance to member countries that are experiencing balance of payments problems with conditions that would not only help resolve the problems but would make the loans more likely to be repaid. Finally, the articles allow the fund to provide technical assistance to members (and others), provided the assistance is consistent with the purposes of the fund.[2]

Given the importance of taxation to each of these three areas, it is not surprising that the fund has a long tradition of attending to tax matters when conducting surveillance, designing conditions for the use of fund financial resources, and providing technical assistance. During the 1980s and '90s, the onshore jurisdictions intimated that they would like the fund to support anti–tax haven activities through its surveillance, conditionality, and technical assistance. With respect to the first two, however—surveillance and conditionality—the IMF (meaning the executive board, management, and staff) apparently concluded[3] that its jurisdiction lay uniquely in how a particular member's tax policies affected *its own* economic and fiscal well-being.[4] The issue of the effects of a member's tax policies on the economic or fiscal well-being *of other* members was not within its jurisdiction. With respect to tax technical assistance, which was strictly voluntary, the question of external implications of domestic tax policy was generally not raised. Had it been, the effects of such voluntary fund-to-jurisdiction advice on curbing OFCs' so-called harmful tax practices would have been, at best, trivial.

The IMF and Prudential Supervision

Beginning in the 1980s, officials from onshore jurisdictions claimed that OFCs destabilized the international financial system by failing to implement prudential regulations, which allowed both offshore institutions and onshore institutions using offshore facilities to avoid onshore regulations, putting them at greater risk of failure. While all prudentially supervised institutions (banks, insurance, and securities firms) were of concern to the onshore jurisdictions, banks were the primary focus of their attention. According to onshore jurisdictions, because OFCs did not either promulgate adequate prudential regulations or implement them effectively through a program of compliance, an OFC-chartered bank could act in ways that would threaten its own soundness. These could include lending in excess of a prescribed capital minimum and failing to control for default and concentration risk. Another allegation was that in granting banking licenses OFC regulators did not vet owners and controllers to see if they were "fit and proper," so as to make poor management and poor compliance with prudential principles less likely. Together, these poor prudential practices would lead to a greater likelihood of banks failing, resulting in losses by creditors, especially depositors. If other, onshore banks were creditors, this could adversely affect those banks, resulting in a chain reaction of defaults that could endanger the entire international financial system.

Also raised in the financial supervisory context were a few money laundering issues. The anti–money laundering measures were not prudential in nature in that they did not have as a goal keeping the bank solvent; but because their implementation in onshore jurisdictions was most typically through the financial supervisor or regulator, they became part of the "poor prudential regulation" indictment. The most important of these measures was a requirement to identify the physical person who owned and controlled a particular customer account. Of course, such information was also critical for providing tax-related information to the major onshore centers.

The regulatory arbitrage provided by offshore centers allowed their financial institutions, or at least their financial institutions with an offshore presence, to operate more profitably by reducing the costs of regulation, rendering completely onshore institutions less profitable and subject to unfair competition.

Domestic bank supervisors had problems supervising domestic banks with foreign establishments (that is, branches and subsidiaries located in foreign jurisdictions) whenever those foreign establishments were domiciled in jurisdictions with strict bank secrecy. Supervisors also had trouble supervising branches and subsidiaries of foreign banks.

Briefly, bank supervisors need an *entire* bank's financial information (for parent and branches or subsidiaries) to determine if the bank is heeding prudential regulations. In 1975, the Basel Committee on Banking Supervision issued a report on the importance of supervising banks' foreign establishments to ensure the safety and soundness of domestic banks; the committee's arguments were extended in a paper in 1979 favoring consolidated supervision of banks' international activities. In 1981, the Basel Committee published a report noting that banking secrecy can impede the flow of information needed by supervisors. While the report did not single out offshore centers, it did note that nonmembers of the committee, "particularly offshore centers," were in broad agreement. The report was followed by a number of others exploring ways in which supervisors should share information about the activities of banks and their foreign branches and subsidiaries.[5] Of great importance, in 1990 the Offshore Group of Banking Supervisors (OGBS), an informal organization consisting of regulators in offshore centers, generally agreed to the various proposals to ensure the flow of information among supervisors.[6]

The bankruptcy of the Bank of Credit and Commerce International (BCCI) in 1991 drew attention to the serious problems that could arise when there was no effective consolidated supervision of banks with foreign operations, especially when an offshore center with allegedly lax supervision and "excessive" secrecy like the Cayman Islands was involved. The following year the Basel Committee issued a report on minimum standards for the supervision of international banking groups.[7] Among the standards were that all international banks be supervised by a home country authority that performs consolidated supervision; that banks and their foreign branches or subsidiaries receive the prior consent of both home country supervisor and host country supervisor; and that home country supervisors have the authority to receive information necessary to conduct consolidated supervision. Finally, if these minimum standards were not met, the report suggested, the host country supervisor should either prohibit the establishment of foreign branches or subsidiaries or impose restrictive measures on them. In other words, hard power could be exercised against resident banks by local regulators. The market would ensure that the foreign jurisdiction would also suffer as a result.[8]

While the 1992 report put into place a process of improved cooperation among supervisors from both onshore and offshore jurisdictions, problems remained. One involved the Meridien Bank International, which was really two banks, with one registered in Luxembourg (though it did no banking business there) and another, its 74 percent owner, licensed in the Bahamas; operational control of much of its activity was located in London. In 1995, Meridien collapsed and was placed into liquidation by the Bahamian Supreme Court. As with BCCI, regulators and commentators concluded that the use of complicated cross-border corporate structures allowed the bank to escape effective prudential supervision.[9]

With little doubt, both the BCCI and Meridien examples showed that effective supervision required better attention to cross-border issues, but it was not clear in either case that offshore centers were to blame for the failure. In both instances, supervisory authorities in the United States and the United Kingdom appeared to be at least partially at fault by not taking effective action after noting clear warning signs that the banks were not complying.

At the same time, other banking problems unrelated to these specific cross-border supervisory issues were gaining attention. Because the international community's eventual response to these issues played such a crucial role in shaping the treatment of OFCs, this discussion now turns to a series of crises and near-crises in a number of emerging markets, the most prominent of which were in Asia, that had particularly adverse effects on domestic banking systems. These macroeconomic crises were largely caused by large external borrowings and significant balance of payments deficits. Many banks had excessive external exposures and foreign exchange risk that resulted in insolvency; if local supervision had been better, some argued, these banks would not have been so vulnerable to economic shocks, and recovery after the crises would have been faster and less disruptive.[10]

The first of these shocks was the 1994–95 Mexican Peso Crisis. The first significant emerging-market sovereign debt crisis since the Brady restructuring of the Latin debt crises in the late 1980s, the Peso Crisis resulted in significant IMF-led intervention. A key analysis by the IMF of the crisis suggested that while macroeconomic variables largely determined the timing of bank failures, it was bank-specific prudential indicators that explain the likelihood of their occurring.[11]

By 1995, the two different issues—the lack of effective, consolidated supervision of cross-border banking and the ineffective domestic supervision in many countries suffering macroeconomic shocks—became conflated.[12] That year, the Group of Seven industrialized nations (G-7) announced that much more work was needed in creating and implementing appropriate prudential supervisory standards in all countries. In particular, they urged that the IMF and World Bank be involved, but that they "concentrate on their core concerns (macro for IMF and structural and sectoral policies for the Bank)." In partial response, a Working Group on Stability in Emerging Market Economies was convened under the sponsorship of the Group of Ten.[13]

The IMF and World Bank also set up staff working groups to consider these issues, while the Basel Committee continued its efforts to refine standards. In 1996 the committee, again with the full cooperation of and participation from the OGBS, released another report that addressed a number of practical considerations in implementing the 1992 report, especially regarding confidentiality of exchanged information.[14] The committee also accelerated its work on creating a set of generally accepted principles for effective banking supervision; these "core principles" were released late in 1997. The core principles require that supervisors practice consolidated supervision and that they "apply appropriate prudential norms to all aspects of the business conducted by these banking organizations worldwide." Supervisors must also "require the local operations of foreign banks to be conducted to the same high standards as are required of domestic institutions and [they] must have powers to share information needed by the home country supervisors . . . for the purpose of carrying out consolidated supervision."[15] In releasing the core principles, the Basel Committee "suggested that the IMF,

World Bank, and other interested organizations use [them] in assisting individual countries to strengthen their supervisory arrangements." There was no mention of offshore centers.[16]

Similar activities with respect to the creation of best practices or standards were under way for the two other key elements of the regulated financial system—securities markets (including broker-dealers) and insurance—to be carried out by the International Organization of Securities Commissions (IOSCO) and the International Association of Insurance Supervisors (IAIS).

In April 1997, the Working Party on Financial Stability issued its report, which urged the creation of "an international consensus on the key elements of a sound financial and regulatory system" by representatives of both developed and developing countries, including the Basel Committee, the IAIS, and IOSCO. It also called for the "promotion by multilateral institutions such as the IMF, the World Bank and the regional development banks of the adoption and implementation of sound principles and practices." More specifically, the report suggested that, as part of its Article IV surveillance activities, the IMF should "take stock of the progress that countries *with clear vulnerabilities* have made in the adoption of sound principles and practices developed by the international groupings." The report went on to state that "the IMF and World Bank should develop modalities for sharing their assessments of financial sector strength and the regulatory and supervisory regimes," and that IMF conditionality could "include steps to correct shortcomings in the financial sector." Nowhere in the report were offshore centers mentioned.[17]

Almost immediately after the report was issued (and just before the Basel Committee issued its core principles) the Asian financial crisis struck, followed by crises in Russia, Ukraine, and Ecuador. There are a number of different views as to what caused Thailand (the financial sector and the government) and then South Korea and Indonesia to move toward a massive default on external (and then internal) obligations. One thing virtually all commentators agree on is that the banking systems in each country were not well run; they were undercapitalized and had taken on far too much risk, including exchange rate risk and credit risk. When the financial crisis hit and investors fled from local currencies, banks were unable to pay their creditors—often foreign banks—resulting in illiquidity and insolvency. Clearly, the banking systems in these countries had not been adequately supervised. Another issue was what was termed "contagion," where a serious loss of investor confidence in one country could spread to other, similar countries. Perhaps more important was the significant evidence that bank illiquidity or insolvency in one country could spread to creditor banks in another, resulting in illiquidity or insolvency in the latter. While the problems in these banking systems were not new, they had not been the subject of IMF attention during the annual Article IV consultations. Yet, when the IMF stepped in to provide financing, the problem of poor banking supervision was brought immediately to the fore; bank restricting, plus new and improved banking regulation, was key to the reform program.[18]

Unlike with the Organisation for Economic Co-operation and Development's (OECD) harmful tax practices initiative, the promulgation of prudential banking standards did not require the IMF to conclude that a country should make a sacrifice for the benefit of another; unsound domestic banking systems, management and staff concluded, adversely affected the well-being of the country itself, as well as potentially having contagion effects on other countries.

What happened next was a multipronged attempt to find ways to prevent future crises, an effort known broadly as "strengthening the international financial architecture." Unlike the OECD's work on harmful tax competition, this work involved not only the IMF and World Bank, but representatives of the developing countries themselves. Among the various prongs was the ongoing work on financial standards—the promulgation of the Basel Core Principles (BCP) (and, to a lesser extent, the analogous standards of IAIS and IOSCO) through the work of the IMF and the World Bank. In theory, at least, the heads of the IMF, the World Bank, the OECD, and the Bank for International Settlements (BIS, another treaty organization) participated in this effort, attending meetings as observers. In practice, however, IMF staff, and to a lesser extent World Bank staff, were most closely involved in the working group's activities.

A little later, in the spring of 1999, a new international group, the Financial Stability Forum (FSF), was created. It included central banks, finance ministries, and financial system supervisory authorities from twelve developed countries, plus the IMF, the World Bank, BIS, the OECD, the Basel Committee, IOSCO, and IAIS, as well as some others. Again, IMF staff, and to a lesser extent World Bank staff, were closely involved in promoting the FSF's research and conclusions.

Clearly, the IMF was going to play a key role in adopting and promulgating any new rules of the road for avoiding future financial crises.[19] The fund published *Toward a Framework for Financial Stability*, which proposed that "the IMF, *with its near-universal membership*, has an important role to play in . . . the broad dissemination of the work of various organizations, particularly that of the Basel Committee [and] . . . with its broad responsibility to engage in surveillance of member countries' economic policies . . . can assist in identifying potential vulnerabilities . . . and help the authorities in formulating corrective policies."[20]

The Group of Twenty-Two's report had few surprises. It announced an "international consensus" on banking and securities supervision, specifically endorsing the Basel Core Principles, including principles on information exchange for supervising internationally active financial groups. It also called on the IMF and World Bank to enhance their work in the area, anchored in IMF surveillance. The IMF and World Bank, in coordination with the G-22 and the new Financial Stability Forum, worked to develop a new international effort to encourage the adoption and implementation of financial standards.[21]

This work led to the Financial Sector Assessment Program (FSAP), a new program piloted in 1998 and adopted the next year. The purpose of the FSAP was to identify strengths and vulnerabilities of a country's financial sector, in part by assessing compliance with key international financial standards, including the Basel Core Principles and related standards on insurance and securities regulations. The IMF and World Bank agreed that they should divide assessment work between them based on their areas of competence (meaning, primarily, the expertise of staff) with some being exclusively IMF, others exclusively World Bank, and others of joint responsibility. Basel Core Principle assessments were to be the responsibility of the IMF, and would be summarized in "Reports on the Observance of Standards and Codes" (ROSCs).

A number of key features of the FSAP and the ROSC program were developed over the first few years, namely, that the adoption and assessment of internationally recognized standards be voluntary, and that assessment be independently conducted and consistently applied. Of great importance, detailed methodologies for assessment were required to make the process as objective as possible and were drafted for the Basel Core Principles with the close cooperation of IMF staff. In other words, the FSAP and ROSC procedures were designed to ensure as uniformly objective a compliance assessment process as possible.

While the FSAP and ROSC programs were being devised, the IMF and the G-7-dominated Financial Stability Forum turned once again to the issue of offshore centers. During the Asian and follow-on financial crises, not a single offshore center experienced a significant problem in its regulated financial sector. Nevertheless, both the IMF and FSF managed to find problems with the operations of offshore banking and made valiant efforts to tie these problems, at least in part, to banking problems in the crisis countries.

In early 1999, the fund issued a staff working paper entitled "Offshore Banking: An Analysis of Micro- and Macro-Prudential Issues."[22] Almost bizarrely, it concluded that "offshore banking has most certainly been a factor in the Asian financial crisis [and has] . . . also played a significant, but not catalytic, role in the recent Latin America crisis," even though the body of the paper identified virtually no role at all. It went on, however, to discuss in general terms the issues raised by offshore banking. Claiming that there are "legitimate" and "illegitimate" reasons for banks to use OFC facilities, the paper, oddly, listed among the legitimate reasons "convenient" fiscal and regulatory regimes which, by lowering explicit and "implicit" taxation, increase net profit margins.[23] The ease of incorporation, legal frameworks for protecting the privacy of the principal–agent relationship, and the freedom from exchange controls offered by OFCs were also characterized as legitimate. Among the illegitimate reasons were bank secrecy ("almost invariably" a selling point[24]), tax avoidance and evasion, and money laundering. The paper suggested that the "greater leeway for balance sheet management, generated by favorable regulatory frameworks in OFCs, make offshore banks potentially more vulnerable . . . to solvency and foreign exchange risks."[25] And yet, the paper also asserted that offshore banks are *less* likely to be unprofitable and *more likely* to be profitable than onshore banks. In an apparently desperate effort to find a way to condemn offshore banking from a prudential perspective, the working paper concluded that, while offshore banks are far more likely to be liquid (since their regulators do not enforce capital standards with the verve of their onshore counterparts), they may be more highly leveraged and therefore less "solvent," although no risk-weighted data were available to back up this claim.[26]

The working paper was followed the next year by a report of the FSF's working group on offshore centers.[27] The FSF report concluded that "OFCs, to date, do not appear to have been a major causal factor in the creation of systemic financial problems."[28] It also concluded, however, that OFCs *could* cause contagion problems in the future due to the growth in assets and liabilities of OFC financial institutions and the suspected growth in off-balance sheet activities. The report distinguished between OFCs with weak supervision and those with strong supervision and went on to distinguish as well between prudential concerns and what it termed "market integrity concerns,"[29] the latter presumably having a meaning similar to the IMF staff paper's "illegitimate purposes." It listed as a key prudential problem the old OFC tax issue of information exchange but added a far more general concern over a lack of prudential supervision. Again similar to the IMF staff paper, the FSF report also noted that lax supervision equaled higher profits, but added that jurisdictions that followed international standards were at risk of losing business to the lax jurisdictions. With respect to market integrity, the report noted that while offshore centers did not pose immediate risks to international financial stability, by hampering international surveillance and law enforcement they eroded the integrity of international financial markets and therefore represented a potential threat to global financial systems. Highlighting "a lack of information on beneficial ownership of corporate vehicles . . . [that] can thwart efforts directed against illegal business activities," the report called for an assessment program similar to the FSAP for all OFCs, suggesting that the assessment program include subsets of the Basel Core Principles and the IAIS and IOSCO standards.[30]

At the time, many IMF staff reacted with dismay to the FSF report. Many concurred with the general conclusion that offshore centers had *not* been a weak link in the world financial system. And while they also agreed that many offshore jurisdictions applied a light supervisory hand, they *did not* believe that the result was a weak banking system; as the staff working paper had contended, they felt that offshore banks were healthy—largely, they did not make risky investments. The proposed offshore center assessment program seemed instead to be addressed more to solving other issues referenced in the report, including the fear on the part of onshore jurisdictions that they could be losing out to offshore ones in the global competition for banking services.

Of greatest concern, however, was that by focusing on information sharing, customer identification, and transparency of ownership, the working group was really focusing on tax evasion and, to a lesser extent, money laundering. And, as discussed above, many staff believed it was illegitimate for the IMF to suggest that one jurisdiction should sacrifice to benefit another. A number of those most closely involved in putting together the new offshore center program expressed their view that the program had little or nothing to do with prudential regulation, which they believed actually was a legitimate subject for IMF involvement. Instead, they wondered if it were all a subterfuge to help the OECD and its member states with the harmful tax practices project.

IMF management moved promptly to propose a pilot assessment program. Interestingly, they also discussed at some length other OFC initiatives, including the OECD tax competition program and the recent anti–money laundering initiative of the Financial Action Task Force (FATF), involving so-called noncooperating countries and territories (NCCT). Like the tax competition program, the NCCT program (which is discussed below) assessed a selected group of jurisdictions, most of which were OFCs, and threatened them with "countermeasures" if they did not comply with a set of anti–money laundering standards created by the FATF. The proposal threw a few bones with respect to anti–money laundering issues, noting that Basel Core Principle 15 included ensuring an effective anti–money laundering program.[31]

As a result, what the FSF had proposed—a selective assessment of the Basel Core Principles and of anti–money laundering principles, with a threat of possible "countermeasures" if the OFC didn't measure up—was replaced with a voluntary extension of the BCP assessment part of the FSAP/ROSC program to offshore centers. In effect, the FSF (and its sponsors in the major onshore jurisdictions) was hoist on its own petard. At least arguably, the FSF wanted the IMF's OFC program to address what was outside the mandate of the fund: the competitive advantage offshore banks had due to a less rigorous regulatory environment (plus issues of unfair tax competition and money laundering). To make the argument for IMF involvement, the FSF had to claim that it was all really an issue of bad prudential regulation. The IMF accepted this argument and proposed that it fold OFCs into its onshore assessment program, all without adopting the proposals that would have targeted the FSF's real concerns.

All offshore centers consented to being assessed. The reasons for this were varied and, no doubt, included a significant amount of lobbying, but there were a number of practical reasons as well. IMF staff heard a number of different comments voiced by officials in offshore jurisdictions as to why they agreed. Certainly, there was a fear that if a particular jurisdiction did not participate it would be assumed to be in serious noncompliance with the Basel Core Principles, which could then be cited by onshore regulators as a reason for restricting banking activities with offshore institutions. Many offshore centers also believed that their banks were safe and sound and that a truly impartial assessment by the international civil servants of the IMF would likely give them at least passing marks. They might not have trusted the onshore jurisdictions to be fair, but they placed faith in the skills and impartiality of the IMF staff (or at least they decided that the IMF staff was more impartial than the substate regulatory members of the Basel Committee on Banking Supervision). Offshore centers were already the subject of essentially involuntary assessments under the OECD's harmful tax practices program (and the FATF's NCCT program, to be discussed below); they might in some instances have hoped that the cooperative and less biased IMF assessment could be used as a tool to counter the work of the G-7 civil servants who dominated the OECD and the FATF.

As it turned out, offshore centers did quite well in their assessments overall. While some of the newer (and less wealthy) offshore centers fared poorly, the older established ones performed better than many onshore centers. The most significant problems lay in the setup and operations of the supervisors themselves, including the examination process, and in particular supervision over credit risk and market risk. While a lack of effective supervisory implementation might result in problems, however, none of the banking systems assessed was in any way actually weak. Frequent discussions among assessors suggested that none was actually concerned about potential bank failures. Although local bank *examination* of credit and market risk was a problem, the banks themselves did not appear to be behaving too riskily, in part because so much of their business was actually intermediation between depositors and other onshore banks, and in part because many of them were also the subject of consolidated supervision by onshore jurisdictions. In that regard, staff assessments had generally found good cooperation with respect to sharing information with onshore regulators. Of particular interest, staff noted that OFCs so far had a better record of compliance with the Basel Core Principles than did onshore jurisdictions.[32]

These first impressions were largely confirmed as the Offshore Financial Center Assessment Program continued forward, eventually covering all offshore centers by 2004. One significant effect of the assessments was that OFCs did work to improve their prudential supervisory programs, including by passing new laws and regulations to bring them into fuller compliance with the Basel Core Principles (especially with respect to the independence of the supervisor, onsite examinations, and a focus on credit and market risk). Not at all clear, however, was that these improvements materially improved the actual safety and soundness of the various banking systems. In a 2003 review of the program, staff did not find much risk posed by poor prudential supervision.[33] An informal review by IMF staff in 2006 found "strong compliance [with the Basel Core Principles], with over 70% compliant with 22 out of 30 principles, with strengthening required for independence, onsite and offsite supervision [and] for credit risk [and] market risk, but," the staff added, "*these [are] less material.*"[34]

There was one more interesting development. Many offshore centers specialize, at least in part, in providing efficient and inexpensive offshore company chartering (meaning that the company, while incorporated in the offshore center, cannot transact business there). Many also specialize in providing trust management services. In part to protect the users of these services and in part to prevent the use of companies for fraudulent or other illegal purposes, many offshore centers required the licensing and even supervision of trust and company service providers. In many offshore jurisdictions, international companies could only be founded by licensed providers, and only after due diligence was performed to ensure that the company would not be used for illegitimate purposes. In 2002 the OGBS established a working group to create an international standard for regulating the sector, together with participation of the OECD, the IMF, and the FATF. In September 2002, the working group issued a statement of best practice, and for two years the OFC program included assessments of compliance with this statement, after which staff concluded there was too much redundancy with the anti–money laundering assessments. But what was most peculiar about the assessment was that no onshore center licensed or supervised this sector. This was a case where offshore centers, through the work of the OGBS and the IMF, were able to show the world that they were doing a *better* job than onshore centers.

The IMF and Money Laundering and Terrorism Financing

In the aftermath of the terrorist attacks of September 11, 2001, the examination of anti–money laundering provisions intensified, culminating in the inclusion of an assessment of compliance with the FATF anti–money laundering standards in both the FSAP and the Offshore Financial Center Assessment Program. Because of the increasing emphasis by the latter on anti–money laundering and terrorism financing beginning at this time, this section will discuss the effects of the OFC program after addressing that development.

Onshore jurisdictions also claimed that, relative to themselves, OFCs assisted criminals by failing to implement anti–money laundering principles, which allowed criminals more easily to retain the proceeds of their crimes. Among the most important rules was a requirement that financial institutions "know their customer," including knowing who controlled the account and whether the source of the funds was likely to be criminal. These principles also required financial institutions to monitor accounts to see if they might indicate criminal proceeds, to report to a government agency when they did, and, finally, to make this information available to other jurisdictions.

By not enforcing such rules, onshore centers claimed, OFCs allowed criminals to hide the fact that they owned or controlled accounts, either because the accounts were actually anonymous (as in the case of numbered accounts), or because the account holder was a company, or because of another legal arrangement in which the owner and controller were not revealed. The criminal could make deposits of his ill-gotten gains to these accounts, often through a transfer from another bank, without any questions being asked as to the origin of the funds. When the criminal wanted use of the money, he would implement a transfer to an account in his own name, typically in a large onshore jurisdiction. Running criminal proceeds through the effectively anonymous offshore accounts prevented onshore banks from discovering the origins of the funds or whether the accounts had been controlled by a criminal, thereby laundering the proceeds. Any request for information by another jurisdiction would be rebuffed either because the information was not available or because of laws protecting financial secrecy.

Besides the requirement that financial institutions monitor and report on accounts, the principles also included having jurisdictions extend cooperation to each other in investigating and prosecuting alleged criminals involved in laundering. Onshore jurisdictions claimed that offshore centers either rebuffed such requests directly or provided such poor cooperation that little assistance was actually given. Following the terrorist attacks of September 11, 2001, the onshore jurisdictions extended their criticism to include inadequate cooperation in the "global war on terror." One requirement of this "war," adopted as international law by the U.N. Security Council, was to seize accounts owned or controlled by known terrorists and terrorist organizations. Most of the complaints by the larger onshore jurisdictions were that a failure to implement "know your customer" rules made it impossible to seize the funds of known terrorists.[35]

Over a decade earlier, the first major efforts to develop a global anti–money laundering strategy had involved the promulgation of international agreements. These included the Vienna Convention in 1988, which required all parties to enact legislation providing for the identification and confiscation of laundered drug money and set out procedures for providing mutual legal assistance, and the Council of Europe's Strasbourg Convention, which included some anti–money laundering measures. The next major international step to enhance global anti–money laundering efforts came with the creation of the FATF in 1989, following the G-7 Summit in Paris. The original task force, which consisted of sixteen OECD countries, with the United States and France taking leadership roles, was intergovernmental in nature, with participants including financial supervisors, criminal investigators, and prosecutors. Less than a year later, the FATF published its first set of forty recommendations, which covered the criminalizing of money laundering and the freezing and seizing of criminal proceeds, preventive measures for banks, such as customer identification and record-keeping, transaction monitoring and the filing of suspicious activity reports when a financial institution suspected money laundering, and cross-border cooperation in investigating and prosecuting money laundering.

In 1991, the FATF began its mutual evaluation program. The mutual evaluations involved onsite assessments of compliance with the recommendations, undertaken by experts drawn solely from other members. The following year, FATF helped set up the Caribbean Financial Action Task Force, the first FATF-style regional body (FSRB) designed to advance adoption of the FATF 40. While membership in regional bodies required a political commitment to implement the FATF 40 and to undergo mutual evaluations, no treaty obligation was involved, and no timetable was set for implementation. The FATF also worked on developing appropriate "countermeasures" to deal with those jurisdictions that failed to implement anti–money laundering policies adequately. The FATF also expanded its membership to include twenty-four members of the OECD, plus a few others.[36]

In 1996, a revised version of the forty recommendations was completed that extended AML preventive measures to nonbank financial institutions. The FATF also agreed to apply "preliminary *sanctions* against certain [FATF] members" that did not comply with the recommendations.[37] By 1997, FATF-style regional anti–money laundering organizations existed for nearly every significant offshore center.

The 1996 revision was, in part, a response to concerns raised by FATF members in the early 1990s about jurisdictions they believed were key weak links in enforcing anti–money laundering rules. At that time, many onshore jurisdictions had few or no AML rules or enforcement. The role played by some key offshore jurisdictions was frequently mentioned as the most troublesome, however. These jurisdictions allegedly had benefits for launderers that the vast number of poorer and developing countries did not: They were usually "tax havens"; they had a first-world financial infrastructure (including branches or subsidiaries of onshore banks or domestic onshore banks that were an accepted part of the international financial system, and trust and company service providers to assist in access to the financial system); and a first-world legal system to protect property rights. The 1996 FATF 40 included Recommendation 21, which stated that financial institutions should give heightened due diligence to business relations and transactions with persons from jurisdictions that "do not or insufficiently apply [the] Recommendations."[38] Such heightened due diligence could result in a financial institution's refusing to undertake transactions with a person from a noncomplying jurisdiction, though the recommendation was vague on this issue. Recommendation 21 was an invitation for local regulators to ensure compliance on the part of nonresident institutions, in a manner quite similar to that recommended for both tax and prudential standards enforcement.

There are a number of reasons offshore centers might not have wished to make full implementation of the FATF's recommendations a priority. The primary purpose of anti–money laundering rules is to reduce criminal activity by reducing the ability to enjoy the profits of crime. The vast majority of criminals and criminal activities, however, were onshore, not off; therefore, implementing such policies was likely to help onshore jurisdictions far more. Because implementation was relatively costly, especially to financial institutions, there may have been relatively few "nonaltruistic" reasons to expend such cash. Also, because anti–money laundering rules required clients of financial institutions to jump through more hoops regarding such matters as identification, implementation might have hurt business.[39]

By 1999, key FATF members determined that diplomatic efforts plus the threat of implementation of Recommendation 21 had not been enough to encourage these allegedly troublesome jurisdictions to change their ways. Taking as their model the OECD's harmful tax competition project (the modest FATF secretariat was physically housed at the OECD's Paris headquarters), FATF delegates began to formulate an analogous anti–money laundering program, putting together the NCCT process. In doing so, the FATF made a number of crucial decisions.

First, analogous to the harmful tax practices program, the FATF delegates chose not to include in the initial review all the jurisdictions that failed to follow the FATF 40, but rather those they believed were causing the most practical problems. For this purpose they put together an ad hoc group to determine which jurisdictions should be included in the initial review. The reasons for doing so were obvious: Most countries in the world had yet to adopt and implement the FATF 40, and to cover all countries would require too many resources. By selecting only a subset of such countries, however, they left themselves open to criticism over the selection. It was also odd that the FATF added countries as uncooperative in subsequent rounds of assessment that were not included in the first round. In part as a result, the FATF members selected a relatively large number of jurisdictions for review, including a number of large onshore jurisdictions, such as Russia. Eventually, a total of forty-seven countries or territories was examined in two rounds of reviews.[40]

As was not the case with the harmful tax practices program or even the prudential supervisory program, the FATF already had a standard formally endorsed by virtually all of the jurisdictions they wished to examine: the FATF 40. Although the jurisdictions had not pledged to implement the FATF 40 by a specific date when they signed onto the FATF-style regional bodies, they had accepted it as the applicable standard against which their anti–money laundering policies should be judged through a mutual evaluation process. Nevertheless, the FATF decided neither to apply the full FATF 40 as the standard by which cooperation would be judged nor to rely on the FAFT-style regional body mutual evaluations to determine compliance. Rather, it chose to create a special set of twenty-five criteria based on a subset of the FATF 40, and to assess compliance with the twenty-five criteria themselves. A "certain subjectivity" in assessments was also contemplated.[41]

Many of the twenty-five criteria focused on the core of the preventive measures in the FATF 40—meaning those focused on financial institutions rather than criminal law enforcement—such as poor regulation and supervision of financial institutions, inadequate fit and proper test rules for the licensing and creation of financial institutions, inadequate customer identification requirements for financial institutions, excessive secrecy provisions regarding financial institutions, and the lack of an efficient reporting system for suspicious transactions. Others focused on law enforcement and on international cooperation. But two criteria were not even included in the 1996 FATF 40: "inadequate commercial law requirements for registration of business and legal entities" and "lack of identification of the beneficial owner(s) of legal and business entities."[42]

For jurisdictions found to be uncooperative, proposed responses could include "specific actions . . . by other multi-lateral organizations. . . . In particular, the World Bank and the International Monetary Fund could examine the consequences of a particular jurisdiction's failure to take appropriate corrective action."[43] And, finally, again reminiscent of the OECD's harmful tax project, the report proposed the application of "countermeasures," including conditioning, restricting, targeting, or even prohibiting financial transactions with uncooperative jurisdictions.[44]

In February 2000, the FATF published its first review. The vast majority of the OFCs listed in the initial forty-seven did not make it to the "non-cooperative" list. While it was not clear from the report why this was the case, a number of persons who were part of the review process reported that the United Kingdom had worked to keep its offshore territories off the list, while Canada also worked to keep off the list a number of territories with which it had close relations and which it represented on the executive board of the IMF. One United Kingdom territory that did make it to the list—one of the most important of all OFCs in terms of total business transacted—was the Cayman Islands. Another important jurisdiction was Liechtenstein. The report noted that neither had a requirement for customer ID and record-keeping, the most essential of the AML preventive measures, and both had little active bank supervision. Other jurisdictions were listed primarily for not providing information on beneficial ownership of legal persons or arrangements, something that most onshore jurisdictions also did not do. Some other relatively minor OFCs (in terms of total business transacted) were on the list and were also uncooperative tax havens. Others with serious shortcomings, including Russia and Lebanon, were not offshore centers at all.[45]

As the NCCT process proceeded in parallel with the OECD's harmful tax project, jurisdictions named as NCCTs complained vociferously and for many of the same reasons. The defensive "countermeasures," they said, were actually coercive sanctions—an illegitimate application of power by the rich and powerful against the small and weak. As with the OECD harmful tax practices project, there was some agreement with this view in the popular press as well as in academia. While the FATF 40 was at least arguably a standard accepted by virtually all of the OFCs on the NCCT list via their membership in an FATF-style regional body, the twenty-five criteria by which they were assessed were not. This allowed the offshore centers to claim that the larger onshore centers were trying to impose standards that were neither internationally accepted nor applied to some of their own members. As with the tax competition program, the NCCT program lacked all the hallmarks of due process; in particular, the assessments were certainly neither uniform nor impartially applied. Objectivity was noticeably absent.[46]

Ever since the mid-1990s, a number of key onshore centers—again most notably the United States and France—had been trying to involve the IMF and World Bank in promoting anti–money laundering principles. In 1996, a staff member in the Monetary and Exchange Affairs Department published a paper on the macroeconomic implications of money laundering. In it he argued that laundering created inaccuracies in macroeconomic data, investment decisions based on ease of laundering rather than on rate of return, erosion of confidence in financial markets, tax evasion, and, finally, an increase in underlying criminal activities (that is, predicate offenses) that would result in the promotion of private economic benefits over social welfare.[47] The IMF's legal department disputed each of these views, suggesting that if a problem existed it was that *anti*-laundering policies resulted in inaccurate macroeconomic data, skewed investment decisions, erosion of confidence in markets, and tax evasion.[48] As for the argument that crime is bad, the article noted that while this was obviously true, it would lead to a conclusion that all anticrime efforts should be within the IMF's mandate, which would be unworkable.[49] Informal discussions among the legal department, executive board offices other than those held by the United States and France, management, and senior staff at other IMF departments confirmed a strong general inclination for the IMF to avoid money laundering issues because they were primarily criminal enforcement–related and therefore beyond the fund's mandate and expertise.

In early 2000, U.S. Treasury secretary Lawrence Summers sent a letter to the IMF and World Bank urging the two to "step up" their efforts to combat money laundering by including money laundering measures in financial sector reform programs.[50] In particular, the United States began lobbying to include the FATF 40 as a standard to be assessed under the FSAP/ROSC and OFC programs. The reaction from most other executive directors, management, and staff was again largely negative. Two staff reports that were discussed by the executive board rejected the idea, suggesting instead that assessment of the anti–money laundering principles in the Basel Core Principles and IOSCO and IAIS standards be enhanced. The staff reports also suggested that the World Bank and IMF recognize the FATF 40 as the anti–money laundering world standard, but that it should be up to the FATF and FATF-style regional bodies to assess compliance. The board went along, noting, however, that the IMF should not become involved in "law enforcement."[51]

A key concern expressed by all the non-OECD executive directors at this time (and privately by a few OECD directors) was that the FATF NCCT process was, in their opinion, anything but voluntary, and therefore anathema to both the fund and the bank's culture and tradition in general, and to the FSAP/ROSC/OFC program specifically. They did not want the two international financial institutions to support in any way the NCCT process and contemplated ways in which the IMF and World Bank might work to soften or eliminate the entire NCCT program.

In spite of criticism, the NCCT process had been continuing without the support of the two international financial institutions. In June 2000 the Bahamas, the Cayman Islands, and Liechtenstein had been removed from the list, while a number of large, developing onshore countries had been added. While the addition of these onshore countries muted somewhat the complaints that the NCCT process involved a ganging up of the powerful on the weakest, it also added the voices of countries with significantly larger populations and political influence to those of parties critical of the process.[52]

Any remaining effort to derail plans for significant IMF and World Bank involvement in promoting compliance with AML principles was rendered nearly moot by the September 11, 2001, terrorist attacks on the United States. Although the attacks were done on the cheap, the U.S. Treasury Department began immediately to push other members of the FATF to include terrorism financing as a central part of its mandate. On October 29 and 30, the FATF adopted eight new recommendations on terrorist financing. Soon after, the IMF managing director created a special task force to consider how to intensify IMF involvement in anti–money laundering and anti–terrorism financing work. On November 5, 2001, the task force issued a report recommending that the IMF and World Bank endorse the FATF 40 plus the eight new special recommendations and begin to include the assessment of compliance with the FATF 40 + 8 in the FSAP and OFC programs, and that AML/Combating the Cost of Terrorism (CFT) ROSCs be prepared once the rules for ROSC assessments could be achieved. The task force managed to find the previously missing mandate for activity in this area in the IMF's role in overseeing the international financial system. Intellectually this was a stretch, but politically the results were unavoidable. The task force report states that the IMF's involvement should be based on the fact that "the Fund is a collaborative institution with near universal membership, *which lends the Fund legitimacy and acceptance*, and makes it a *natural forum for sharing information and developing common approaches to issues.* These strengths also make the Fund *a vehicle for actively promoting desirable policies and standards* in member countries." The report also noted that the IMF already had experience in assessing compliance with other standards.[53]

While the task force members were drafting the report, the U.S. and French executive directors made clear that they wanted not only for all offshore center assessments to include money laundering assessments, but for the offshore program to be accelerated. There was some resistance to this on the part of many members of the task force, who felt that the events of 9/11 had nothing to do with offshore centers, and that resources could be better used elsewhere. Nevertheless, the task force report proposed increasing the number of OFC assessments from a target of ten to a target of twenty per year so that two-thirds of the forty-two OFCs on the Financial Stability Forum's list would be assessed by the end of 2002, and the executive board agreed.

The report noted a number of other issues. For instance, for assessments of compliance to be as objective and uniform as possible, the FATF 40 + 8 needed an assessment methodology. The report also suggested that the IMF and World Bank should not be involved in assessing compliance with criminal law matters and discussed the NCCT process, which clearly breached the rules of the game for producing ROSCs: The NCCT process was not voluntary and not independently applied across countries (for example, there was no methodology for assessment), and there were pass–fail ratings. While not explicitly mentioning the NCCT process, the executive board agreed that these issues had to be resolved before AML ROSCs could be prepared, and, in particular, that the process be "compatible with the uniform, voluntary, and cooperative nature of the ROSC exercise."[54]

An intense series of discussions began among key FATF members and senior staff with respect to the continuation of the NCCT process. In effect, management at the IMF and World Bank had concluded that the executive board would not endorse an AML ROSC while the FATF continued the NCCT process, while key FATF members insisted that the NCCT process was working and should be allowed to continue. Another issue was the assessment methodology document. The FATF had delegated the job to the U.S. delegation, but they failed to complete the task. As a result, IMF and World Bank staff agreed to complete the methodology, with IMF staff taking the lead. They produced a highly detailed set of criteria which, one staff member noted, would "make it very hard for the FATF to be easy on themselves and hard on others." IMF staff began to use the draft methodology to make AML assessments in the OFC program. By April the fund's International Monetary and Finance Committee called on the fund to complete the

AML/CFT methodology and the development of "assessment procedures compatible with the uniform, voluntary, and cooperative nature of the ROSC process."[55]

In June 2002, the FATF released its next NCCT report; fifteen jurisdictions were still listed, just under half of which were offshore centers, and none of which was particularly important in terms of total business. A number of the remaining onshore jurisdictions (including Egypt, Indonesia, Nigeria, the Philippines, Russia, and Ukraine) were, however, influential with respect to the IMF executive board; indeed, they elected four executive directors or alternates.[56]

The next staff paper proposed a pilot program of AML assessments based on the new methodology to be undertaken by the IMF and World Bank and the FATF and regional bodies set up to undertake assessments based on the FATF recommendations, also known as FATF-style regional bodies. However, the authors insisted that all assessments embrace a process that was

> *uniform*, including using the same methodology for all assessments (the FATF's NCCT process uses a different methodology from those of mutual evaluations), *voluntary* (the FATF NCCT process is mandatory and can result in the imposition of sanctions) and *cooperative*, including not using a pass–fail approach (the FATF NCCT process labels jurisdictions either "cooperative" or "noncooperative") and giving the jurisdiction the opportunity to publish a right of reply alongside the ROSC (the FATF NCCT process does not allow such a right of reply).[57]

The FATF flatly refused to give up the current NCCT round. After additional negotiations, Germany, then the president of the FATF, agreed only that the FATF was prepared to indicate that it had no plans, at present, to undertake a further round of the NCCT exercise. A majority of executive directors opposed to the NCCT process still favored accepting the FATF's offer; they felt it was the best they could get, and that having an impartial IMF assessment of NCCT countries would act as a significant counterbalance to the "partial" and "unfair" NCCT assessments.[58] Some, including those representing the constituencies headed by Nigeria, Egypt, and Russia, felt that such benefits could be outweighed by the legitimacy that an IMF/World Bank–endorsed FATF ROSC would confer on the FATF and therefore on the NCCT process. In the end the board was split, with a majority deciding to go ahead with a twelve-month pilot of AML assessments, with IMF/World Bank doing some, including OFCs, and the FATF and FSRBs continuing to assess their own members. They insisted, however, that the FATF agree to undertake mutual evaluations of its own members in a manner consistent with the ROSC process, and that it agree "not [to] undertake a further round of the [NCCT] initiative, at least during the period of the 12-month pilot project."[59] A number of directors, however, expressed their disapproval, saying that those conditions did not go far enough. They said that reports on observance associated with FATF-led assessments should not be designated ROSCs "unless the FATF undertook a blanket commitment not to undertake any further [NCCT assessments] and acknowledge that it would accept the results of any Fund/Bank-led assessments."[60]

As the pilot program went forward, by the end of 2002 the eight offshore centers assessed, which included the formerly listed Liechtenstein, did quite well, with only Vanuatu showing significant problems. The assessments showcased how effective jurisdictions were in implementing their AML programs, in most cases noting great improvement in recent years. The remaining OFCs on the FATF NCCT list, however, did not request an immediate assessment. The following year the Cook Islands requested and received an assessment from the IMF, with the staff report noting that the authorities "have strengthened the AML/CFT legal and institutional framework mainly in response to the FATF's listing of the Cook Islands as a non-cooperative" but that "the efforts remain uneven," noting that the FATF had not removed the jurisdictions from the list.[61] While the IMF provided free technical assistance to the Cook Islands, they remained on the NCCT list until 2005.[62] If one theory was that involving the IMF in assessing AML compliance would help get OFCs off the NCCT list, it did not appear to be playing out.

An unanticipated effect on the onshore jurisdictions resulted from the involvement of the IMF in the AML project. In agreeing to allow the FATF and FATF-style regional bodies to produce ROSCs, the IMF/World Bank insisted that they ensure uniformity through review of the FATF's assessments. This did not go entirely well for the FATF and FATF-style regional bodies, where a major review found "a high degree of variability in the quality and consistency of reports" prepared by the FATF and FATF-style regional bodies.[63] A large majority of reports were found to be of high or medium quality with respect to key components of the assessments, but the report also suggested that the quality and consistency of assessments by all assessor bodies needed improving, including the standardization of documentation and the strengthening of peer/internal reviews.[64]

IMF staff's review of the OFC program in 2003 generally gave OFCs high marks in both supervision and anti–money laundering, noting that they "compared favorably" with onshore jurisdictions of similar wealth.[65] The review again found no serious systemic risk; the review the following year actually found that compliance levels for OFCs were, on average, more favorable than those for other jurisdictions assessed by the IMF in its financial sector work.[66] Not surprisingly, the IMF's OFC program began to wind down, with fewer assessments and with AML assessments increasingly undertaken by FATF-style regional bodies. By early 2005, forty-one of the forty-four OFC jurisdictions had been assessed under the first phase of the OFC program. The second phase was to focus on monitoring compliance though assessment updates every four to five years, with a focus on providing technical assistance to less wealthy jurisdictions to help improve their compliance.[67] Finally, in 2008, the Offshore Center Assessment Program was merged with the FSAP program, treating offshore centers, in essence, like their onshore counterparts.[68]

Recent Developments

Recent news suggests that many key onshore centers are once again ratcheting up at least their rhetoric against OFCs. The Stop Tax Haven Abuse Act, originally introduced by Senators Carl Levin, Barak Obama, and others in 2007, was reintroduced in 2009.[69] During his campaign for president, Obama blasted "tax havens," stating that "there's a building in the Cayman Islands that houses supposedly 12,000 US-based corporations. . . . That's either the biggest building in the world or the biggest tax scam in the world, and we know which one it is."[70] And, in much the way many onshore countries tried to blame OFCs for the Asian financial crisis, United Kingdom prime minister Gordon Brown recently tried to shift at least some

100   OFFSHORE FINANCIAL CENTERS

blame to OFCs for the current financial meltdown.[71] French and German leaders have made similar comments, even though no offshore bank has yet failed or been implicated in an onshore bank's failure.[72] No doubt, criticism of offshore centers' anti–money laundering efforts will also follow. It obviously makes some significant political sense for leaders whose countries are in the depth of serious financial problems to blame others. OFCs tend to be small and weak, and therefore good targets.

Some Conclusions

It is easy to understand why most offshore centers were not interested in the 1980s and 1990s in helping onshore centers enforce their income tax laws or keep their banks from engaging in poor lending policies or fight their problems with drug addiction and crime. On the other hand, offshore centers were under considerable pressure from the onshore centers, which could impose domestic tax, prudential, and money laundering rules on their own residents that would shut down much of the work performed by offshore centers. Offshore centers decided to cooperate on prudential and money laundering issues, even though allegedly bad prudential supervision or anti–money laundering policies did not pose risks to the offshore centers themselves. Here the participation of the IMF (and the World Bank) actually helped the offshore centers. By helping ensure the implementation of generally accepted standards in a uniform fashion, the IMF exposed the apparent hypocrisy of at least some onshore centers. Whether this will continue in the current financial crisis remains to be seen. The IMF did not participate in the OECD's tax competition program because it was not accepted as part of the fund's mandate. Had it been, perhaps the worst excesses of the OECD program would have been mitigated in a similar fashion.

Some question still remains as to why onshore jurisdictions chose to formulate and prosecute the three programs the way they did, acting in concert rather than individually. The advantages included maximizing pressure, but the negatives included some bad publicity and, eventually, the IMF's heavily moderating influence. There would, however, be another reason for choosing to act in concert, a reason that may be found somewhere else than in promoting a safe financial system and a world with fewer criminals. The use of offshore centers offered the potential cost-savings benefits of avoiding or evading taxes and the costs imposed by prudential regulation and anti–money laundering policies. While any one onshore center could have prevented its own residents from taking advantage of such cost savings, they could not, at least acting alone, have prevented the residents of other onshore countries from doing so. The three OFC programs may have been created largely to ensure that if one onshore country's residents were denied such cost savings, all would be so denied. That way, no onshore resident would gain the competitive advantage of lower costs from using an OFC. While there is no smoking gun, the fact that some onshore centers are now blaming OFCs for the current international financial crisis—and with no plausible evidence to support the charge—suggests that the real reason for attacking OFCs, and seeking more coordinated action to oppose them, may lie here.

5

The Role of Offshore Financial Centers in Regulatory Competition

Andrew P. Morriss

A standard part of the debate over the impact of offshore financial centers (OFCs) on onshore countries' policies is the assertion that the offshore and onshore governments are engaged in a competition and that, from the onshore perspective, the offshore jurisdictions engage in "unfair" competition which results in a "race to the bottom," or some other negative outcome. Offshore jurisdictions are accused of everything from enabling money laundering of criminal proceeds[1] to undermining onshore governments' regulatory efforts to ensure sound banking, insurance, and financial practices.[2] Oxfam argues that OFCs are "an increasingly important obstacle to poverty reduction" because they are "depriving governments in developing countries of the revenues they need to sustain basic services and the economic infrastructure upon which broad-based economic growth depends."[3] Raymond Baker, one of the most thoughtful critics of offshore financial centers, contends that "tax havens and offshore jurisdictions permit operations outside the rule of law and outside the process of regulation" and so contribute to corruption and poverty in developing countries.[4]

In particular, most critiques presuppose that OFCs have few beneficial impacts on the legal systems of democratic governments and only ill effects on corrupt regimes. These attacks presume the financial structuring made possible by offshore financial centers has no legitimate uses, and also that any revenue lost by onshore governments due to tax and regulatory competition would be put to productive uses if collected. What if these assumptions are not true? What if the impacts of regulatory competition differ across jurisdictions?

We should begin by accepting that regulatory competition is an inevitable result of a world made up of many jurisdictions. No amount of harmonization or number of treaties, multilateral organizations, or other measures will completely stifle it. As Erin O'Hara and Larry Ribstein note,

> governments often fail to effectively control everyone everywhere. Any state can make rules, but not every state legitimately can enforce them in all circumstances, especially those involving people or assets outside the state. Because no single government can extend its courts and enforcement powers to cover the world, multiple states end up competing with no state able to exercise effective monopoly power over mobile entities. In the end, the states compete for mobile parties and their assets by attempting to provide the laws people want.[5]

That is not to say that such efforts at control cannot damage particular jurisdictions' efforts to provide competition, for they can; but while those jurisdictions that do not like regulatory competition can make it harder or more expensive, they cannot eliminate it. This is good news: The existence of regulatory competition is a feature of our world, not a bug.

Assessing the impact of international regulatory competition requires asking and answering three questions:

- For what do jurisdictions compete?
- How do jurisdictions compete?
- Does regulatory competition affect jurisdictions in different ways?

The answers to these questions can help us assess the impact of regulatory competition, and the role of offshore jurisdictions in particular, by illuminating the advantages of regulatory competition in disciplining corrupt onshore jurisdictions and spurring innovation in transactions costs–reducing legal "technologies" among both corrupt and benevolent jurisdictions.

The first question is important because understanding what jurisdictions are competing *for* suggests differences among them that are relevant to understanding the impacts of regulatory competition by offshore financial centers. By tracing the competition to the benefits to individuals and interests within governments, we can clarify its impacts.

The second question allows us to expand our analysis beyond the dimensions cited by opponents of offshore financial centers. Jurisdictions compete on the basis of more than secrecy and tax rates. Understanding the full range of competition is crucial to understanding its impact.

The third question asks whether offshore jurisdictions are different *in kind* from onshore jurisdictions. Competition among states for economic activity exists among onshore governments as well as between onshore and offshore governments. Does it matter whether international regulatory competition takes place among the United States, the European Union, Japan, China, Bermuda, Barbados, the Cayman Islands, and the Channel Islands, or would it look the same if it involved only the first four jurisdictions? Adding the last four increases the total population of the jurisdictions competing by less than half a million from the 2,240,851,389 combined population of the first four (less than 0.03 percent); does this have a disproportionately large impact compared to that on the population numbers? In other words, does adding offshore jurisdictions to the mix result in a change in the character of the competition? If so, how? Is there an effect on regulatory competition comparable to the entry of Wal-Mart into a town's retail market, or is it a case of just another "firm" selling a product similar to that offered by existing firms? This chapter argues that adding offshore jurisdictions does make a difference, and that the role of offshore financial centers is to push regulatory competition in beneficial directions.

We can also ask whether the impact of regulatory competition differs depending on whether the states involved are constrained by democratic institutions or are autocracies lacking such constraints. For simplicity of exposition, let us divide governments into two groups: democratically constrained and autocratic governments. Democratically constrained governments are those subject to significant degrees of constraint as a result of their need to win relatively open and fair elections, although the degree of constraint will obviously vary with the competitiveness and fairness of the political system. Autocratic governments are constrained by the possibility of extraconstitutional regime change.[6] A jurisdiction's government may move from one category to another as a result of changes to the political system. Critics of OFCs have focused exclusively on looting by autocrats, which regulatory competition can facilitate. This chapter argues that such competition is particularly important in restraining autocratic regimes.

Having made the argument that regulatory competition is sometimes beneficial, and that offshore jurisdictions add an important element to that competition, the chapter then briefly examines the rise of regulatory competition after World War II and the appearance of offshore financial centers. Using two examples to illustrate the impact of regulatory competition—the rise of Eurodollar corporate financing and the spread of captive insurance law—the chapter then examines the impact of regulatory competition on domestic U.S. legislation and argues that offshore financial centers played an important role in generating transactions costs–lowering legal innovations internationally and in the United States.

Finally, the existence of limits on governments imposed by regulatory competition can be beneficial from the point of view of limiting government overreaching, but problematic if they prevent governments from undertaking beneficial activities. Whether the impact of regulatory competition is desirable on net depends on whether the beneficial effects are more significant than the problematic ones. The chapter concludes by offering a framework for considering whether regulatory competition is likely to be beneficial in particular areas.

For What Do Jurisdictions Compete?

In general, jurisdictions compete for economic activities. Almost all politicians, regardless of ideology and in all forms of governments, seek to have wealth created within their jurisdictions. Of course, politicians of different types may prefer different forms or amounts of wealth creation,[7] and I will argue below that there are important distinctions between politicians and bureaucrats who are subject to the constraints imposed by contested elections and those who are not. But the key premise of the argument set out in this chapter is that politicians and bureaucrats need wealth created within their jurisdictions to enable them to accomplish their goals. In economic terms, wealth creation is necessary to maximize government officials' utility, and economic activity creates wealth.

Politicians' and bureaucrats' need for economic activities within their jurisdictions can be broken down into three motives: (a) increased wealth for their citizens (the public interest motive) and creation of a pool of resources that can be captured and devoted to pursuit of government officials' priorities, including (b) the production of public goods (the public good motive) and (c) enhancement of the officials' personal well-being (the personal interest motive), including both tangible personal benefits (through corruption) and the psychic benefits of being in a position to satisfy personal policy preferences.[8] Criticisms of offshore financial centers generally presume that OFCs reduce the ability of onshore governments to produce public goods (by reducing available tax revenue) while increasing the ability of corrupt politicians and criminals to loot their jurisdictions (by enabling opaque financial transactions). They do not address whether or not OFCs (or even competition among onshore jurisdictions) facilitate increased wealth in the onshore jurisdictions as well as in the OFCs.

These criticisms are partially correct. Considerable looting is occurring in developing and post-Communist regimes. And at least *some* of this looting is made easier on the margin by some of the services provided by some of the OFCs.[9] (Of course, it is made easier by *some* services provided by *some* onshore countries, as well.[10]) In particular, corrupt officials have made use of bank secrecy, bearer bonds and shares, and other strong forms of financial privacy to conceal their identities. Because little scholarly or public attention has focused on the impact of regulatory competition on increasing wealth or differences in impacts on various types of governments (except in arguments advanced by offshore jurisdictions themselves), the net impact of OFCs has rarely been considered, and discussions of looting and money laundering dominate the policy debates.[11] Since history offers evidence suggesting that subjecting political elites to market forces can lead to increased liberty for their subjects,[12] this omission neglects an important potential contribution of offshore jurisdictions and regulatory competition. To assess it requires us to consider the different motives of public officials.

Increasing Wealth. To the extent they are motivated by the public interest in increasing the wealth of their citizens, politicians and bureaucrats will seek those economic activities that provide larger value added within their jurisdictions over those that provide relatively little, enabling their citizens to benefit from the increased economic activities. This type of distinction among various categories of economic activities is important for the assessment of the role of offshore jurisdictions, because different types of offshore activities yield different levels of benefits to the domestic economy. If a jurisdiction simply operates a company registry, charging a fee for listing a company and doing little else, little value is added to the local economy other than the fee. If a jurisdiction can secure high value-added transactional work creating and managing business entities, however, it can secure greater benefits to the local economy.[13] The most successful offshore jurisdictions today have evolved from an initial focus on company registries and similar activities to a mix of financial center activities that include legal, accounting, and other services in an attempt to expand the portion of the economic activity occurring within their borders.[14]

Politicians seeking to increase wealth within their onshore jurisdictions may also find that at least some OFC activities are beneficial. For example, the United States used Curaçao's OFC as a means of enabling U.S. firms to gain access to the Eurodollar markets from the mid-1960s to the mid-1980s, eliminating the need for changes in U.S. tax law.[15] At least initially, this activity was encouraged by the U.S. Treasury Department.[16] Similarly, the United States amended federal insurance law to allow access by Bermudan and Caymanian insurance companies to the U.S. market in an effort to lower insurance costs for U.S. insureds.[17] Onshore politicians and regulators thus sometimes see the benefit of increasing regulatory competition for their own jurisdictions and so are sometimes willing to allow entities to opt for foreign laws to govern important aspects of their behavior.[18]

Providing Public Goods. Government officials may also seek economic activity to finance the provision of public goods by increasing government revenues without increasing domestic taxation. Revenue from additional economic activity can be a substitute for domestic tax revenue, reducing distortions introduced by domestic tax regimes or simply shifting tax burdens off voters and onto foreigners seeking to "rent" the jurisdiction's legal system to conduct a transaction. For an OFC, a company registry could serve this purpose even without producing domestic value-added activities.

When they compete for such business, OFCs often lower the cost of doing business by charging lower fees or offering better services, as Dionne and Macey argue in this volume. (This is, of course, what Delaware does within the United States with respect to corporate charters.) Competition from such jurisdictions for economic activity is thus seen as a negative by onshore government officials because it reduces the prices their governments can charge individuals and firms engaged in the economic activity for some of the services governments provide. For example, the United States competes for bank deposits by exempting foreign nationals with U.S. bank accounts from federal taxes on the interest paid on those accounts; foreign governments dislike this activity because it locates the deposits beyond their reach.[19]

Of course, regulatory competition does not equally affect all the dimensions of the price charged. Jurisdictions with substantial wealth remain able to charge economic actors for access, which explains the persistence of the high prices charged by European Union economies for access to their markets through expensive labor law provisions (which constitute an implicit tax) and high tax rates in places like New York City, which offer a wide range of amenities and business advantages. Economic actors may respond to such prices by shifting some activities to lower-cost jurisdictions, but to the extent activities cannot be completely removed or authorities are able to insist on a portion being conducted locally, government authorities are able to maintain relatively high prices. The nonmarket access portion of the "price" is subject to regulatory competition, however, and, on the margin, competition matters.

The criticism of OFCs for offering tax competition generally presumes that onshore governments would have devoted the "lost" revenue to high-value public goods (education, highways, park facilities, hospitals) rather than low-value or negative-value goods and services (monuments to dictators, corruption). It is true that some of the "lost" tax revenue might be used for high-value public goods, but it is far from certain that even in the least corrupt states marginal tax revenues would be devoted to high-value public goods. In less successful states, where fewer high-value public goods are provided, there is reason to think the same obstacles to good governance that render those states generally unsuccessful might hinder the efficient spending of the additional marginal tax revenues. Moreover, as O'Hara and

Ribstein point out, competition for law can benefit even the states with bad laws, since it enables affected persons and firms to avoid relocating outside those states in an effort to escape the bad laws' reach.[20] As a result, in the absence of data on the revenue losses and the uses to which the revenue would be put, we are left with an ambiguous answer to the question of the net impact of the competition provided by OFCs.

Corruption. Government officials may seek economic activity within their jurisdictions to create opportunities to feather their own (or their supporters') nests through corruption. This can occur by charging economic actors directly for access to the local market (as in Ghana, where the former dictator Kwame Nkrumah "often awarded contracts personally, without reference to the cabinet, the appropriate minister, or the cabinet's contracts committee"[21]); by demanding inclusion of favored local partners in the profits (as in Zimbabwe, where a protégé of the dictator Robert Mugabe boasted, "I am rich because I belong to [ruling party] Zanu-PF. . . . If you want to be rich you must join Zanu-PF"[22]); by demanding bribes (a common practice in Indonesia under the Suharto regime, which ranked first in Transparency International's 2004 list of corrupt regimes[23]); or by manipulating exchange controls and rates to subsidize favored interests and penalize disfavored ones (as happens routinely in a wide range of autocracies[24]). It can also occur by allowing illegal activities to occur for a fee (bribe), as with illegal drug–related production and distribution.

Treating corruption costs conceptually as an implicit tax, we see that legitimate economic actors will seek to avoid paying the "corruption" tax by avoiding these jurisdictions.[25] Only if the jurisdiction has an advantage unavailable elsewhere (for example, access to a large market, as is the case with China) or a resource that produces rents (as in countries like Equatorial Guinea, subject to the "resource curse") will legitimate economic actors seek to be involved in jurisdictions where corruption is a serious problem.

In the first case, legitimate business entities or other transactions costs–reducing legal technologies are unavailable to the corrupt economic actor, and any jurisdiction willing to accept the proceeds will have an advantage in the competition for such business. If entrepreneurs' activities are themselves illegal, these entrepreneurs may be drawn to corrupt jurisdictions. OFCs can play an important role in illegal activities, particularly in allowing laundering of the proceeds. They generally cannot play an important role in the commission of the underlying criminal activity, however, since they tend to be small jurisdictions with correspondingly small "domestic markets" for crime. A drug dealer selling illegal substances in the Cayman Islands would have a domestic market of only fifty thousand and face the higher costs of doing business on an island (where entry is readily controlled) and in a small, homogeneous society (where criminal activity is relatively easy to detect, compared to larger, heterogeneous societies). Criticism of OFCs thus centers on their role in failing to prevent money laundering, which occurs after onshore criminal activity. It may be true that criminal activity is most efficiently stopped by focusing on the proceeds rather than the underlying crime. There is also a case that law enforcement efforts should be focused on the criminal activity. Where to focus law enforcement attention within a jurisdiction is properly a question for each jurisdiction to make. It does not follow, however, that Jurisdiction A is entitled to excuse its failure to control criminal activity by blaming Jurisdiction B for failing to stop the laundering of the proceeds of the activities occurring within Jurisdiction A.

Rent Extraction. Not all economic activities are equal in the eyes of political leaders. A public-spirited political leader will prefer activities that have fewer negative externalities (preferring a service sector business to a toxic waste processing facility, for instance) or that require highly paid, highly skilled labor rather than rely on low-paid, unskilled labor.[26] More importantly, where a leader has available valuable natural resources (for example, oil, gas, or mineral deposits[27]) or agricultural commodities,[28] he can take advantage of the rents associated with these resources to obtain revenues without allowing productive economic activity to take place within his jurisdiction. Thus, where natural resources can generate considerable revenues which can be exploited by a government, corrupt regimes may not be particularly interested in fostering economic activities outside the natural resource sector. This was the case, for example, in Zaire under the Mobutu regime, and it has been true in Nigeria for much of the time since the discovery of oil there. Indeed, the predatory natural resource state is a clear example of what happens when a government is unconstrained by competitive political or economic forces.[29] The slow disintegration of the

Zairian state under Mobutu led to considerable chaos and suffering for the Zairian people but served the autocrat's purposes by making it easier for him to allocate rewards to supporters and disable opponents.[30]

Even outside natural resource–rich autocracies, political leaders may prefer to engage in activities that reduce economic activity rather than increase it if they see such actions as necessary to maintain their hold on power (for example, Robert Mugabe's ruinous economic policies in contemporary Zimbabwe). Agricultural subsidies in the developed world fall into this category, as well. Neither of these circumstances means that there is not competition for economic activity. They suggest that when political leaders are able to focus on maximizing the size of their share of the economic pie, they may prefer a larger share of a smaller pie to a smaller share of a larger pie. Where rents are large from natural resources or commodities, or the rent-dissipating activity is seen as necessary to maintaining power, important limits on politicians' interest in maximizing their nations' wealth may restrict the influence of regulatory competition.

The Role of Competition. Regulatory and tax competition play an important role in limiting the excesses of both autocracies and democratically constrained governments. George Ayittey's exhaustive critique of African autocracies found that the lack of political freedom and "the defective economic system of statism" were "interdependent" problems.[31] By fusing the economic and political systems, he argued, the state had become "a mafia-like bazaar, where anyone with official designation can pillage at will."[32] Under these circumstances, adding economic competition to the ruling elites is virtually a prerequisite for developing political competition. Ayittey's point applies to autocracies that have fewer totalitarian ambitions, as well. By creating alternative centers of power, economic freedom undermines autocratic control. Even in democratically constrained states, regulatory competition restrains efforts to redistribute through regulation and erodes regulatory inefficiencies.

The crucial point is that jurisdictions are engaged in a competition for economic activity. Depending on the motives of those engaged in the activity and the motives of the politicians controlling a jurisdiction, this competition may take a variety of forms. It occurs along a wide range of fronts, just as firms engage in competition for customers along a similarly broad range. And just as the money price is only one component of firms' competition for customers, so the tax "price" of a jurisdiction is only one component of jurisdictions' competition for economic activity. Furthermore, the motive of the politicians and bureaucrats in seeking economic activity will affect the type of economic activity they prefer to encourage. In the next section, I turn to the question of how jurisdictions compete for economic activity.

Competition among Jurisdictions

What does it mean to compete for economic activities? Much of the discussion of such competition focuses on whether there is a "race to the bottom" for tax rates or cost-lowering measures dealing with environmental and labor standards, and whether or not government aid to businesses (such as tax abatements and grants) that locate economic activities in a jurisdiction is permissible under trade agreements. There are many other forms of competition, however, and many of these are equally or more important. As O'Hara and Ribstein argue, "Territorial thinking about the law is becoming increasingly outmoded because rapid transportation, instantaneous communication, and free trade have shrunk the world and people no longer stay put."[33] This section examines how jurisdictions compete, and the impact of their competition on different types of states.

How Jurisdictions Compete. In addition to competing on tax rates, jurisdictions compete by offering high-quality infrastructure, educated workforces, stable legal regimes, efficient judiciaries, and political stability. Of particular interest here, jurisdictions compete by offering transactions costs–reducing legal innovations. Professor Saskia Sassen argues that "one of the marking features of the financial era that begins in the 1980s is its drive to produce innovations."[34] The rapid spread of the limited liability company (LLC) business entity within the United States after Wyoming passed the first LLC statute in 1977, followed by all the other states and the District of Columbia by 1996, is an example of such competition;[35] the spread of international business corporations (IBCs) and segregated cell insurance entities internationally also illustrates this phenomenon. Indeed, "because it is so hard to identify a single location for every person and transaction, deciding which laws to apply to a legal problem is becoming increasingly arbitrary,"[36] making competition easier to engage in. Governments thus compete for economic activities along a wide range of margins, not simply on tax rates or stringency of environmental and labor regulations. Those things matter, of course, but it is important to remember they are not the only, or even the main, margins of competition.

Regulatory competition also differs according to the type of law that applies where it is occurring. To assess the impact of regulatory competition on law, we can divide laws into four categories:

- laws that raise revenue for the public sector;

- laws that organize the public sector (that is, laws governing the organization of government and management of public assets);

- laws that seek to change private behavior by altering incentives (for example, laws governing emissions of pollutants, or non-neutral tax laws that seek to encourage or discourage particular behaviors); and

- laws that facilitate transactions by offering the means of reducing transactions costs (for example, laws providing for official property registries that permit registration of secured interests, or laws that provide for generic corporate formation).

Of course, a particular statute or regulation may have characteristics from more than one of these categories.

Laws that raise revenue for the public sector are an important part of the price of doing business in particular jurisdictions. Jurisdictions compete in this area primarily by offering reduced tax rates for particular types of transactions. The Channel Islands, for example, began their histories as offshore jurisdictions relative to Britain by charging lower customs duties on items such as tea, luring British pensioners seeking a lower cost of living to the islands.[37] In the financial sector, jurisdictions such as Barbados offer reduced tax rates for international business corporations through a network of tax treaties, and jurisdictions such as the Cayman Islands offer zero-tax regimes,[38] with both sorts of jurisdictions charging fees for specific services (for example, company registration) as a way of earning government revenues. Domestically, U.S. jurisdictions engage in similar competition. Alaska, Florida, Nevada, South Dakota, Texas, Washington, and Wyoming have no state income taxes, for example, and the top marginal rates in states with income taxes range from 3.0 percent to 9.3 percent.[39]

Laws that organize the public sector are also a part of the package of goods, services, and costs offered by jurisdictions. A jurisdiction that requires multiple permits and approvals by authorities with discretionary power imposes different costs on economic entities than one that offers a "one-stop shop" regulator capable of handling all issues, and in which decision-makers have less discretion to challenge a transaction. Providing efficient government services is an important margin of competition. It is also an active one: Offshore financial centers routinely tout the speed and efficiency of their regulatory processes, as do jurisdictions like Delaware or Britain that play analogous roles within larger jurisdictions like the United States or the European Union.

Regulatory laws that aim to change private behavior by altering incentives (through discriminatory taxation, restrictions on transactions, and so forth) also affect the cost of operating within a particular jurisdiction. European Union jurisdictions provide far greater job security for employees than do the United States, India, or China by restricting employers' ability to discharge employees. These laws operate as an implicit tax on employment in the European Union (EU). A firm creating a multinational production and distribution network might therefore be inclined to minimize the more costly employment in EU jurisdictions in favor of employment in one of the cheaper jurisdictions. Jurisdictions compete on these margins not simply by reducing regulation, but also by increasing the cost-effectiveness of the regulatory package. For example, Europe's more statist employment law regimes were well suited to European economic conditions in the 1950s and 1960s, when employee wage restraint was crucial to producing the investment necessary to rebuild European industry.[40] Competition on this margin thus will not automatically yield fewer regulations, although it will tend to produce less costly forms of regulation, as Dionne and Macey argue in this volume. More generally, O'Hara and Ribstein argue that it will cause legal regimes to shift away from mandatory rules toward "quasi-mandatory" rules that individuals and firms accept as part of a total package of laws, which are, on net, desirable.[41]

Transactions costs–reducing laws lower the cost of locating economic activity within a jurisdiction. Examples of transactions costs–reducing laws range from efficient default rules within the law to the availability of expert neutral decision-makers for resolving disputes. All these are features of the state-level competition for corporate charters in the United States. For example, Delaware, the market leader in corporate charters within the United States, has a reputation for providing both efficient default rules in corporate law and a judiciary expert in resolving corporate legal issues.[42] Captive insurance laws, discussed later in this chapter, are a further example. By offering insurance companies corporate structures such as the segregated portfolio company, jurisdictions lower the transactions costs of organizing insurance vehicles suitable for use as captives.

With respect to transactions costs–reducing legal innovations, competition often takes the form of mimicking and adapting the successful concepts of other jurisdictions.[43] Jurisdictions that do not adopt successful transactions costs–reducing innovations will lose business to those that do. For example, insurance business shifted to Bermuda from the United States when Bermuda pioneered new forms of insurance company organization,[44] and hedge fund business shifted to the Cayman Islands from other jurisdictions when Cayman adopted a more efficient hedge fund regulatory regime.[45] Delaware attacked New Jersey's then dominant position in corporate charters by seeking "to assure potential customers that its corporate law, like that of New Jersey, had been the 'result of a conservative, steady and progressive growth,' and . . . therefore '[would] not be subject to any radical changes.'"[46]

Mistakes can harm a jurisdiction's competitive position. For example, New Jersey suffered a blow to its once dominant position in corporate charters within the United States, losing business to Delaware when New Jersey damaged its reputation for consistency and reliability by passing the "seven sisters" corporate law changes in 1913;[47] and the Bahamas lost its dominant position in offshore banking to the Cayman Islands when the post-independence Pindling government attempted to renegotiate the government's bargain with the offshore sector for a larger share of the profits.[48]

Just as landlords compete by offering prospective tenants different price–location bundles, so governments compete for economic activity by offering economic actors different bundles of prices and services for the opportunity to do business within their jurisdictions. The explicit components of these prices are the requirements of taxes and fees that the economic actors must pay to locate their transactions within the jurisdiction. The implicit costs are the regulatory costs imposed on economic activities in the jurisdiction. These can be direct or indirect. Direct implicit costs affect transactions by mandating particular features of the transaction. For example, German firms must have a supervisory board on which employees have representation, while American firms do not (a cost which, at least for a time, had some efficiency benefits).[49] A direct implicit cost of doing business in Germany through a German corporate entity is thus some sharing of information and control with employee representatives. Indirect implicit costs are the additional costs of doing business in a jurisdiction with regulatory regimes that increase transactions costs. For example, when utility regulation increases the cost of utility services to fund cross-subsidization of residential customers, economic transactions in those jurisdictions pay an implicit tax through the higher prices for the utility services.[50]

Competition is likely to have different effects in different areas of the law, and we cannot consider any particular area in isolation. Further, law is simply one of many technologies available to individuals to use to achieve their objectives. (Outside the realm of expressive laws, there is rarely a preference for law as a good in and of itself.) What people desire is to accomplish a particular end, and that end can be accomplished by the use of multiple technologies, including various legal technologies.[51]

Consider this simple example from property law. A developer wishes to subdivide a parcel into individual lots and a central park, with ownership of the park shared among the owners of the lots. The developer reasons that by doing so, he will increase the aggregate value of the lots by more than he will lose by not being able to sell the land used for the park. Prior to the development of equitable servitudes, the developer would have found creating such a transaction to be costly, since contract law was inadequate to bind future owners of the lots with a transaction that would persist past the first owner. A new technology—equitable servitudes—solved the problem and created a general legal technology capable of being applied to a multitude of other circumstances through the continued evolution of the law.[52]

Once we consider law as a technology to accomplish economic objectives, we can analyze the impacts of regulatory competition on the production and diffusion of the various forms of technology produced by different types of jurisdictions. The next section addresses whether or not jurisdictions competing for economic activities are affected differently based on the jurisdictions' characteristics.

Does Regulatory Competition Affect Jurisdictions in Different Ways?
We have different concerns about democratically constrained and autocratic regimes. With respect to democratically constrained regimes, the primary danger of a lack of regulatory competition is increased rent-seeking by interest groups. If restrictions on trade, capital flows, and activity by foreign entities can be used to insulate an area of economic activity from international competition, the business entities involved in that area will be able to generate rents. Those rents can then be partially captured by politicians. The classic example of pure rent-seeking through protectionism is the use of tariff and nontariff barriers to insulate domestic sugar production from international competition. U.S. domestic sugar producers earn an estimated $1 billion in rents as a result.[53] Some of this is shared directly with politicians through campaign contributions (sugar interests have contributed more than $20 million to campaigns since 1990).[54] Some is also made available to politicians to use in funding either public good or rent-seeking government activities via taxes on sugar producers.

Democratically constrained governments must resort to such subterfuges to permit interest groups to rent-seek; autocratic governments can directly restrict trade.[55] Insurance regulation is an example of how democratically constrained governments may make use of a lack of regulatory competition to distribute benefits to favored groups. By restricting insurers' risk classifications, governments can cross-subsidize the favored group. Since U.S. state governments can control access to their markets for insurance, state insurance regulators are able to force insurers seeking to sell policies into profitable markets within the state also to sell them in less profitable sectors.[56]

The General Agreement on Tariffs and Trade (GATT) and the World Trade Organization (WTO) are examples of measures designed, albeit imperfectly, to reduce the opportunities available to domestic politicians to insulate areas of their economies from competition. Regulatory competition can similarly limit such rent-seeking because it facilitates exit by those harmed by the rent-seeking.[57] To the extent that it reduces the ability of domestic interest groups to rent-seek by making it more difficult to insulate areas of the economy from competition, international regulatory competition serves a valuable role in reducing deadweight losses due to rent-seeking.

When insulated from regulatory competition, democratically constrained governments have two alternative methods of achieving the personal and policy goals of the individuals in them. First, they may tax their populations (or borrow money with the promise to repay from future tax revenue) and spend the money raised on the goals ("the direct method"). Second, they may conceal the cost of the measures by incorporating it into an opaque regulatory competition, as with cross-subsidization measures in the insurance or telecommunications market ("the indirect method"). Such efforts introduce distortions into prices and impose deadweight losses. The total social cost of indirect efforts to achieve goals are thus higher than the total social cost of direct efforts, particularly if the revenues to accomplish the direct goals are raised through the least distortionary form of taxation available. Direct efforts at policy implementation are thus almost certainly less costly than indirect efforts.

Regulatory competition can limit both forms of policy implementation. It limits the direct method by reducing the opportunity to use certain forms of taxation, at least at some levels. If a government has reached the level of taxation that maximizes the total tax revenue, regulatory competition (particularly in tax matters) may result in reduced total tax revenue, as highly taxed, mobile economic activities shift to other jurisdictions.[58] Jurisdictions may have to shift their mix of taxes toward a heavier reliance on taxation of less mobile factors of production (for example, away from capital and labor and toward land), or toward consumption taxes and away from income taxes, to maintain a particular level of revenue as international regulatory competition increases. This can make addressing certain policy goals, such as redistribution, more expensive.

Regulatory competition imposes even greater limits on the indirect method. Because the indirect method is at least as costly as the direct method, the equivalent revenue effect is likely to be at least as large. But because it is less cost-efficient to proceed through cross-subsidization and other indirect means of policy implementation, the cost of achieving any particular policy goal is likely to be higher to the regulated firm when the goal is sought through indirect means. When economic actors are regulated through the indirect method, therefore, they have a greater incentive to seek an opportunity to engage in regulatory arbitrage to avoid the indirect regulation.[59]

International regulatory competition thus has a different effect on each of the two forms of policy implementation. Direct implementation of policy goals is constrained by limits on the revenue available to a government and by the increasing cost of obtaining that revenue through forms of taxation less susceptible to international arbitrage. While indirect implementation of policy goals is also constrained by the greater arbitrage opportunities produced by the availability of competing legal regimes, it is constrained to a greater degree than direct implementation because the inefficiencies associated with indirect regulation make international arbitrage more likely to be cost-saving.

These impacts may be considered beneficial or detrimental, depending on how one views the underlying government activity. To someone who thinks that the marginal dollar of government spending will be spent on socially desirable public goods, or for whom a policy like redistributory taxation is desirable, the impact will be seen as negative. To someone who thinks that the marginal dollar of government revenue will go to wasteful rent-seeking, or that the types of policies made more costly are undesirable, the impact will be seen as positive. Clarifying which set of assumptions is in use can make debates over regulatory competition clearer.[60]

Regulatory competition has additional effects on governments which are unambiguously beneficial. Economist J. R. Hicks argued that, in private sector competition, "the best of all monopoly profits is a quiet life," because "people in monopolistic positions will very often be people with sharply rising subjective costs; if this is so, they are likely to exploit their advantage much more by not bothering to get very near the position of maximum profit, than by straining themselves to get very close to it."[61] Governments are in a similar position to firms with respect to competition. The existence of alternative jurisdictions in which to locate a transaction reduces onshore governments' freedom of action, just as the existence of competitive firms reduces a prospective monopolist's freedom of action with respect to pricing on investments in research and development. When a government has a monopoly with respect to the organization of economic transactions within its borders, it has little reason to keep its price (regulatory costs and tax rates) low, devote resources to innovating its product offerings (by providing new legal vehicles for the organization of transactions), or offer efficient services (by reducing the costs of organizing a transaction by providing speedy responses).

For example, state-controlled firms are often granted monopolies that enable them to engage in inefficient, lucrative transactions. The 1980s Tanzanian state monopolies are dramatic instances of this. The government sisal board had overhead in 1980 that was greater than the total export earnings from the sale of sisal; the pyrethrum board spent more in 1980 on administrative costs than the total value of the crops it purchased.[62] This type of state activity was not limited to commodities; after the turn toward socialism in 1967, the Tanzanian state "became predominant in all spheres" taking over "all commercial banks, insurance companies, grain mills, and the main import–export firms, and [acquiring] a controlling interest in the major multinational corporation subsidiaries and the sisal industry."[63] Some benefited from these transactions; most suffered due to the inefficiencies and corruption that state ownership introduced. International regulatory competition limits the abilities of states to engage in such corrupt and grossly inefficient behavior. This is important, because the impact of these entities goes well beyond the losses they themselves incur. As trade economist Anne O. Krueger notes, the resulting state sector in Tanzania produced "overstretching of governmental capabilities" that contributed to inefficient tax regimes, neglect of infrastructure, and growth of the deficit-ridden, state-controlled entities that crowded out efficient firms.[64] The entities also distort prices, creating inefficiencies and deadweight losses throughout the economy as a whole.

Of course, governments have at least partial monopolies over certain types of transactions. Buying and selling land is difficult and expensive without the acquiescence of the government with jurisdiction over the parcel in question. But even in an area as closely tied to geographic jurisdiction as land sales, economic activity does occur without official government sanction.[65] It simply does so at a higher cost. Monopolistic behavior by a government, whether of the direct price-raising variety or the indirect quiet-life variety, similarly raises the cost of economic activity.

Competition from other jurisdictions can reduce a jurisdiction's ability to raise prices directly or indirectly. For example, the ability of a firm in

Jurisdiction A to shift intellectual property assets to an entity located in Jurisdiction B and shift revenue to that entity via licensing payments allows profits to be shifted out of A and into B, escaping taxation in A. Similarly, the ability of a firm in Jurisdiction A to use a captive insurance company located in Jurisdiction B to provide insurance services to itself not only allows relocation of profits, but allows the Jurisdiction A firm access to a form of insurance company organization available only in Jurisdiction B. The ability to choose different types of entities is increasingly important for firms. Trade economist Douglas Irwin recently noted how firms are increasingly making use of foreign affiliates, with almost $100 billion in net revenue flowing to U.S. firms' foreign affiliates in 2002.[66] Similarly, Professor Sassen notes, trade in services can occur "directly, through the movement of people . . . through foreign affiliates in which the service provider has equity participation, licensing, or other nonequity mechanisms, and through commercial means, such as sales or representatives' offices."[67] These examples illustrate the point that private actors have choices in how they organize their transactions, and these choices embody choices among jurisdictions.

Criticism of offshore financial centers tends to concentrate on OFCs' ability to undercut the price charged by onshore governments through taxes, as well as to facilitate types of transactions that onshore governments dislike (such as Internet gambling). Thus, an offshore jurisdiction offering lower tax rates for a particular transaction (for example, capital gains tax) enables tax avoidance if the transaction producing the gain can be moved to the offshore jurisdiction. In doing so, the offshore jurisdiction imposes a limit on the ability of the onshore jurisdiction to set its tax rates on that class of transaction. But, as noted above, tax rates are only a small part of the dimensions on which jurisdictions compete. While London and New York are engaged in vigorous competition for financial transactions, this competition is largely not conducted through tax rates but on other regulatory costs, as both cities are jurisdictions with relatively high taxes and high costs of doing business. Indeed, as Dionne and Macey note in this volume, some of the competition is conducted through creating value-adding regulations. Because the ability of offshore jurisdictions to compete with onshore jurisdictions differs from policy area to policy area—compare competition in income taxes to competition in real estate taxes—an additional impact of regulatory competition is to change the mix of policies available to onshore jurisdictions. Regulatory competition thus both limits governments' freedom of action in specific areas and alters the mix of government policies by changing the relative costs of various policies in terms of economic activity forgone. In addition to limiting regulatory efforts, regulatory competition can spur positive changes in onshore law, creating incentives for onshore jurisdictions to respond to legal innovations introduced in offshore jurisdictions. This is an important benefit for those firms and individuals unable to relocate to escape an inefficient or otherwise costly legal regime.[68] Competition requires that taxpayers be able to relocate a transaction from the onshore jurisdiction to the offshore one, and barriers to competition may exist under some circumstances.

Governments can provide legal environments that facilitate economic activity by providing contract enforcement, secure property rights, honest and efficient courts, registries for forms of property from land to security interests, and other services. The price of the legal environment is the cost of compliance with the conditions necessary to bring a transaction under the coverage of a jurisdiction's laws (for example, payment of taxes and compliance with regulations).

Some aspects of the marketplace are not competitive with respect to law. Competition regarding land laws, for example, is limited by the immobility of land and can take place only indirectly with respect to competition for real estate investment capital. Similarly, individuals and firms intending to do business in a particular physical location are limited in their ability to use competitive forces to negotiate new regulatory bargains with jurisdictions. Jurisdictions that control attractive markets like New York City can use their advantages to charge higher prices for market access, just as a firm with a desirable location may be able to charge more for its products than one with an undesirable location. For example, New York City is able to charge businesses operating there substantially higher taxes while maintaining a high level of business activity relative to other American cities, because being located in New York offers sufficient advantages to make paying the taxes worth the value added by locating in New York. Of course, on the margin, even desirable locations are limited by market forces, as can be seen from New York's recent interest in restoring its competitiveness in the face of international competition for financial transactions.[69] The decreasing costs of conducting many transactions internationally due to declining communications and transportations costs, increasing mobility of capital due to reductions in barriers to trade and financial transactions, and globalization of the legal and finance professions have expanded the areas of law in which jurisdictions may compete.

The Rise of Competition and the Role of Offshore Jurisdictions

Regulatory competition has expanded significantly since the 1960s, and the role played by financial centers (both onshore and offshore) has increased. "Globalization dramatically increased the size and depth of international capital markets," writes Daniel W. Drezner. "From 1994 to 2002, the valuation of all international debt securities almost quadrupled, from $2.3 trillion to $8.3 trillion. Over the past twenty years, the size of all banks' cross-border positions increased from $1.4 trillion to $12.7 trillion."[70] This section briefly surveys the expansion of competition and explains the entrepreneurial rise of offshore jurisdictions.

The International Marketplace. Before World War I, the division of the world into colonial empires, with trade occurring primarily within them, meant that regulatory competition was relatively weak. Although by some measures trade volume was at similar levels to the present, the level of global economic integration is significantly higher today.[71] Since World War II, "tariffs, import quotas, and exchange controls that originated in the interwar period have been gradually relaxed," and average tariffs on manufactured goods have fallen sharply in both developed economies like the United States and developing economies.[72] Sociologist Saskia Sassen argues that the 1980s saw an intensification of globalization "through the development of a wide array of innovations, which had the effect of transforming more and more components of finance or financial assets into marketable instruments."[73] Together with a shift of foreign direct investment from "raw materials, other primary products, and resource-based manufacturing" into "technology-intensive manufacturing and services"—a shift from less than 20 percent in services in the 1950s to over 60 percent by 1999—financial services trade exploded,[74] increasing the opportunities for offshore centers. The global liberalization of trade was facilitated in part by the General Agreement on Tariffs and Trade and the World Trade Organization, which "fostered the creation of pro-free-trade coalitions" and increased "the costs of *ex post* opportunistic and nationalistic behavior."[75]

Trade agreements also played an important role in locking in such reforms, as they made it harder for governments to defect from their part of the deregulatory bargain.[76] Trade barriers fell unevenly, with developed countries removing them in the 1950s and 1960s, a time when most developing countries were pursuing import substitution development policies that required raising trade barriers.[77] Not until the 1980s were most developing nations' economies opened to world competition.[78] As a result, the higher volume of trade has had significant benefits for the developed economies, both large (for example, the United States, European Union, and Japan) and small (for example, Canada, New Zealand, and Australia), while the benefits for many developing economies have been slower to appear.

As a result of the network effects of the GATT/WTO liberal trade regime, the costs of not participating in the global economy have risen, and more governments have joined,[79] expanding the opportunities for regulatory competition. These opportunities have also significantly expanded with the growth in the number of jurisdictions following the breakup of colonial empires and Communist federations. In 1900 there were 49 independent countries; today there are 192 (or as many as 196, depending on how one treats the Vatican, Taiwan, South Ossetia, and Abkhazia), with 32 new countries appearing just since 1990. In addition, there are a significant number of British overseas territories (Anguilla, Bermuda, British Virgin Islands, Cayman Islands, Gibraltar, Montserrat, and the Turks and Caicos Islands) and crown dependencies (Jersey, Guernsey, and the Isle of Man), and territories associated with the Netherlands (Aruba and the Netherlands Antilles, which is in the process of subdividing into several new jurisdictions), New Zealand (the Cook Islands), and the United States (Guam and Puerto Rico), which are not independent but are effectively separate jurisdictions for many aspects of regulatory competition. This expansion in the number of jurisdictions undermines the ability of jurisdictions to maintain regulatory cartels that restrict competition.

Communications and transportation costs have plummeted over the past fifty years; according to Francis Cairncross, "The death of distance as a determinant of the cost of communicating will probably be the single most important force shaping society in the first half of the [twenty-first] century."[80] This facilitates relocation of transactions. One critical step taken by early offshore centers was the creation of reliable transportation and communications links with their target markets. Cayman, for example, invested heavily in building an airport and upgrading its telecommunications facilities in the 1960s,[81] and some attribute part of Bermuda's success to the ease of access to the island from New York.[82] Such investments continue. For example, in the wake of Hurricane Ivan, Cayman improved its off-island data backup capabilities to ensure that weather could not shut down its financial center operations.[83] Competitive forces are thus still pushing even successful offshore jurisdictions to continue to attempt to improve their offerings.

Another reason for the opening of these economies is that experience demonstrated the failure of closed and socialist economic development strategies. The pressure on developing economies to open their markets was, thus, in part due to the success of the more open economies, a success attributable at least in part to the impacts of regulatory competition. But the delay in opening their markets meant that autocrats in countries like Zaire and Tanzania were able first to make use of the international financial mechanisms developed by the competitive process to loot their countries' economies. For example, capital flight by African elites in recent decades has exceeded the total foreign investment and foreign aid to African nations combined.[84] In addition, potential rivals to the autocrats used these same channels to secure their assets beyond the autocrats' reach. Thus, the most visible aspect of financial market openness was, at first, the flight of capital from the decaying economies of autocracies. Only later—and in less obvious ways—did those autocracies, unable to subsist on natural resource and commodity rents, experience the efficiency-enhancing aspects of financial openness.

The Structure of Competition. The rules of this liberalized trade regime created the opportunity for increases in regulatory competition. As Craig Boise and I argue elsewhere at greater length, onshore jurisdictions themselves engage in the same behavior for which they criticize offshore financial centers.[85] One reason international trade rules foster the conditions that allow regulatory competition is that it suits the interests of the United

States and the European Union to have such competition because they are successful competitors of developing countries in many dimensions. Both offer foreign investors access to major capital markets, stable political regimes, rule of law, efficient courts and other dispute resolution fora, and other advantages. As a result, from the perspective of Latin American governments, Miami's extensive banking industry has a remarkably similar appearance to that of Cayman's banks as viewed from the United States, and from the perspective of many former British colonies, London's financial sector has a remarkably similar appearance to that of Liechtenstein's finance industry as viewed from Britain. The relative volume may be even larger in the former cases than in the latter; some estimate that up to a third of deposits in Miami banks are from Latin America,[86] a much larger share of Latin American capital than the share of U.S. capital that flows through the Cayman Islands. Perhaps the main distinction between, respectively, foreign deposits in Miami or London and foreign deposits in the Cayman Islands or Liechtenstein is that a higher percentage of the deposits in the former two are likely invested within the jurisdiction where they are deposited than is the case for the latter two. This is a distinction without a difference that reflects the relative sizes of the economies involved. The location of the ultimate investment vehicle's market is irrelevant to the impact on the country providing the investment and the provision of the professional services surrounding the investment.

Of course, competition can occur regardless of the "onshore" or "offshore" nature of the jurisdictions involved. London vigorously competed with New York for "international financial center" business, originally holding the advantage, in part because prior to World War II much world trade was conducted in sterling.[87] After World War II, New York gained advantages over London due to differences in laws and the rise of the dollar as an international unit of account.[88] More recently, London once again gained some advantages over New York as a result of post-Enron changes in American law.[89] Such competition is vigorous in the financial sector but is present in many areas.[90] If we can have regulatory competition among states without participation by offshore jurisdictions, the question then becomes whether the offshore jurisdictions add something important to the competition that would be lacking without them (a question addressed in the next section).

The liberal trade regime created by the major economies allows regulatory competition in a variety of sectors, in part because, as noted above, the developed economies are effective competitors and so have an interest in creating the conditions in which they can compete, and in part as a byproduct of general trade rules.[91] One need not accept that the choice is between the "free market vanilla" and North Korea to see that the opportunity cost of not participating in the global economy is sufficiently high that most jurisdictions will opt to participate.[92]

Maintaining competition in law requires meeting three conditions.[93] First, the combination of the physical and financial transactions costs of conducting an economic activity in Jurisdiction A together with the total price charged by Jurisdiction A for access must be below the cost of conducting the economic activity in Jurisdiction B for Jurisdiction A to compete with Jurisdiction B for the activity. If jurisdictions A and B are able to maintain a cartel in areas of potential competition (for example, the European Union's various harmonization drives), these differences can be kept small enough that the additional transactions costs of operating in Jurisdiction A prevent some competition from occurring.

Second, the legal environment in Jurisdiction B must allow the transaction to be located in Jurisdiction A. If the area of competition is labor market regulation, Jurisdiction B must allow imports of goods manufactured in Jurisdiction A at cheap enough tariffs (and nontariff costs) that the goods can be manufactured in A and shipped to B rather than manufactured in B. In financial transactions, Jurisdiction B must recognize legal entities organized in Jurisdiction A. Thus, if XYZ Co. in Jurisdiction B transfers its intellectual property assets to XYZ IP Holdings Co. based in Jurisdiction A, the latter jurisdiction will not be competitive unless Jurisdiction B recognizes XYZ IP Holdings Co. as a separate entity legally resident in Jurisdiction A and so not subject to Jurisdiction B taxes and regulations. The advantages of a regime that treats business entities in this manner are sufficiently large to the dominant trading powers that they include such treatment within the global trade regulatory regime.[94] When the large economies wish to do so and work together, however, they can coerce changes in offshore jurisdictions. For example, of the fifteen jurisdictions identified by the Financial Action Task Force (FATF) as "noncooperative," four "acquiesced completely" in the FATF demands, seven "made significant concessions," three "passed laws that addressed enough FATF demands to temporarily avoid sanctions," and "73 percent ... made major concessions prior to the implementation of any economic sanctions."[95] Remarkably, this was done without any commitment by FATF members to meet the standards themselves.[96]

Third, the jurisdiction seeking the business must be able to commit credibly to honoring the regulatory bargain offered to economic actors long enough to make relocating the economic activity to Jurisdiction B worthwhile, taking into account the transactions costs of the relocation. A regulatory difference may exist today, and the difference may be capable of being exploited profitably through a reorganization of an economic activity. But to lure business, the jurisdiction seeking to entice individuals to incur the costs of relocating the transactions must convince economic actors, first, that it will not renege in the future on the bargain to allow the transactions to continue on current terms; second, that it will adapt its rules in the future to preserve the regulatory arbitrage opportunity in the face of efforts by the other jurisdictions involved to raise the costs of operating across jurisdictions; and, third, that the regulatory arbitrage will be eliminated by changes in the other jurisdictions' rules. The offshore banking sector's experience in the Bahamas after independence illustrates this.

The Competition. Elected politicians want private decision-makers to locate economic activities within their jurisdictions. Economic activity increases the wealth of the jurisdictions' citizens, an effect the citizens are likely to attribute to the politicians at election time. Economic activity that creates wealth also enables the politicians to use revenue measures and regulations to divert some portion of the wealth to their preferred policy ends. Autocratic politicians lack the concern of democratic politicians for election returns and popular opinion. Autocracies may even prefer not to have significant private wealth creation occurring within their jurisdictions (assuming they have alternative sources of wealth, such as natural resources), because private wealth creates alternative centers of power within the jurisdiction that could lead to challenges to their authority. For example, Guinea's former dictator Sekou Touré "extended state control to every sector of the economy" in an effort to "prevent the rise of an elite entrepreneurial class."[97] Zaire's Mobutu, Venezuela's Hugo Chávez, and Russia's Vladimir Putin are other autocrats with policy preferences for redistribution of natural resource–based wealth over fostering wealth creation through economic growth. As noted earlier, legal competition is therefore likely to have different effects on governments subject to some degree of democratic constraints than it will on autocracies.

Both democratically constrained governments and autocracies have commitment problems. The current government in a democratically constrained jurisdiction has difficulty restricting successor governments. Uncertainty over whether the next government will honor the current regulatory bargain affects the value of the bargain to the private parties. Autocracies have both a current commitment problem, since the greater degree of power the autocrat holds, the less trustworthy his commitment is, and a future commitment problem, since succession is a major problem, and the life of an autocratic regime is difficult to predict with certainty. Furthermore, just as firms prefer not to compete in the marketplace, governments of both the democratic and autocratic varieties would prefer not to be constrained by regulatory competition in pursuit of their policy objectives (whether motivated by a public-spirited approach to policy or by more venal considerations), as can be seen by the virulent complaints from a range of French and German governments in recent years about the detrimental nature of "Anglo-Saxon" competition.[98]

In looking for the impacts of regulatory competition, we therefore have to look at multiple policy dimensions. Competition may affect

- the mix of measures available for governments to fund themselves;
- the explicit rates governments can charge through taxes and fees;
- the extent to which governments can use implicit taxes imposed through regulations;
- the types of regulatory objectives that governments can achieve; and
- the extent to which particular regulatory objectives can be achieved.

Different types of governments may be affected differently, and increasing the degree of regulatory competition may give a competitive advantage to particular forms of government over other forms.

Offshore Jurisdictions as Competitors. Offshore jurisdictions share six characteristics that make them qualitatively different from onshore jurisdictions.

First, offshore jurisdictions tend to be small in size, resources, and population. The Bahamas (13,940 sq. km., 300,529 population), Barbados (432 sq. km., 280,946 population), Bermuda (53.3 sq. km., 66,163 population), the Cayman Islands (262 sq. km., 46,600 population), Jersey (116 sq. km., 91,321 population), Guernsey (78 sq. km., 65,573 population), Hong Kong (1,092 sq. km., 6,980,412 population), the Isle of Man (572 sq. km., 75,831 population), the Netherlands Antilles (960 sq. km., 223,652 population), Lichtenstein (160 sq. km., 34,247 population), Luxembourg (2,586 sq. km., 480,222 population), Switzerland (41,290 sq. km., 7,554,661 population), and Singapore (693 sq. km., 4,553,009 population) are all jurisdictions with few, if any, natural resources, and limited population and land area compared to the size of onshore economies. Their small size leaves them with few alternatives for viable economies.[99] The Cayman Islands explicitly developed their offshore sector in response to the lack of alternative development strategies.[100] Similarly, the Netherlands Antilles developed an extensive offshore financial center in the 1960s and 1970s in large part because it had few alternative development strategies available to it.[101] Moreover, these jurisdictions are so small that their internal markets are insufficient to support any degree of self-sufficiency in any economic sector, and so they must turn to trade as a means of economic development.

Larger jurisdictions may have a choice in how open to make their economies, since a relatively closed (if not prosperous) economy is possible for them, but even small states much larger than the typical offshore jurisdiction have little choice in the matter. Lacking a large labor supply, natural resources, and significant domestic market, these small jurisdictions have few options beyond financial services and tourism other than exporting their populations to find work elsewhere. Offshore jurisdictions thus differ from many onshore jurisdictions in that they are credibly committed to an open economy. One measure of this credibility is that one does not observe politicians seeking office on protectionist platforms in such economies, whereas many larger economies have strong protectionist strains to their political discourse, regardless of ideology.

Second, also as a consequence of the lack of domestic resources or economic activity, the primary opportunity of offshore jurisdictions' governments to secure revenue comes from fees paid by offshore sector participants. Much as Delaware's dependence on corporate charter fees is thought to help that state credibly commit to maintaining the corporate law regime on which its market position depends,[102] so the dependence of offshore sectors makes their commitments more credible. Moreover, much of the offshore financial business is not dependent on physical assets. Unlike industries with substantial fixed assets within jurisdictions (for example, mining), financial firms are capable of relocating quickly and relatively cheaply. And the development of flight clauses enables the financial industry to threaten credibly to leave in the event that the offshore jurisdiction reneges.

Third, offshore jurisdictions' limited alternatives motivate them to be more aggressive in innovating in law. Their small size makes their governments more flexible and responsive in adopting legislation and regulations to facilitate transactions by reducing the transactions costs of government action.

Fourth, their publics' awareness of the importance of the offshore business to local prosperity depoliticizes measures related to offshore business. The benefits of trade liberalization generally can be difficult for politicians in large economies to sell to their populations. Populations of successful offshore financial centers appear to have less trouble grasping the connection between their prosperity and international trade in financial services than the residents of larger onshore jurisdictions do in understanding that link for their own economies.

Fifth, many offshore jurisdictions are relatively new; even older ones like the Isle of Man are relatively new players on the international financial scene. As these jurisdictions lacked established reputations when they entered the international markets, they were forced to develop innovative means of demonstrating commitment to the regulatory bargains they proposed to outside economic entities. The Cayman Islands adopted a statute providing exceptionally strong financial privacy protections, expanding on what was available under the applicable English common law by adding criminal sanctions for violations.[103] This was done to enhance the jurisdiction's credibility; given the small size of the islands' economy during the early years, the Caymanian supporters of the statute argued that investors needed additional reassurance.[104]

Finally, the small size of offshore financial centers allows them to innovate in development of regulatory regimes. For example, financial sector regulation in Cayman is primarily the responsibility of the Cayman Islands Monetary Authority (CIMA), an independent regulatory body whose board includes numerous non-Caymanian members, many of whom have brought significant expertise to the regulator that was not available within the islands.[105] By comparison, onshore regulators in the United States are more often chosen under conditions that involve political considerations. Delaware's lucrative corporate charter business is overseen by a political appointee with no significant financial sector experience; even when the choice of powerful federal financial regulators results in appointees with financial sector experience, the political dimensions of the choices are considerable.[106]

Compared to U.S. financial regulators, Cayman regulators have broader, more extensive powers, and financial entities in Cayman have fewer due process protections during the course of regulatory investigations than financial entities in the United States. For example, a former Caymanian financial secretary described how he handled complaints about a banker in the 1970s: "I called [the banker] to my office, locked the door behind him, and seriously questioned his involvement [in the activities], while reminding him of his moral and official obligations in the community as a Class A banker." After listening to the banker's explanation, the regulator decided that the banker's "side of the story had merits and I accepted it. However, before unlocking my door for his exit, I impressed on him the fact that if at any time he should slip out of his bounds as a banker and hurt people or the local banking community, I would see him behind bars."[107] As I have noted elsewhere, it is impossible to imagine an equivalent interview between any major regulator in the United States and the head of an American bank without also picturing the presence of a vast number of lawyers (on both sides), the absence of such a frank discussion, and a subsequent press conference held on the agency's front steps, during which the aggrieved banker and his lawyers denounce the heavy-handed efforts of the regulator.[108] On the other hand, financial entities in Cayman are well protected by the Confidential Relationships (Preservation) Law against leaks of confidential information accumulated in the course of investigations.[109] And Cayman regulators are constrained by their need to maintain Cayman's reputation in the competitive marketplace for offshore financial business.

These jurisdictions are, therefore, qualitatively different competitors in the international marketplace for transactions. Adding competition by offshore jurisdictions to the mix thus brings to the marketplace a group of competitors insulated from some of the domestic political pressures that undermine larger jurisdictions' commitments to openness. This role is particularly important, as onshore governments have strong incentives to find ways to limit competition to provide themselves with additional freedom in economic policy. Economist Barry Eichengreen's account of the evolution of the twentieth-century international monetary system notes the increasing difficulty governments had in maintaining fiscal stability over the course of the twentieth century. Prior to World War I, the major trading nations maintained a system of pegged exchange rates, which, Eichengreen argues, was possible only because governments were under relatively little domestic political pressure to "subordinate currency stability to other objectives."[110] (Their insulation from such political pressure was due to the impact of restricted franchises on politicians' calculations about the impact of economic policy on their reelection chances.[111]) After World War II, expanding democracy increased such pressures, diminishing "the credibility of the authorities' resolve to defend the currency peg," and governments resorted to exchange controls as a means of preventing market pressures from punishing them for defecting from the prior regulatory bargain.[112] Such controls were not a sustainable policy in the face of increasing international capital flows: "The conjunction of free trade and fettered finance was not dynamically stable."[113] There is widespread agreement with Eichengreen's assessment of the impact of global capital flows as a disciplinary force: "The sheer amount of capital residing in or passing through OFCs and tax havens is now so great that it is beyond the ability of any single government to—in Mrs. Thatcher's famous words—'buck the market.'"[114]

A similar dynamic takes place with respect to regulatory competition by offshore financial centers. Consider the development of the Caymanian offshore sector. Cayman had little financial, physical, or communications infrastructure in 1959. Once the islands decided to make an effort to develop an offshore financial center, they invested in upgrading their physical and legal infrastructures. The legislature passed statutes governing banks, trust companies, and corporations. By being prepared, Cayman profited from the flight of capital from the Bahamas after Bahamian independence produced a government that reneged on the regulatory bargain with offshore interests.[115] Cayman developed new products, expanding beyond a company registry and banking to hedge funds and captive insurance.[116]

Offshore financial centers are thus a different type of "firm" in the market for legal rules, because their vulnerability to competition and dependence on the financial sector make their politicians' and voters' incentives differ from those of politicians and voters in onshore jurisdictions. Adding offshore financial centers to the regulatory competition mix changes the mix of "legal products" present in the world market for economic activity.

Eurobonds and Finance Subsidiaries. After World War II, the United States poured dollars into European reconstruction, creating a large pool of dollars on deposit outside the United States.[117] As these dollar balances grew in European banks, they became the subject of a separate market in "Eurodollars," and parallel markets in other currencies on deposit outside the issuing country also appeared ("Europounds," "Euromarks," and so forth).[118] Because these currencies were deposited outside their countries of issue, regulators in the issuing country had no jurisdiction over banks' treatment of the deposits. At the same time, most countries' banking regulators did not regulate lending by the foreign subsidiaries of their countries' banks in foreign currencies. As a result, the Eurocurrency markets were largely unregulated, which reduced banks' operating costs. For example, London-based subsidiaries of U.S. banks accepting dollar deposits were not required by U.S. regulators to purchase deposit insurance, maintain reserve ratios on those deposits, or be subject to limits on the interest paid.[119]

Meanwhile, by the mid-1960s, the United States was experiencing a shortage of dollars as a result of the fiscal pressures created by the rise in social spending and the financing of the Vietnam War.[120] The federal government took steps to discourage firms from financing their non-U.S. operations through U.S. capital markets, including imposition of the interest equalization tax.[121] As the pool of Eurodollars grew, the price of borrowing in Eurodollars fell below the price of borrowing in dollars in the U.S. capital markets. American firms increasingly sought access to them not only for financing non-U.S. operations, but for financing their domestic operations.

Blocking U.S. firms' Eurodollar borrowing was the U.S. withholding tax, which applied to interest payments to a foreign entity or individual. Despite its name, the tax was not a means of collecting a payment that could later be refunded if the recipient had a lesser American tax liability than the amount withheld (as with income tax withholding), but a nonrefundable 30 percent tax collected from the payor. Foreign lenders reacted by requiring that the U.S. payor "gross up" the interest payments to cover the taxes (and the taxes on the additional amount paid to cover the taxes), increasing the real interest rate sufficiently to destroy the cost advantage offered by the Eurodollar market.

A 1950s tax treaty with the Netherlands, later extended as a matter of routine to the Dutch islands in the Caribbean known as the Netherlands Antilles, contained language that allowed interest payments by U.S. borrowers to Dutch or Netherlands Antilles lenders without payment of the withholding tax, making it possible to gain access to the Eurocurrency markets. U.S. Internal Revenue Service (IRS) commissioner Roscoe Egger Jr. noted in 1983 that the treaty's inclusion of such language was "largely by accident," as most of the treaties signed in the same period did not include it.[122] When the Netherlands Antilles adopted one of the first "ring-fenced" tax regimes, which allowed companies legally resident in the Antilles but not conducting business there to pay income tax at an effective rate of between 2.4 percent and 3.0 percent, an opportunity to get access to the Eurocurrency markets appeared.[123] Since the Antilles did not have a withholding tax of its own, a foreign lender could receive payments from an Antilles subsidiary of a U.S. firm tax-free (except for any domestic tax obligations of the lender).

After the IRS began routinely issuing opinion letters approving the transactions as exempt from the withholding tax, U.S. borrowers began creating Netherlands Antilles subsidiaries that borrowed funds on the Eurocurrency markets and re-lent the money to the parent in the United States.[124] Because of the low Antilles tax rate applied inside the ring-fenced regime, the Antilles subsidiaries owed minimal taxes on the paper profits created by relending the money to their U.S. parents at a slightly higher rate than that at which they had borrowed the funds (to cover their operating expenses). The business grew dramatically, with billions of dollars annually flowing through Antillean finance subsidiaries into the United States economy.[125] The Antilles finance subsidiary business provided substantial benefits to the United States economy, lowering the cost of borrowing funds and making available to U.S. firms a substantial pool of capital that would have been otherwise unreachable. It also provided a significant benefit to the Antilles, which by the mid-1980s derived more than a third of its government revenue from the offshore sector.[126]

The United States canceled the U.S.–Netherlands Antilles tax treaty in 1984 (grandfathering existing bonds to prevent chaos in financial markets) after unsuccessfully attempting to negotiate a tax information agreement with the Antilles that would have provided the IRS with access to information on Antillean corporations (many of which were used by third-country nationals to hold U.S. real estate and other assets) and to limit the benefits of the tax treaty to Antillean individuals.[127]

To retain access to the Eurodollar market, the United States reformed tax law to eliminate the withholding tax and to make it possible for U.S. firms to borrow directly without the use of finance subsidiaries.

Captive Insurance. The spread of captive insurance structures demonstrates the impact of regulatory competition by offshore financial centers on onshore governments. Captive insurance companies are limited-purpose insurance companies which provide insurance to insureds who are the owners of the company. Generally, a subsidiary is organized that insures the parent company's activities. Companies could achieve the same insurance function by self-insuring; the captive structure allows the insured additional cost-reducing benefits, primarily by making premiums tax deductible under some circumstances and by allowing the captive to purchase reinsurance at wholesale prices. Captives are also used as risk management devices, reducing costs by lowering losses. In addition, captives can be used to insure against risks where a market for a particular type of insurance does not exist. Captives entail additional costs, however, as the insurance subsidiary must be created and maintained.

The availability of captive insurance structures is a beneficial development in insurance law. Captives expand the scope of the insurance market, making it possible for economic actors to obtain insurance products otherwise unavailable. They increase the competition for readily available forms of commercial insurance, and so make the market for insurance more competitive. Captives allow insureds access to the reinsurance market. Captives also allow for a greater range of business structures dealing with insurance, allowing creative risk management, investment, and other strategies otherwise unavailable in the marketplace.

Captives first became popular in the late 1970s and early 1980s.[128] Because many captives were located offshore, we have only estimates of the total amounts, but by 1986 an estimated $8.5 billion in premiums was being paid to captive insurance companies (for comparison purposes, note that commercial insurers collected approximately $100 billion in premiums that year).[129] Much of this involved entities domiciled in Bermuda, although the Cayman Islands, Channel Islands, and Isle of Man also were involved in captives early. Captives evolved from primarily dealing with medical malpractice to covering "general liability, automobile liability and physical damage, workers' compensation, business owners' packages, small property cover, professional liability and other lines of insurance for manufacturers, contractors, distributors, wholesalers, retailers and professional consultants."[130]

Offshore jurisdictions offered insurance laws specifically tailored for captive insurance companies, flexible (not lax) regulatory environments in which the insurance industry had regular access to regulators to discuss concerns, and political stability. Domestically, Vermont aggressively sought captive business, starting in 1979.[131] Vermont offered "low initial capital requirements, an annual audit, and a hefty dose of self-regulation." By 1989, it had as many captives as the rest of the states combined and was collecting $4 million annually in taxes on premiums.[132] According to a flattering 1989 *Business Week* profile, Vermont kept other states from luring away its captive business with "its telling combination of attractive laws, efficient insurance department, and plenty of skilled insurance professionals."[133] And Vermont offered "image conscious companies" a "base free of any offshore, tax ducking connotations."[134] Perhaps the most striking thing about this description of Vermont's efforts is that it could have readily been written by the public relations department of any of the offshore jurisdictions. Administrative efficiency, low fees and taxes, and the supply of professionals all are features regularly touted by high-end offshore jurisdictions in their quest for business. Even the avoidance of "tax ducking connotations" is similar to the claims by the reputable offshore jurisdictions that they provide a solid reputation for legitimate business operations.

One response to the rise of offshore captives was federal legislation in the United States to enhance the ability of states to create insurance entities capable of competing across the country. The Product Liability Risk Retention Act (PLRRA) was enacted in 1981 in response to the mid-1970s liability insurance crisis as a means of expanding the availability of insurance in a market in which Congress perceived too little supply.[135] The PLRRA explicitly allowed Caymanian and Bermudan companies to participate for a limited time, as well as overriding state restrictions on risk retention groups (RRGs) and purchasing groups (PGs).[136] The two offshore jurisdictions "were included as chartering jurisdictions . . . to discourage obstructionism in state legislatures by interests opposing the formation of risk retention groups."[137] This initial attempt to create competition was unsuccessful, as the PLRRA did not produce many new insurance groups, with a total of only seven of both types formed. Its failure was due to changes in market conditions that made traditional insurance sufficiently available to deter use of the new forms.[138] Nonetheless, a captive insurance industry did grow up offshore as Bermuda and Cayman responded to the identification of the market opportunity by creating their own captive insurance laws.

When the insurance market again produced a "liability crisis" in the mid-1980s, Congress amended the PLRRA with the 1986 federal Risk Retention Act (RRA)[139] and significantly expanded the range of insurance services available from RRGs and PGs to "nearly all nonpersonal lines of liability insurance."[140] The 1986 RRA allowed the use of RRGs and PGs organized under the laws of any domestic jurisdiction, but this time excluded new companies organized under Caymanian or Bermudan law and all other companies organized in foreign jurisdictions. At the time of passage, the amendments were expected to spur adoption of new captive insurance statutes beyond those previously passed in Colorado (1972), Tennessee (1978), Vermont (1981), and Virginia (1980).[141] In addition to the 1986 amendments to the RRA, the 1986 Tax Reform Act amended the Internal Revenue Code to eliminate the tax advantages of organizing a captive offshore, but failed to stem the growing success of offshore captives based on nontax considerations.[142] In particular, Cayman and Guernsey pioneered the "cell captive" structure in 1997–98, which lowered administrative costs for captives with multiple risk pools.[143]

Since then, more than ten states (and most recently the District of Columbia) have adopted captive insurance legislation,[144] although Vermont remains the domestic leader. Vermont's lead rests largely on its proactive efforts to keep its statutory framework up to date and on its vigorous competition with Bermuda and Cayman. And it seems clear that the competition with Bermuda and Cayman has played an important role in spurring Vermont to compete for captive insurance business. Captive insurance thus exemplifies the benefits of regulatory competition.

The Impact of Regulatory Competition

How does regulatory competition affect governments? In this section, I argue that the impacts are different for democratically constrained governments and autocratic governments. In both cases, I contend that there are substantial positive impacts which have been undervalued in the policy debate over regulatory competition.

Impacts on Democratically Constrained Governments. Regulatory competition constrains democratic governments in several important ways. First, with respect to public finance laws, in a world with relatively few barriers to capital mobility, the existence of tax competition makes discriminatory taxes costly for governments. Whenever a tax or fee structure creates an opportunity for arbitrage, some transactions on the margin will shift to an alternative jurisdiction offering lower taxation. When offshore financial centers participate in the competition, they will seek to expand arbitrage opportunities. For example, the growth of "open registry" jurisdictions for shipping, particularly Panama and Liberia, spurred considerable change in taxation of shipping by Greece, Britain, and Japan.[145]

Second, with respect to the laws organizing the public sector, democratic governments will face some competitive pressures from offshore financial centers, but these will be relatively minimal.

Third, regulatory competition will likely have a significant impact on laws that seek to change private behavior by altering incentives. Because of offshore financial centers' focus on maximizing their revenue from the sum total of transactions occurring within their jurisdictions, they are less likely to seek to change regulated entities' behavior in ways unrelated to that goal. Competition from offshore financial centers is thus likely to exert greater pressure on indirect efforts at regulation, forcing democratically constrained onshore governments to shift their regulatory efforts to direct regulation methods or to reduce them. This does not mean that offshore financial centers have an incentive to ignore financial shenanigans such as fraud, as the offshore jurisdictions must be concerned with their reputations. Indeed, they have much more reason to be concerned with reputation than do large onshore economies like the United States. Just as China's market is sufficiently large that foreign investors are willing to tolerate levels of corruption and uncertainty that they would not accept in a much smaller jurisdiction, so, too, are investors willing to accept regulatory costs or poorly designed regulatory schemes in giant economies like the United States or the European Union.

Finally, because offshore jurisdictions have a greater incentive to win market share in transactions, their innovations will create regulatory competition for onshore jurisdictions to match the reduced transactions costs.

Offshore regulatory competition offers some advantages for democratically constrained governments, as well. Governments may wish to price-discriminate among economic activities to enhance their citizens' opportunities for participation in economic activities outside their jurisdictions. For example, suppose Jurisdiction A uses relatively high corporate and personal income tax rates as part of the funding mechanism to provide a generous social welfare system to its citizens. If Jurisdiction A taxes its citizens at the same rate for their domestic and international investments, it will disadvantage its businesses in international competition with firms and citizens from a lower-tax jurisdiction. If Jurisdiction A has a tax treaty with Barbados, however, its firms and citizens can participate in international business through Barbadian entities and secure a lower tax rate on the profits from the international venture. In essence, the offshore jurisdiction's lower tax rate and the tax treaty network allow Jurisdiction A to offer one "price" to firms conducting activities occurring within its jurisdiction and another price for activities conducted elsewhere. By making its firms competitive internationally, and allowing repatriation of the profits at the lower tax rate, Jurisdiction A benefits by increasing the wealth available to its citizens. Substitute "Canada" for "Jurisdiction A," and we have a compelling picture of why Canada tolerates its multinationals' making use of Barbados's network of tax treaties despite the losses of tax revenue this entails.

Despite frequent protests by governments, the existence of regulatory competition can serve their interests by creating opportunities to pursue policies through offshore vehicles.[146] One example of this is the creation of the Panamanian ship registry during the early days of World War II to enable the reflagging of American vessels to neutral flags, allowing them to transport war materials to Britain. After passage of the Neutrality Act in November 1939, U.S.-flagged ships were barred from the ports of the European belligerents and many other European ports, as well. "Between September 1939 and June

1941 the U.S. Maritime Commission approved the transfer of sixty-three U.S.-flag vessels to Panamanian registry, which provided a convenient way around the Neutrality Act."[147] Another shipping deal done with government participation was the *shikumisen* system of shipbuilding utilized by Japanese merchant shipping firms in the 1960s and 1970s. A Japanese firm would contract with a Japanese trading company, which in turn would contract with a Hong Kong ship owner. The Hong Kong and Japanese shipping companies agreed on the ship specifications, and the ship was ordered through a Japanese shipyard, with a 70 percent loan at a low interest rate through the Japanese Export–Import Bank, 25 percent from a Hong Kong bank, and 5 percent down by the Hong Kong shipping company. This system "originally arose in order to circumvent the Japanese regulations that controlled the supply of credit, currency transfers, etc., but it also took place under the supervision of the Japanese state and with its approval. . . . The *shikumisen* deal was an elegant way of getting round the Japanese currency and credit regulations while allowing the Japanese state full insight and control."[148]

Impacts on Autocratic Governments. Regulatory competition has a different set of impacts on autocratic governments. Actors in autocratic governments express their preferences under different constraints than they do in democratically constrained governments.[149] Autocrats need to keep economic activity at a level sufficient to prevent a revolt, but that level need not be particularly high if the autocrat is willing to engage in high levels of repressive behavior (for example, North Korea or Zimbabwe today, Zaire under Mobutu, Albania under Communist rule). But the need to attract investment can be a significant constraint where more than a subsistence level of existence for the population at large is desired or necessary for regime preservation. For example, "the tyrannical instincts of [South Korean dictator] Park Chung Hee's government, and its successors, were somewhat curbed by the need to maintain the friendship of the United States, to keep Japanese investments flowing in, and to maintain markets abroad. There were no such restraints in the North."[150]

What often matters most to autocrats is avoiding the creation of alternative centers of power within their societies that threaten their continued rule. Autocrats are often blunt about their ambition to prevent any institution they do not control from acquiring influence. Malawi's former dictator,

Hastings Banda, declared, "Everything is my business. Everything. The state of education, the state of our economy, the state of our agriculture, the state of our transport, everything is my business," and, "Anything I say is law. Literally law."[151] Similarly, Tunisia's former dictator Habib Bourguiba, when asked about the country's political system, replied, "System? What system? I am the system!"[152] Economic activities the autocrat does not control not only provide centers of power but create demand among those involved in such economic activities for greater rule of law and security of property rights.

Exchange controls, access to credit, and similar measures are important levers of control of economic activities for autocratic regimes. Zaire is a typical example. Under the Mobutu regime, the official rate for the local currency fell from an exchange rate of Z50 per U.S. dollar in 1985 to Z719 in 1990; a devaluation in August 1991 attempted to match the black market rate of Z114,291 to the dollar; and the free fall continued to Z8,000,000 per dollar in October 1993.[153] As a result, access to hard currency became critical for individuals and firms seeking to maintain their wealth and continue their businesses.[154] But during the period of currency free fall in the early 1990s, "the Zairian government accelerated its attempts to acquire hard currency and to control foreign exchange transactions. In October 1993, the regime required all Zairian exports to be paid for in advance in foreign currency. In addition, all incoming foreign exchange had to be 'sold' to the central bank for domestic currency within forty-eight hours of receipt."[155] To evade these controls, "it was common practice to ask bankers to deliver foreign currency receipts to another customer, who would then pay the exporter zaires at the parallel rate minus a commission."[156] The same facilities criticized as enabling autocrats to loot their countries by funneling cash out into foreign investments thus enabled those with access to them to preserve their wealth.[157]

For an entrepreneur in an autocratic jurisdiction, the autocratic state poses three related problems. First, the entrepreneur is likely to lack the ability to structure his economic activities freely within the autocratic state. For example, it may be necessary to hire the autocrat's supporters or give them a share of the firm.[158] Those hired in response to political pressure are problematic not simply because they may lack the requisite skills; because of the political uncertainties of autocracies, such individuals have the incentive to focus on short-term efforts to gain rents.[159]

Second, the autocratic state is less likely than a democratically constrained government to be responsive to the entrepreneur's need for innovations that reduce transactions costs, because it is less interested in maximizing economic activity. Further, if the autocrat's goal is maximizing his personal returns, imposing (rather than reducing) transactions costs allows him to collect either the transactions costs or a bribe to remove them. Zaire's dictator Mobutu Sese Seko famously encouraged his followers to engage in such behavior when he told an audience in 1976: "If you want to steal, steal a little cleverly, in a nice way. Only if you steal so much as to become rich overnight, you will be caught."[160]

Third, entrepreneurs want to keep the returns from their entrepreneurial efforts. Failing to comply with the autocrat's demands puts these gains at risk.[161] Indeed, one of the most effective techniques autocrats use to eliminate opposition is to pauperize it through "a whole battery of controls on prices, exchange rates, interest rates, and other economic variables . . . [which are] exactly the controls the strongmen [need] to punish their rivals and enrich themselves."[162] Not only do these tools enable the autocrat to punish his opponents, but they also enable him to enrich himself and his friends. Where "every permit has its price," there is an enormous incentive to invent new requirements for permits.[163]

Competition from jurisdictions outside the autocratic state reduces its ability to limit entrepreneurs. Using a combination of domestic and international business entities can provide the entrepreneur in an autocratic state with the ability to evade the autocrat's grasping hand, keeping more of the business entities involved under the entrepreneur's control. In particular, regulatory competition with jurisdictions that have strong confidentiality laws limits autocratic regimes in their efforts to discover the value of entrepreneurs' holdings. (Of course, the autocrat may also be able to use entities in jurisdictions with strong confidentiality laws to conceal wealth obtained by looting his country.) Where the rule of law is missing, shifting transactions to another jurisdiction may be the only way an entrepreneur can obtain the application of a fair set of rules to his business.

Regulatory competition has a greater impact on autocratic states than on democratically constrained ones in inducing innovation, as well. In general, democratically constrained states seek to increase wealth by encouraging economic activity (with the caveat that rent-seeking may limit this).

This is not necessarily true of autocratic states, however, as the threat posed by accumulation of private wealth is problematic for the autocrat's maintenance of power. Autocratic states are less likely to be responsive to market demand in innovating to reduce transactions costs. Regulatory competition from other jurisdictions thus both increases the market pressure to respond and provides an outlet for entrepreneurs in autocratic states to create transactions cost–reducing legal entities outside their home jurisdictions. This competition is important because it reduces autocrats' freedom of action.

Finally, the existence of outside legal entities protected by strong confidentiality laws is important for citizens of autocratic states. Entrepreneurial activity always includes a risk of loss, but entrepreneurial activity in an autocratic state includes the additional risk posed by the weaker restrictions on government confiscation of property under autocracies. Providing vehicles that allow entrepreneurs in autocratic states to conceal their wealth thus promotes the creation of alternative centers of power within autocracies.

Conclusion

Offshore financial centers are routinely denounced as "outside the rule of law"[164] for enabling tax evasion, money laundering by criminals, looting by autocrats, and, most recently, as potential avenues for the financing of terrorism. Even setting aside the hypocrisy and inconsistency of neglecting the role of onshore jurisdictions' financial centers, particularly New York and London, in exactly the same activities that the onshore governments find so alarming when conducted in Georgetown, Grand Cayman, or Liechtenstein, such a view of these jurisdictions neglects the crucial roles they play in the world economy. It is not a trivial contribution to the world economy to lower the cost of borrowing funds by 2–3 percent, as the Netherlands Antilles finance subsidiaries did for American firms from the 1960s to 1985, or to make insurance available for risks routinely not insurable on the commercial market or at a lower cost, as Bermuda, Cayman, Guernsey, and the Isle of Man do for firms in North America and Britain. Most important, the regulatory competition—which is not limited to tax competition—provided by offshore financial centers qualitatively changes the larger market for law, introducing a new class of jurisdiction into the market.

I have argued in this chapter that this competition has a significant impact on autocratic governments. The criticism of offshore financial centers for enabling the looting of jurisdictions by autocrats puts the cart before the horse. Consider Meredith's description of African autocracies:

> Time and again, [Africa's] potential for economic development has been disrupted by the predatory politics of ruling elites seeking personal gain, often precipitating violence for their own ends. . . . After decades of mismanagement and corruption, most African states have become hollowed out. They are no longer instruments capable of serving the public good. Indeed, far from being able to provide aid and protection to their citizens, African governments and the vampire-like politicians who run them are regarded by the populations they rule as yet another burden they have to bear in the struggle for survival.[165]

This problem is not unique to Africa or even postcolonialist regimes. Professor Dan Chirot describes the post-Stalin Soviet Union as "little more than a group of organized racketeers who lied, stole, and plundered their society into ruin."[166] While OFC critics like Raymond Baker are correct that many of these autocrats have used bank secrecy and foreign businesses to shift considerable wealth out of their countries (including using banks and businesses in the United States and Europe), we must also consider the impact on corrupt autocrats of the competition to which their states are exposed by the existence of those same financial channels. Ayittey argues that the business empires of African autocrats "will collapse if economic reform strips them of state controls,"[167] and that this can bring about political as well as economic change for the better.

Both democratically constrained and autocratic governments are affected by regulatory competition in important ways. Democratically constrained governments find the cost of inefficient policies increased by more vigorous regulatory competition, and so engage in less of it. Autocrats find that regulatory competition in financial matters makes many of the measures they have traditionally used to impoverish opponents too expensive to maintain in the long run. Indeed, only autocrats with significant rents available from commodities and natural resources have been able to maintain their economies above the subsistence level in recent decades, while those without such rents have been forced to liberalize or forgo the rewards of economic growth. This competition is a significant benefit of the regulatory competition provided by offshore financial centers. If we are to avoid losing these benefits, we must ensure that the policy debate over measures aimed at restricting regulatory competition, such as the American proposal for the Stop Tax Haven Abuse Act and the European Union's Savings Directive, be expanded to a more complete understanding of the benefits of international regulatory competition and the important role of offshore financial centers in that competition.

Notes

Introduction

1. Alex Barker, "Turks and Caicos Premier Hits Out at UK Moves," *Financial Times*, March 18, 2009; Rensselaer W. Lee III, *The White Labyrinth: Cocaine and Political Power* (Piscataway, N.J.: Transaction Publishers, 1991), 183.

2. Jan Rogozinski, *A Brief History of the Caribbean: From the Arawak and the Carib to the Present*, rev. ed. (New York: Plume Books, 2000), 282.

3. Joanna Chung, "Stanford Accused over $1.6bn 'Ponzi' Scheme," *Financial Times*, February 28, 2009.

4. Joanna Chung, "Former UBS Banker Expected to Plead Guilty in Tax Evasion Case," *Financial Times*, May 30, 2008 (describing Swiss bank's tax evasion issues); Hugh Williamson, "Mammoth Tax Evasion Probe Widens," *Financial Times*, February 21, 2008 (describing Liechtenstein probe).

5. S. 509, 111th Congress (2009–10).

6. Associated Press, "Text of the Communiqué of the G-20," April 2, 2009.

7. Organisation for Economic Co-operation and Development, "Following G20 OECD Delivers on Tax Pledge," April 2, 2009, available at http://www.oecd.org/document/57/0,3343,en_2649_34487_42496569_1_1_1_1,00.html.

8. Jean Eaglesham and Alex Barker, "UK Premier Calls for Crackdown on Tax Havens," *Financial Times*, February 19, 2009; Alex Barker, "Brown Warns Tax Havens to Comply," *Financial Times*, April 10, 2009; Robert M. Morgenthau, "Too Much Money Is Beyond Legal Reach," *Wall Street Journal*, September 30, 2008; Grant McCool, "More Offshore Tax Probes in the Works: NY's Morgenthau," Reuters, April 24, 2009.

Chapter 1: Offshore Finance and Onshore Markets

1. See Roberta Romano, *The Genius of American Corporate Law* (Washington, D.C.: AEI Press, 1993); Ralph Winter, "State Law, Shareholder Protection, and the Theory of the Corporation," *Journal of Legal Studies* 6 (1977): 251–92; Jonathan Macey and Geoffrey Miller, "Toward an Interest Group Theory of Corporate Law," *Texas Law Review* 65 (1987): 469–524.

2. Hilton McCann, *Offshore Finance* (Cambridge: Cambridge University Press, 2006), xiii.

3. See Rose-Marie Belle Antoine, *Confidentiality in Offshore Financial Law* (New York: Oxford University Press, 2002), sec. 1.34–45.

4. See, for example, G. Scott Dowling, Comment, "Fatal Broadside: The Demise of Caribbean Offshore Financial Confidentiality Post USA PATRIOT Act," *Transnational Lawyer* 17 (2004): 263, 271–72; Kathleen A. Lacey and Barbara Crutchfield George, "Crackdown on Money Laundering: A Comparative Analysis of the Feasibility and Effectiveness of Domestic and Multilateral Policy Reforms," *Northwestern Journal of International Law and Business* 23 (2003): 277–78.

5. See Dowling, "Fatal Broadside," 281–82; Frank C. Razzano, "So You Want to Be an International Financial Center. . . . Are You Prepared to Spit in the Giant's Eye?" *Securities Regulation Law Journal* 28 (2000): 334.

6. U.S. Senate, Committee on Government Affairs, Permanent Subcommittee on Investigations, *Crime and Secrecy, Use of Offshore Banks and Companies*, Senate Report No. 99-130 in Serial Set vol. 13621 (Washington, D.C.: Government Printing Office, 1985), 1.

7. U.S. Senate, Committee on Homeland Security and Governmental Affairs, Subcommittee on Investigations, *Tax Haven Abuses: The Enablers, the Tools and Secrecy: Minority and Majority Staff Report*, August 1, 2006, http://levin.senate.gov/newsroom/supporting/2006/PSI.taxhavenabuses.080106.pdf (accessed August 24, 2009).

8. See, for example, Reuven S. Avi-Yonah, "Globalization, Tax Competition, and the Fiscal Crisis of the Welfare State," *Harvard Law Review* 113 (2000): 1576; Organisation for Economic Co-operation and Development, *Tax Co-operation: Towards a Level Playing Field*, OECD Publishing, 2006). Oxfam International estimated the amount of lost revenue by industrialized nations due to tax havens at $50 billion annually. Alexander Townsend Jr., Comment, "The Global Schoolyard Bully: The Organisation for Economic Co-operation and Development's Coercive Efforts to Control Tax Competition," *Fordham International Law Journal* 25 (2001): 234.

9. James P. Springer, "An Overview of International Evidence and Asset Gathering in Civil and Criminal Tax Cases," *George Washington Journal of International Law and Economics* 22 (1988): 281.

10. U.S. Department of State, Bureau for International Narcotics and Law Enforcement Affairs, *2000 International Narcotics Control Strategy Report*, issued March 1, 2001, http://www.state.gov/p/inl/rls/nrcrpt/2000 (accessed August 24, 2009).

11. This figure refers to the estimated offshore assets of high-net-worth individuals. Tax Justice Network, "Briefing Paper: The Price of Offshore," http://www.taxjustice.net/cms/upload/pdf/Price_of_Offshore.pdf (accessed August 24, 2009).

12. Aline Sullivan, "Tax Havens/Going, Going, Gone?: World Watchdogs Make Life Unpleasant Offshore," *International Herald Tribune*, March 15, 2003.

13. William Brittain-Catlin, *Offshore: The Dark Side of the Global Economy* (New York: Macmillan, 2005), 72–73.

14. Amos N. Guiora and Brian J. Field, "Using and Abusing the Financial Markets: Money Laundering as the Achilles' Heel of Terrorism," *University of Pennsylvania Journal of International Economic Law* 29 (2007): 59–104. This concern animates Title III of the USA PATRIOT Act, the International Money Laundering Abatement and Anti-Terrorist Financing Act of 2001, which empowers the Treasury secretary to order domestic financial institutions to take special measures in response to money laundering and to heighten the requirements for financial disclosure. See 31 U.S.C. § 5318a (2006).

15. See Dowling, "Fatal Broadside," 272. "The level of illegal activity in offshore banking is greatly overstated and sensationalized. . . . Many offshore centers are well regulated, have enacted measures to reduce criminal activity and view misuse of confidentiality as a threat to their economic stability. In fact, the Bahamian money laundering statute may be more modern than those of most nations, including the United States. Ironically, many nations with highly regulated banking systems have been victims of elaborate money laundering schemes." Ibid. (internal citations omitted).

16. It is important to bear in mind that companies and individuals that utilize OFCs still are required to comply with all applicable laws in the jurisdictions in which they operate. Thus, the utilization of OFCs simply is part of a legitimate tax planning strategy, so long as the firms and individuals involved are in compliance with all applicable laws.

17. For a discussion of the examples of Enron, which used Caribbean tax havens to pay U.S. corporate federal income tax only once in a five-year period when its profits were near $2 billion and its tax liabilities just $17 million, and Stanley Works, which estimated a reduction from 32 percent to 24 percent in domestic taxes, saving $30 million per year, by reincorporating in Bermuda, see Brittain-Catlin, *Offshore: The Dark Side*, 55, 91–92.

18. Joanne Ramos, "On or Off?" *Economist*, March 1, 2007, http://www.cfo.com/article.cfm/8792331/c_8771072 (quoting European bank regulators; accessed August 24, 2009).

19. Marshall J. Langer, *How to Use Foreign Tax Havens* (New York: Practising Law Institute, 1975), 4.

20. Ibid.

21. See notes 33–47 and accompanying text.

22. Vanessa Houlder, "Financial Standards Come under Fire," *Financial Times*, May 1, 2007, http://www.ft.com/cms/s/0/38b1ff06-f781-11db-86b0-000b5df10621.html (accessed August 24, 2009).

23. See below, note 67 and accompanying text.

24. Langer, *Foreign Tax Havens*, 4. "When a large company needs to borrow money from abroad by issuing bonds or notes, no one will buy them unless they are free of tax. The country into which the borrowed money is flowing must either permit direct borrowing without imposing tax or it must tolerate the use of a tax haven company

to make the interest tax-free. Otherwise there would be no funds available to borrow." Ibid.

25. See notes 61–66 and accompanying text.

26. See notes 67–70 and accompanying text.

27. See, generally, Richard Anthony Johns, *Tax Havens and Offshore Finance: A Study of Transnational Economic Development* (London: Pinter Publishers, 1983); McCann, *Offshore Finance*, 10–257; see also International Monetary Fund, Monetary and Exchange Affairs Department, "Offshore Financial Centers IMF Background Paper," http://www.imf.org/external/np/mae/oshore/2000/eng/back.htm#1.

28. Joanne Ramos, "Places in the Sun," *Economist*, February 24, 2007, 3–5.

29. Johns, *Tax Havens and Offshore Finance*, 225.

30. See, for example, Hoyt Barber, *Tax Havens Today: The Benefits and Pitfalls of Banking and Investing Offshore* (Hoboken, N.J.: John Wiley and Sons, 2007), 15–17; Dowling, "Fatal Broadside," 271–80.

31. See Barber, *Tax Havens Today*, 18.

32. See Dowling, "Fatal Broadside," 275–76; see also Antoine, *Confidentiality in Offshore*; and Antoine, this volume.

33. See *International Money Marketing*, "G-7 Sets Goals for Onshore Gains," June 2000, 3; see also Gordon, this volume. For an explanation of anti–money laundering measures in the Caribbean offshore community, see Jason Ennis, "Cleaning Up the Beaches: The Caribbean Response to the FATF's Review to Identify Non-Cooperative Countries or Territories," *Law and Business Review of the Americas* 8 (2002): 637. OFC supporters have alleged that anti–money laundering efforts are reaching and deterring more conduct than is appropriate. See, generally, Barber, *Tax Havens Today*, 21–22. For support for the proposition that the root concern is really revenue loss, see Antoine, *Confidentiality in Offshore*, sec. 2.63–65.

34. FATF is an ad hoc group of countries that collaborate on anti–money laundering measures and measures to combat terrorist financing. It was formed in 1989.

35. See "Offshore Issues: Synopsis of International Policy Initiatives," in International Monetary Fund, "IMF Background Paper," pt. III, table 3.

36. See Organisation for Economic Co-operation and Development, *Harmful Tax Competition: An Emerging Global Issue* (Paris: OECD Publishing, 1998).

37. For a recent progress report, see Organisation for Economic Co-operation and Development, *Tax Co-operation*.

38. See Financial Action Task Force, *Financial Action Task Force on Money Laundering: Review to Identify Non-Cooperative Countries or Territories: Increasing the Worldwide Effectiveness of Anti–Money Laundering Measures*, June 22, 2000, http://www.fatf-gafi.org/dataoecd/56/43/33921824.pdf (accessed November 25, 2009).

39. For an in-depth analysis of international efforts generally, see McCann, *Offshore Finance*, 259–331.

40. See, for example, Antoine, *Confidentiality in Offshore*, sec. 11.10–13. "Offshore countries . . . question whether the OECD, as an institution, has the right to define

any tax reform process which involves the sovereignty of independent nations, in particular, non-members of the institution. For some states, the OECD position is a crude intervention in the affairs of offshore states." Ibid. "Recently . . . the G7 nations began a campaign that uses the threat of sanctions to coerce cooperation from offshore financial centers in the areas of money laundering and tax competition. The use of sanctions to force compliance is problematic because, although sanctions would be available to remedy a violation of an international obligation, there has been no attempt to identify any such obligation for the Object States. Instead the Financial Action Task Force (FATF) and the Organization for Economic Cooperation and Development (OECD), in accordance with the agenda of the G7, have set forth self-referential criteria that assess compliance of the offshore financial centers with presumed international 'standards' against money laundering and harmful tax competition." Benjamin R. Hartman, "Coercing Cooperation from Offshore Financial Centers: Identity and Coincidence of International Obligations against Money Laundering and Harmful Tax Competition," *Boston College International and Comparative Law Review* 24 (2001): 253.

41. See International Tax and Investment Organisation and Society of Trust and Estate Practitioners, *Towards a Level Playing Field: Regulating Corporate Vehicles in Cross-Border Transactions*, 2002, 14–16, http://www.itio.org/documents/TowardsaLevel.pdf (accessed August 24, 2009).

42. Ibid., 11–12.

43. Timothy Ridley (chairman, Cayman Islands Monetary Authority), "The Future of Offshore Financial Centers: Reading the Tea Leaves from a Cayman Perspective" (background paper to personal remarks to the University of Illinois Law School, Champaign, Ill., March 19, 2008), http://www.cimoney.com.ky/uploadedFiles/Media_Centre/Speeches/TimRidleyFutureofOffshoreCentres.pdf (accessed August 24, 2009).

44. See Vaughn E. James, "Twenty-First Century Pirates of the Caribbean: How the Organization for Economic Cooperation and Development Robbed Fourteen CARICOM Countries of Their Tax and Economic Policy Sovereignty," *University of Miami Inter-American Law Review* 34 (2002): 1–50.

45. Organisation for Economic Co-operation and Development, *Tax Co-operation*.

46. Antoine, *Confidentiality in Offshore*, sec. 4.09.

47. See, generally, Sullivan, "Tax Havens Going."

48. For a brief discussion of the international political economy of OFCs' evolution, see International Monetary Fund, "IMF Background Paper," pt. II.C. For a good discussion of the origins of tax competition, see Townsend, "Global Schoolyard Bully," 219–27.

49. Other scholars have identified a link between increased capital mobility and tax competition. See, for example, Avi-Yonah, "Fiscal Crisis of the Welfare State," 1575.

50. Sullivan, "Tax Havens Going."

51. See *Lawyer*, "The Offshore Puzzle," May 5, 2008; Andrew P. Morriss, "The Role of Offshore Financial Centers in Regulatory Competition," University of Illinois Law

and Economics Research Paper No. LE07-032, University of Illinois at Urbana-Champaign, 2007, 6.

52. Antoine, *Confidentiality in Offshore*, sec. 1.28–29.

53. Ibid.

54. *Bermuda Insurance Quarterly*, "US and Bermuda Battle over Taxes," January 2008, 2, http://www.pwc.com/extweb/ncinthenews.nsf/docid/4083732A6568084F852571AA004A47C9/$file/BIQJan08.pdf (accessed August 24, 2009).

55. See Bermuda Market Solutions, "Welcome to the Bermuda Insurance Market," http://www.bermuda-insurance.org (accessed August 24, 2009).

56. Matt Piotrowski, "SEC Regulation Concerns Hedge Funds," *Oil Daily*, April 12, 2005.

57. Mark Chapman, "The Diverse Face of Investment Success in the British Virgin Islands," *Hedgeweek*, June 28, 2006, http://www.hedgeweek.com/articles/detail.jsp?content_id=27221&livehome=true (accessed August 24, 2009).

58. Ibid.

59. An extensive practitioner "how-to" literature provides instruction on the effective use of OFCs. See, for example, Barber, *Tax Havens Today*; Langer, *How to Use Foreign Tax Havens*. There is also an extensive academic literature concerning the history and development of particular offshore jurisdictions. See, for example, Michael Craton, *Founded upon the Seas: A History of the Cayman Islands and Their People* (Kingston, Jamaica: Ian Randle Publishers, 2003); Richard Anthony Johns and C. M. Le Marchant, *Finance Centres: British Isle Offshore Development since 1979* (New York: St. Martin's Press, 1993); David G. Kermode, *Offshore Island Politics: The Constitutional and Political Development of the Isle of Man in the Twentieth Century* (Liverpool, U.K.: Liverpool University Press, 2001).

60. See, for example, Dale D. Murphy, "The Business Dynamics of Global Regulatory Competition," in *Dynamics of Regulatory Change: How Globalization Affects National Regulatory Policies*, ed. David Vogel and Robert A. Kagan (Berkeley and Los Angeles: University of California Press, 2004), 84–117.

61. *Louis K. Liggett Co. v. Lee*, 288 U.S. 517, 557–60 (1933) (Brandeis, J., dissenting). "The removal by the leading industrial States of the limitations upon the size and powers of business corporations appears to have been due, not to their conviction that maintenance of the restrictions was undesirable in itself, but to the conviction that it was futile to insist upon them; because local restriction would be circumvented by foreign incorporation. Indeed, local restriction seemed worse than futile. Lesser States, eager for the revenue derived from the traffic in charters, had removed safeguards from their own incorporation laws. Companies were early formed to provide charters for corporations in states where the cost was lowest and the laws least restrictive. The states joined in advertising their wares. *The race was one not of diligence but of laxity.*" Ibid. (emphasis added).

62. See, for example, William L. Cary, "Federalism and Corporate Law: Reflections upon Delaware," *Yale Law Journal* 83 (1974): 663–705; David Charny, "Competition

among Jurisdictions in Formulating Corporate Law Rules: An American Perspective on the 'Race to the Bottom' in the European Communities," *Harvard International Law Journal* 32 (1991): 423–56; Murphy, "Business Dynamics," 13.

63. See Organisation for Economic Co-operation and Development, *Harmful Tax Competition*.

64. See Organisation for Economic Co-operation and Development, *Tax Co-operation*; see also Organisation for Economic Co-operation and Development, "OECD Reports Progress in Fighting Offshore Tax Evasion, But Says More Efforts Are Needed," October 12, 2007, http://www.oecd.org/document/48/0,3343,en_2649_201185_39482288_1_1_1_1,00.html (accessed August 24, 2009).

65. See Murphy, "Business Dynamics." For an argument that tax competition from offshore jurisdictions leads to undertaxation in onshore jurisdictions, see Avi-Yonah, "Fiscal Crisis of the Welfare State."

66. See Richard A. Johnson, "Why Harmful Tax Practices Will Continue after Developing Nations Pay: A Critique of the OECD's Initiatives Against Harmful Tax Competition," *Boston College Third World Law Journal* 26 (2006): 351–440.

67. See Antoine, *Confidentiality in Offshore*, sec. 3.06–14, 12.17–18; Dowling, "Fatal Broadside"; Michael Littlewood, "Tax Competition: Harmful to Whom?" *Michigan Journal of International Law* 26 (2004): 411–88; Townsend, "Global Schoolyard Bully."

68. See, for example, Antoine, *Confidentiality in Offshore*, sec. 2.62, 4.14–21, 6.60–8; Dowling, "Fatal Broadside."

69. See, for example, Rajiv Biswas, ed., *International Tax Competition: Globalisation and Fiscal Sovereignty* (London: Commonwealth Secretariat, 2002); James, "Twenty-First Century Pirates."

70. See, for example, Joshua D. Moore, "The Economic Importance of Tax Competition for Foreign Direct Investment: An Analysis of International Corporate Tax Harmonization Proposals and Lessons from the Winning Corporate Tax Strategy in Ireland," *Pacific McGeorge Global Business and Development Law Journal* 20 (2007): 345–82; Andrew K. Rose and Mark M. Spiegel, "Offshore Financial Centers: Parasites or Symbionts?" *Economic Journal* 117 (2007): 1310–35; Javier G. Salinas, "The OECD Tax Competition Initiative: A Critique of Its Merits in the Global Marketplace," *Houston Journal of International Law* 25 (2003): 531–60; Morriss, "OFCs in Regulatory Competition."

71. Ridley, "Future of OFCs," 4.

72. See Rafael La Porta, Florencio Lopez-De-Silanes, Andrei Shleifer, and Robert Vishny, "Legal Determinants of External Finance," *Journal of Finance* 52 (1997): 1131–50.

73. Rafael La Porta, Florencio Lopez-De-Silanes, Andrei Shleifer, and Robert Vishny, "Investor Protection and Corporate Governance," *Journal of Financial Economics* 58 (2000): 3–27.

74. McCann, *Offshore Finance*, 481–82, 490 (emphasis added).

75. *Amanda Acquisition Corp. v. Universal Foods Corp.*, 877 F.2d 496, 507 (7th Cir. 1989).

76. For a similar interpretation of Judge Easterbrook's argument in another context, see Charny, *Competition among Jurisdictions*, 431–32.

77. See, generally, Alison S. Fraser, Note, "The SEC's Ineffective Move toward Greater Regulation of Offshore Hedge Funds: The Failure of the Hedge Fund Registration Requirement," *Cornell Law Review* 92 (2007): 795–832.

78. Ibid., 801–12.

79. "International companies raised more by listing on [the London Stock Exchange's] markets in 2007 than the New York Stock Exchange and Nasdaq combined.... The LSE has been the principal beneficiary of the onerous US Sarbanes Oxley governance rules." Philip Aldrick, "Stock Exchanges: London Stays Top of the Bourses," *Daily Telegraph*, December 28, 2007; see also Paul Sweeney, "Rough Sledding for IPO Market: More Companies Are Looking for Alternatives; Will the VISA Offering Help?" *Investment Dealers Digest*, March 24, 2008.

80. Harvard Law School professor Hal Scott found that "in 1996, eight of the 20 largest global initial public offerings were listed on a U.S. exchange. In 2006, one listed here, and so far in 2007, not one of the top 20 global IPOs listed in the USA." Greg Farrell, "Group Wants Less Stringent Market Rules; Panel Says More Companies Snub U.S. Financial Centers," *USA Today*, December 6, 2007.

81. Morriss, "OFCs in Regulatory Competition," 31.

82. See Antoine, *Confidentiality in Offshore*, sec. 1.20.

83. Ibid.

84. Morriss, "OFCs in Regulatory Competition," 18.

85. Ravi Aron, "Financial Services," in *Innovation in Global Industries: U.S. Firms Competing in a New World*, ed. Jeffrey T. Macher and David C. Mowery (Washington, D.C.: National Academies Press, 2008), 342.

86. Ibid., 362–63.

87. Ibid.

88. Rose-Marie Antoine has argued that this interest is manifest in offshore courts' opinions and administrators' comments. See Antoine, *Confidentiality in Offshore*, sec. 2.60–61.

89. For an explanation of the idea of law as a product, see, generally, Roberta Romano, "Law as a Product: Some Pieces of the Incorporation Puzzle," *Journal of Law, Economics and Organization* 1 (1985): 225.

90. See La Porta et al., "Legal Determinants."

91. La Porta et al., "Investor Protection."

92. Christian Leuz, Dhananjay Nanda, and Peter D. Wysocki, "Earnings Management and Investor Protection: An International Comparison," *Journal of Financial Economics* 69 (2003): 505–27.

93. Macey and Miller, "Toward an Interest Group Theory."

Chapter 2: The Legitimacy of the Offshore Financial Sector

1. While the argument on legitimacy applies across the board, this chapter will focus more particularly on certain areas in the offshore sector—that is, the legal institution of the trust, confidentiality, and tax issues.

2. Rose-Marie Belle Antoine, *Trusts and Related Tax Issues in Offshore Financial Law* (New York: Oxford University Press, 2005), 5.

3. For example, Peter Willoughby maintains that "trusts have always concerned asset protection." Peter G. Willoughby, "International Trusts under Fire: The Increasing Scope for Litigation," in *Law Lectures for Practitioners*, ed. Peter Wesley-Smith (Hong Kong: Hong Kong Law Journal Limited, 1997), 16.

4. See, for example, David Pallister, Ed Harriman, and Jamie Wilson, "Looted Dollars 1bn Sent through London," *Guardian*, October 4, 2001; T. Fogarty, "Hill Tackles Russian Loan Scandal," *USA Today*, October 8, 2000.

5. See, for example, the Money Laundering and Financing of Terrorism (Prevention and Control) Act, 2002 CAP. 129, of Barbados.

6. See Financial Intelligence Unit, http://www.barbadosfiu.gov.bb/.

7. As demonstrated in the *locus classicus* of *Gov't of India v. Taylor* [1955] A.C. 491, 497 (H.L.) (U.K.).

8. *Inland Revenue Comm'rs v. Duke of Westminster* [1936] A.C. 1, 19–20 (H.L.) (U.K.).

9. For example, the beneficiaries of nonresident trusts before they receive income and the settlors of such trusts may now be taxed. See, for example, the Taxation of Chargeable Gains Act of 1992, c. 12 (U.K.).

10. Ibid.

11. See, for example, *Bank of Nova Scotia v. Tremblay* [1998–99] ITELR 673.

12. Ibid.

13. See, for example, *In re Colin Douglas 1990 Settlement* [2000] ITELR 682 (Royal Court) Jersey.

14. See, for example, *In re Green GLG* [2002] JLR 571, where the *Hastings-Bass* rule was used to void a transaction which would have created additional tax liabilities for the trust.

15. See, for example, the Confidential Relationships Act of 1995 of St. Kitts and Nevis, the Confidential Relationships (Preservation) Law of 1979, rev. 1999, of Cayman Islands, and sec. 61 of the International Trusts Act of 1999 of St. Lucia.

16. See Rose-Marie Belle Antoine, "The Comity Principle and Confidentiality," in *Confidentiality in Offshore Financial Law* (New York: Oxford University Press, 2002), 282–92.

17. *Tournier v. Nat'l Provincial Bank* [1924] 1 K.B. 461 (C.A.) (U.K.).

18. See *Schmidt v. Rosewood Trust Ltd.* [2003] UKPC 26 (P.C.) (U.K.).

19. No. 70 of 2000, decided October 18, 2002, C.A. The Bahamas.

20. See, for example, *Mailhe v. France* [1993] 16 EHRR 332.

21. See, for example, *Bethel v. Douglas* [1995] 1 WLR 794; *Citibank Ltd v. Commissioner of Taxation* (1988) 88 ATC 4712.

22. For example, *United States v. Bank of Nova Scotia* 691 F.2d. 1384 (11th Cir. 1982); *United States v. Field* 532 F. 2d. 405 (5th Cir.) cert. denied 429 U.S. 940 (1976).
23. *Mackinnon v. Donaldson Lufkin & Jenrette Securities* [1986] All ER 553, at 658.
24. See, for example, *Garpeg Ltd. v. US* 583 F Supp 789 (SDNY 1984); see also *United States v. Field* 532 F 2d 405 (5th Cir) cert denied 429 UD 940 (1976).
25. States including Nevada and Delaware in the United States have adopted such principles. See, for example, the Spendthrift Trust Act of 1999 (Nevada) and the Qualified Dispositions in Trusts Act of 1996 (Delaware).
26. See Antoine, *Trusts and Related Tax Issues*.
27. The name coined for trusts established under the Virgin Islands Special Trusts Act of 2003.
28. For a fuller discussion on VISTA trusts, see Antoine, *Trusts and Related Tax Issues*, chap. 12.
29. For an in-depth discussion of the importance of the confidentiality ethic to offshore financial law and investment in general, see Rose-Marie Antoine, *Confidentiality in Offshore Financial Law* (Oxford: Oxford University Press, 2003). Specifically in relation to the trust, see Antoine, "Disclosure and Confidentiality Obligations," in Rose-Marie Antoine, *Trusts and Related Tax Issues in Offshore Financial Law* (Oxford: Oxford University Press, 2005), chap. 7.
30. See Morriss, this volume.
31. See Antoine, *Trusts and Related Tax Issues*.
32. Ibid.
33. The protector acts as a liaison officer between the beneficiaries and the trustee, while the enforcer exists to regulate purpose trusts.
34. See, for example, sec. 9 of the Belize Trusts Act of 1992, rev. 2000, and sec. 13 of the Trusts Law, rev. 2001, of the Cayman Islands.
35. See, for example, *FTC v. Affordable Media, LLC*, 179 F.3d 1228 (9th Cir. 1999).
36. Convention on the Law Applicable to Trusts and on their Recognition, The Hague, 1 July 1985, UKTS 14 (1992) Cm 1823; 23 ILM 1388.
37. *Saunders v. Vautier* [1841] EWHC Ch J82.
38. See, for example, sec. 9 of the International Trusts Act of 1996 of St. Vincent and the Trusts (Amendment) (Immediate Effect and Reserved Powers) Law of 1998 of the Cayman Islands.
39. Given life on the principle that control by the settlor discredits the trust as a sham. *Rahman v. Chase Bank Trust Co. Ltd.* [1991] JLR 103.
40. *In re Abacus C.I. Ltd. (trustee of the Esteem Settlement) Grupo Torras v. Al Sabah* [2003] 6 ITELR 368 (Royal Ct. Jersey).
41. See, for example, *Lawrence (Stephen Jay), Re* [2002] 5 ITELR 1.
42. See Antoine, *Trusts and Related Tax Issues*.
43. See, for example, the Belize Trusts Act of 1992, rev. 2000, the International Trusts Act of 2002 of St. Lucia, the International Trusts Act of 1996 of St. Vincent,

the Trusts (Amendment) (Jersey) Law of 1996 of Jersey, and the Special Trusts (Alternative Regime) Law of 1997 of the Cayman Islands.

44. D. Hayton [2001] 117 LQR 96.

45. See, for example, Manitoba Law Reform Commission, "Non-Charitable Purpose Trusts," report no. 77, September 1992.

46. Flight clauses enable offshore trusts to be relocated to other offshore jurisdictions expediently where the need arises. Similarly, duress clauses are written into the trust instrument and come into effect where the trust is threatened with some potentially adverse event. For example, if a beneficiary is to be sued for his or her assets, the trust instrument may allow that beneficiary's interest to be severed, thus protecting the trust.

47. [2003] UKPC 26 (P.C.) (U.K.).

48. See, for example, *Eurovest Ltd. v. Segall* 528 S 2d 482 [1988] 483; see also Robert T. Danforth, "Rethinking the Law of Creditors' Rights in Trusts," *Hastings Law Journal* 53 (2002): 360–62.

49. See, for example, the International Trusts Act of 2002 of St. Lucia, the International Exempt Trusts Act of 1997 of Dominica, the Fraudulent Dispositions Law of 1989 of the Cayman Islands, and the International Trusts Ordinance of 1994 of Nevis.

50. See, for example, the International Trusts Act of 1984 of the Cook Islands.

51. [1999] 2 ITELR 95 (H.C. Isle of Man).

52. See, for example, *Stone v. Stone* (2002) 4 ITELR 671, where the court affirmed that an existing claim of action is required.

53. See, for example, *Grupo Torras,* above, note 40. Mareva injunctions are court orders freezing assets so that a defendant cannot move them beyond the court's jurisdiction. They are named for *Mareva Compania Naviera SA v. International Bulk Carriers SA* [1975] 2 Lloyd's Rep 509.

54. See, for example, the Belize Trusts Act of 2000 of Belize, the Trustee (Amendment) Act of 1993 of the British Virgin Islands, and the Trusts Law, rev. 2002 of the Cayman Islands.

55. [2003] 6 ITELR 330.

56. See, for example, sec. 13 of the Trusts Ordinance 1990 of the Turks and Caicos; sec. f 7(1) of the Trusts (Choice of Governing Law) 1989, as amended 1996 of the Bahamas; sec. 13H of the International Trusts Act of 1984 of the Cook Islands, and sec. 90 of the Trusts Law (2001 rev.) of the Cayman Islands.

57. See, for example, sec. 4 of the International Exempt Trust Act of 1997 of Dominica, which precludes the application of foreign law to the offshore trust where it will have the effect of voiding capacity and related rights conferred by that statute.

58. [1998–99] 1 ITELR 925; see also *In re an Isle of Man Trust* [1998–99] 1 ITELR 103.

59. See, for example, *Casani v. Mattei* [1998–99] 1 ITELR 925; *Re Lemos, Trust Settlement* [1992–93] CILR 26; *Garner v. Bermuda Trust Co.* (Sup Ct. Bermuda) No. 318 of 1991, decided March 2, 1992.

60. See, for example, *Casani v. Mattei* [1998–99] 1 ITELR 925.

61. Evidenced, for example, in *In re Brooks* 217 BR 98 101 (Bankr D Conn 1998). There is, of course, a dichotomy here. The rest of the United States adheres to the rule that it is against U.S. policy, but in U.S. offshore trust states, it is allowed for nonresidents. This, to my mind, raises the question whether it can remain a rule of U.S. public policy, but that subject is beyond the scope of this chapter.

Chapter 3: Regulating Tax Competition in Offshore Financial Centers

1. There is no universally accepted definition of either "offshore financial center" or "tax haven." See Ahmed Zoromé, "Concept of Offshore Financial Centers: In Search of an Operational Definition" (IMF Working Paper WP/07/87, International Monetary Fund, April 2007), http://www.imf.org/external/pubs/ft/wp/2007/wp0787.pdf (accessed September 3, 2009); Council of the Organisation for Economic Co-operation and Development, "Recommendation on Tax Avoidance and Evasion," 1977, in OECD, *International Tax Avoidance and Evasion, Four Related Studies,* Annex I, 1987, para. 8. In this chapter, "OFC" is used to describe those (generally offshore) jurisdictions that have low or no income taxation and bank confidentiality. Although such jurisdictions historically were (and frequently still are) referred to as "tax havens," that term has acquired a pejorative connotation as a result of its link in popular media and culture to tax evasion and organized crime. "Onshore jurisdiction" in this chapter refers to a developed country with a mature economy that taxes income at relatively high rates.

2. See U.S. Department of the Treasury, Internal Revenue Service, *Tax Havens and Their Use by United States Taxpayers—An Overview: A Report to the Commissioner of the Internal Revenue, the Assistant Attorney General (Tax Division), and the Assistant Secretary of the Treasury (Tax Policy)*, by Richard A. Gordon (Washington, D.C.: Special Council for International Taxation, Internal Revenue Service, 1981), 3.

3. See Michael S. Kirsch, "Taxing Citizens in a Global Economy," *New York University Law Review* 82 (2007): 443, 446.

4. See Reuven Avi-Yonah, "Globalization, Tax Competition, and the Fiscal Crisis of the Welfare State," *Harvard Law Review* 113 (2000): 1575–76; Organisation for Economic Co-operation and Development, *Harmful Tax Competition: An Emerging Global Issue*, 1998, 13, http://www.oecd.org/dataoecd/33/0/1904176.pdf (accessed September 3, 2009).

5. The OECD is an intergovernmental organization based in Paris and comprised of about thirty of the world's most economically powerful countries (plus the European Commission as a member international organization). Member states share a stated commitment to democracy and the market economy and, through the OECD, share expertise and exchange views with more than one hundred other countries. See, generally, http://www.oecd.org.

6. The EU is an economic and political partnership of twenty-seven European democracies that seeks to create a single economic market and provide for the free movement of people, goods, services, and capital among member states. See http://europa.eu.

7. See Martin A. Sullivan, "Lessons from the Last War on Tax Havens," *Tax Notes* 116 (July 30, 2007): 327.

8. See Nancy H. Kaufman, "Fairness and the Taxation of International Income," *Law and Policy in International Business* 29 (1998): 147–49. The only practical limitation on a state's taxing power is its ability to collect the taxes it levies.

9. Ibid., 148.

10. In most jurisdictions, residence is based on physical presence within the jurisdiction for roughly half of the taxable year. The United States and a handful of other countries also assert the right to tax the income of their citizens, whether or not they reside within the country during the taxable year. See U.S. Internal Revenue Code (I.R.C.), sec. 7701(a)(30)(A) and (b)(1)(B). All references herein to the Internal Revenue Code or "I.R.C." are to the Internal Revenue Code of 1986 (as amended).

11. Technological advances have made the source of some types of income difficult to ascertain. For example, the income from an Internet sales transaction might have several potential sources, including the buyer's and seller's countries of residence, as well as the country in which the computer server facilitating the transaction is located. Similarly, although income from the provision of services generally is sourced in the country where the services are provided, the application of this rule is ambiguous where, for example, a physician in one country examines X-ray images of a patient in another country in real time via remote computer access.

12. Although OFCs generally do not impose direct (income) taxes, they nonetheless exact duties to raise revenue for government operations. See "Infringement of National Tax Sovereignty."

13. Many OFCs limit the ability of foreign persons to work within them. In the Cayman Islands, for example, an annual work permit for non-key employees may have a term of no more than seven years, while such a permit for key employees may be no longer than nine years. Immigration Law of the Cayman Islands, 2007 revised version (Cayman Is.).

14. In the Maldives, for example, Islam is the official state religion, and government regulations are based on Islamic (Shari'a) law. Non-Muslim foreigners may not practice their religions publicly, nor encourage local citizens to practice any religion other than Islam. See U.S. Department of State, Bureau of Democracy, Human Rights, and Labor, *International Religious Freedom Report Maldives*, 2007, http://www.state.gov/g/drl/rls/irf/2007/90231.htm (accessed November 25, 2009).

15. Worldwide taxation is the imposition of tax on the income of residents regardless of where such income is earned.

16. Territorial tax systems generally tax their residents only on income that arises within the jurisdiction and exclude foreign income from taxation. Because a pure

territorial system creates an enormous incentive for residents to shift income offshore (particularly mobile, passive-type income like dividends, interest, and royalties), most territorial jurisdictions tax their residents on their worldwide *passive* income and exclude only *active* foreign income from taxation.

17. Countries imposing this type of purely formal test include the United States, the United Kingdom (post-1988), and Sweden. The Commonwealth countries generally use a "place of management and control" test. Germany and the Netherlands base corporate residence on the jurisdiction of incorporation or the place of management.

18. Onshore jurisdictions with robust antideferral regimes might nonetheless assert indirect claims on the income of the corporation in the OFC by treating shareholders resident in the developed country as receiving on a current basis a proportionate share of some types of income earned by the corporation, even if the income is not distributed to onshore shareholders. See, for example, I.R.C., sec. 951–59.

19. Inversion transactions—popular in the late 1990s—excluded foreign earnings of U.S. multinationals from U.S. residence-based taxation by shifting ownership of foreign assets to newly formed OFC "parent" corporations, while effecting no meaningful change in operations. See Craig M. Boise and James C. Koenig, "Practical and Policy Considerations in Corporate Inversions," *Corporate Business Taxation Monthly*, September 2002. Such transactions are now largely precluded by rules that treat the new parent as a U.S. corporation for tax purposes. In addition, a corporation in an onshore jurisdiction might be required to recognize and pay income tax on gain recognized on the offshore asset transfer. Long-term tax savings might still make such transactions feasible.

20. Here again, an antideferral regime in the parent corporation's country of residence might defeat the tax avoidance strategy. See I.R.C., sec. 951–59.

21. See above, note 11 and accompanying text.

22. For example, a U.S. multinational might sell a product to a subsidiary in an OFC for an artificially low price, thus reducing profits earned and taxed in the United States while increasing the subsidiary's lightly taxed or untaxed profits on final sales of the product abroad.

23. The share of pharmaceutical companies' profits derived from foreign jurisdictions increased from 37.6 percent in 1994 to over 65 percent in 2003, without any corresponding increase in physical presence in those jurisdictions. See Martin A. Sullivan and John A. Almond, "Economic Analysis: Drug Companies Park Increasing Share of Profits in Low-Tax Countries," *Tax Notes* 104 (2004): 1336. For discussion of deferral of U.S. corporate profits through use of subsidiaries in OFCs, see Craig M. Boise, "Breaking Open Offshore Piggybanks: Deferral and the Utility of Amnesty," *George Mason Law Review* 14 (2007): 667.

24. For discussion of the optimal regulatory structures in OFCs, see Dionne and Macey, this volume.

25. Merriam-Webster's Online Dictionary, s.v. "Competition," http.//www.merriam-webster.com/dictionary/competition (accessed September 3, 2009).

26. New regulatory efforts may be imminent, however, following Germany's discovery in 2008 of widespread tax evasion by wealthy residents utilizing a secretive bank in Liechtenstein, a country considered a tax haven under most definitions of the term. See *International Herald Tribune*, "EU Considers Toughening Offensive on Tax Havens," May 14, 2008.

27. See Council of the Organisation for Economic Co-operation and Development (OECD), "Recommendation on Tax Avoidance and Evasion."

28. Council of the Organisation for Economic Co-operation and Development, *International Tax Avoidance and Evasion*, 10. The four-part 1987 study addressed: (1) the reasons for, and measures introduced by, OECD member countries to combat international tax avoidance and evasion through tax havens; (2) resident taxpayer use of tax haven subsidiaries to avoid residence-country taxation; (3) the problem of treaty-shopping; and (4) taxation and the abuse of bank confidentiality laws.

29. Ibid., 22.

30. See U.S. Department of the Treasury, Internal Revenue Service, *Tax Havens and Their Use*.

31. Council of the Organisation for Economic Co-operation and Development, *International Tax Avoidance and Evasion*, 22.

32. See Organisation for Economic Co-operation and Development, *Harmful Tax Competition*, para. 2.

33. The Group of Seven countries includes Canada, France, Germany, Italy, Japan, the United Kingdom, and the United States.

34. See Organisation for Economic Co-operation and Development, *Harmful Tax Competition*, para. 2. Achieving the highest sustainable economic growth and employment and a rising standard of living in its member countries is the OECD's first priority. See "Convention on the Organisation for Economic Co-operation and Development," December 14, 1960, art. I, http://www.oecd.org/document/7/0,3343,en_2649_201185_1915847_1_1_1_1,00.html (accessed May 15, 2008). Representatives of the G-7 had earlier attempted to involve the International Monetary Fund in tax haven issues. Both the IMF staff and a large majority of its executive board concluded, however, that tax haven issues were beyond the organization's mandate, if not beyond its expertise. See Gordon, this volume.

35. The one bit of empirical data cited in the report was a fivefold increase in foreign direct investment by G7 countries in certain Caribbean and South Pacific island states over the period 1985–94. The report states that this rate of increase was well in excess of the growth of overall outbound foreign direct investment. See Organisation for Economic Co-operation and Development, *Harmful Tax Competition*, para. 35.

36. Ibid., para. 23 (emphasis added).

37. Ibid., para. 52.

38. Ibid.

39. Although the effects of both regimes are the same, they differ in that harmful preferential tax regimes may exist in onshore jurisdictions, including OECD member

countries. The OECD's analysis in this regard had ramifications for the way in which the tax competition problem ultimately was addressed.

40. "Ring-fencing" regimes either exclude resident enterprises from taking advantage of the tax benefits given to foreign investors, or insulate the domestic economy from the effects of the preferential regime by preventing foreign investors from participating in domestic markets.

41. As noted above, harmful preferential tax regimes, which have the same effect as tax haven regimes, exist in onshore OECD member countries. The OECD reserved its harshest regulatory sanctions, however, for nonmember tax haven countries. Organisation for Economic Co-operation and Development, *Harmful Tax Competition*, para. 128–32. Moreover, the 1998 report specifically excluded consideration of the tax treatment of interest on cross-border saving instruments, an issue that might have exposed the United States and other OECD member countries to criticism. See ibid., para. 12.

42. These are the so-called four freedoms at the core of European Union economic and social policy. See Treaty Establishing the European Economic Community, March 25, 1957, amended by Single Europe Act, 1987 O.J. (L 169) 1 (effective July 1, 1987); Treaty of Lisbon Amending the Treaty Establishing the European Community, Treaty on the Functioning of the European Union, April 15, 2008, 2008 O.J. (C 321) (Title II and IV).

43. Council of the European Union, *Council Resolution on the Measures to be Taken by the Community in Order to Combat International Tax Evasion and Avoidance*, 1975 O.J. (C035) 1, 2 (European Council).

44. Ibid.

45. See EC treaty, art. 113.

46. Council of the European Union, *Conclusions of the ECOFIN Council Meeting on 1 December 1997 Concerning Taxation Policy—Taxation of Savings*, under Annex 1 Code of Conduct, June 1, 1998, 1998 O.J. (C 002), 1–6.

47. Ibid., para. A. The code also lists factors to be considered in determining whether tax competition is harmful, including whether the favorable tax regime is ring-fenced, whether real economic activity is required within the member state offering the favorable tax regime, and whether the tax regime lacks transparency. Ibid.

48. Ibid., annex 2.

49. See European Commission, *European Commission Directive on Tax Savings*, 2003/48/EC, June 26, 2003, 2003 O.J. (L 157), 38–48.

50. Ibid., para. 52.

51. This can occur "if the ability to relocate taxable profits into low-tax jurisdictions increases the return to investing in high-tax areas, if low-tax jurisdictions facilitate deferral of home-country taxation of income earned elsewhere, or if affiliates in low-tax areas offer valuable intermediate goods and services to affiliates in high-tax areas." Mihir A. Desai, C. Fritz Foley, and James R. Hines Jr., "Do Tax Havens Divert Economic Activity?" (Ross School of Business Working Papers Series), http://hdl.handle.net/2027.42/39145 (accessed August 24, 2009).

52. Organisation for Economic Co-operation and Development, *Harmful Tax Competition*, para. 55.

53. Ibid., para. 14.

54. See U.S. Senate, Committee on Homeland Security and Governmental Affairs, Subcommittee on Investigations, *Tax Haven Abuses: The Enablers, the Tools and Secrecy: Minority and Majority Staff Report*, August 1, 2006, http://levin.senate.gov/newsroom/supporting/2006/PSI.taxhavenabuses.080106.pdf (accessed September 8, 2009).

55. See Avi-Yonah, "Globalization, Tax Competition, and the Fiscal Crisis," 1575–76.

56. Of course, high-tax jurisdictions have the option of attacking this problem by reducing the spending side of the equation. Indeed, OFCs argue that the prospect of competition from low-tax jurisdictions forces onshore jurisdictions to be more prudent in their spending policies.

57. See Ruben P. Mendez, *International Public Finance* (New York: Oxford University Press, 1992), 54.

58. See David Hume, *A Treatise of Human Nature*, ed. Ernest C. Mossner (London: Penguin, 1991), 589–90.

59. Ibid.

60. See Robert J. Peroni, "Back to the Future: A Path to Progressive Reform of the U.S. International Income Tax Rules," *University of Miami Law Review* 51 (1998): 981–86.

61. See, generally, Walter J. Blum and Harry Kalven Jr., *The Uneasy Case for Progressive Taxation* (Chicago: University of Chicago Press, 1963), 103.

62. See Avi-Yonah, "Globalization, Tax Competition, and the Fiscal Crisis," 1575–76.

63. See Maureen B. Cavanaugh, "Democracy, Equality, and Taxes," *Alabama Law Review* 54 (2003): 422–28. But compare J. S. Mill, *Principles of Political Economy*, ed. W. J. Ashley (London: Longmans, Green and Co., 1923), 805: "It cannot be admitted that to be protected in the ownership of ten times as much property is to be ten times as much protected."

64. See Organisation for Economic Co-operation and Development, *Harmful Tax Competition*, para. 24.

65. See Steven M. Sheffrin and Robert K. Triest, "Can Brute Deterrence Backfire? Perceptions and Attitudes in Taxpayer Compliance," in *Why People Pay Taxes: Tax Compliance and Enforcement*, ed. Joel Slemrod (Ann Arbor: University of Michigan Press, 1992), 214.

66. See Julie Roin, "Competition and Evasion: Another Perspective on International Tax Competition," *Georgetown Law Review* 89 (2001): 597.

67. See Vaughn E. James, "Twenty-First Century Pirates of the Caribbean: How the Organization for Economic Cooperation and Development Robbed Fourteen CARICOM Countries of Their Tax and Economic Policy Sovereignty," *University of Miami Inter-American Law Review* 34 (2002): 1.

68. To the extent that an OFC has a general income tax but "ring-fences" (excludes) from that tax corporate entities engaged in business abroad, a stronger case can be made that the OFC is affirmatively engaged in tax competition.

164 NOTES TO PAGES 62–63

69. See Organisation for Economic Co-operation and Development, Committee on Fiscal Affairs, *Towards Global Tax Co-operation: Progress in Identifying and Eliminating Harmful Tax Practices*, 2000, 9, http://www.oecd.org/dataoecd/9/61/2090192.pdf (accessed September 3, 2009). The report listed thirty-five countries as tax havens. Six other countries initially were identified as tax havens but were not included in the 2000 progress report because, prior to its release, they committed to eliminating their harmful tax practices. See Organisation for Economic Co-operation and Development, *The OECD's Project on Harmful Tax Practices: The 2001 Progress Report*, 2001, 7–8, http://www.oecd.org/dataoecd/60/5/2664450.pdf (accessed September 3, 2009).

70. The combined landmass of the forty-one jurisdictions labeled by the OECD as "tax havens" is 252,976 sq. km; New Zealand's landmass is 268,680 sq. km. Their combined GDP is $108.1 billion; New Zealand's GDP is $112.6 billion. See Central Intelligence Agency, *CIA: The World Factbook*, https://www.cia.gov/library/publications/the-world-factbook (accessed May 20, 2008).

71. The population of the forty-one jurisdictions labeled by the OECD as "tax havens" is 10,819,586; the population of the state of Illinois is 12,831,970. See ibid.

72. In the Cayman Islands, for example, the primary source of government revenue is a 20 percent duty levied against imported goods, with few exemptions. Duty on automobiles may be as high as 40 percent for expensive models. The government charges a flat licensing fee to financial institutions that operate in the islands, and each tourist who arrives on the islands is also charged a small fee, including a 10 percent government tax added to all accommodations. See Cayman Islands official website at http://www.gocayman.ky/content/view/22/65 (accessed August 11, 2008). It may be more difficult for an OFC to sustain itself on these types of duties and fees as its economy matures, however. For fiscal year 2009, the Cayman Islands posted a deficit of US$100 million (£63 million), which necessitated an emergency loan of US$61 million (£38 million) from the United Kingdom (of which the Cayman Islands is an overseas territory), and prompted talk of imposing direct (income) taxation in Cayman. See Gillian Tett, "Fiscal Storm in Caymans Is Set to Spread," *Financial Times FT.com*, October 4, 2009, http://www.ft.com/cms/s/0/152ef518-b104-11de-b06b-00144feabdc0.html (accessed October 22, 2009); Michael Klein, "Government Finances—New Revenues Sought," *Cayman Financial Review*, October 5, 2009, http://www.compasscayman.com/cfr/cfr.aspx?id=7170 (accessed October 22, 2009).

73. For example, in Switzerland, the bank confidentiality statute provides that "whoever divulges a secret entrusted to him in his capacity as officer, employee, mandatory or liquidator of a bank . . . shall be punished by imprisonment for not more than six months or by a fine." Federal Law on Banks and Savings Banks of November 8, 1934, article 47 at 23 (Switz.).

74. See discussion of confidentiality in Antoine, this volume.

75. Confidential Relationships (Preservation) Law, 1995, Law 16 of 1976, consolidated with Laws 26 of 1979 and 22 of 1993 (Cayman Is.).

76. 1 K.B. 461 (1924).

77. In fact, even in the United States, part of the 1970 Bank Secrecy Act is administered by the tax authority—the Internal Revenue Service. See Monetary Transactions, Part II, Records and Reports on Monetary Instruments Transactions, 31 U.S.C. §§5311–32.

78. For example, see Cayman confidentiality law, sec. 4.

79. See Organisation for Economic Co-operation and Development, *Harmful Tax Competition*, para. 29.

80. See discussion above.

81. See Charles M. Tiebout, "A Pure Theory of Local Expenditures," *Journal of Political Economy* 64 (1956): 416.

82. See, for example, discussion of the application of Tiebout's theory to tax competition in John Douglas Wilson, "Theories of Tax Competition," *National Tax Journal* 52, no. 2 (1999): 270.

83. See David E. Wildasin, "Interjurisdictional Capital Mobility: Fiscal Externality and a Corrective Subsidy," *Journal of Urban Economics* 25 (1989): 193.

84. See Organisation for Economic Co-operation and Development, Committee on Fiscal Affairs, *Towards Global Tax Co-operation*.

85. See Organisation for Economic Co-operation and Development, *Harmful Tax Competition*, para. 6.

86. Marshal J. Langer, *How to Use Foreign Tax Havens* (New York: Practising Law Institute, 1975), 4.

87. See International Tax and Investment Organization and the Society of Trust and Estate Practitioners, *Towards a Level Playing Field: Regulating Corporate Vehicles in Cross-Border Transactions*, 2002, 42.

88. See Organisation for Economic Co-operation and Development, *Harmful Tax Competition*, para. 149–51.

89. See ibid., para. 85–89; and Organisation for Economic Co-operation and Development, Committee on Fiscal Affairs, *Towards Global Tax Co-operation*, 24. The OECD here echoed the conclusion of the United States' Gordon report, which cautioned, "The United States alone cannot deal with tax havens. The policy must be an international one by the countries that are not tax havens to isolate the abusive tax havens." U.S. Department of the Treasury, Internal Revenue Service, *Tax Havens and Their Use*, 10.

90. Ibid.

91. See Organisation for Economic Co-operation and Development, *The OECD's Project on Harmful Tax Practices: The 2001 Progress Report*, para. 23.

92. See Alex Easson, "Harmful Tax Competition: An Evaluation of the OECD Initiative," *Tax Notes International* 34 (2004): 1037, 1043.

93. See Organisation for Economic Co-operation and Development, *The OECD's Project on Harmful Tax Practices: The 2001 Progress Report*, para. 23.

94. Ibid., para. 32.

166 NOTES TO PAGES 67–70

95. Ibid., para. 48.
96. Ibid., para. 33.
97. Ibid., para. 36 (emphasis added).
98. Ibid., para. 37.
99. Ibid., para. 38.
100. See Easson, "Harmful Tax Competition," 1045.
101. See Organisation for Economic Co-operation and Development, Centre for Tax Policy and Administration, *The OECD's Project on Harmful Tax Practices: The 2004 Progress Report*, 2004, http://www.oecd.org/dataoecd/60/33/30901115.pdf (accessed September 3, 2009).
102. Ibid., 19.
103. Ibid.
104. Ibid., 20.
105. Ibid., para. 22–23.
106. The main task of the Joint Ad Hoc Group on Accounts was to "make sure there [was] a proper balance between the requirement to ensure access to reliable financial information and the need to avoid placing unnecessary compliance burdens on tax payers and administrations." Ibid., para. 25.
107. See J. C. Sharman, *Havens in a Storm* (Ithaca, N.Y.: Cornell University Press, 2006), 8–11.
108. Because the EU defined harmful tax competition as low-tax jurisdictions' seeking to attract mobile capital, it did not address other forms of tax competition.
109. See Council of the European Union, *Conclusions of the ECOFIN Council Meeting*, annex 2.
110. See European Commission, *European Commission Directive on Tax Savings*.
111. Ibid.
112. Austria has the right to secret bank accounts written into its constitution. See Geoff Winestock, "EU Reaches Compromise on Savings Tax But Defers Action for Another Decade," *Wall Street Journal*, June 21, 2000, A23.
113. See European Commission, *European Commission Directive on Tax Savings*.
114. Ibid. Non-EU countries that agreed to comply with the savings tax directive by exchanging information included the OFCs Anguilla, Cayman Islands, Montserrat, and Aruba. Non-EU countries agreeing to withhold tax in lieu of exchanging information on the recipients of interest payments included the OFCs British Virgin Islands, the Channel Islands, the Netherlands Antilles, the Isle of Man, Liechtenstein, and Switzerland. These nonmember states all complied with the directive because of their ties to EU member states
115. The OECD's 1998 report states that it "is not intended to explicitly or implicitly suggest that there is some general minimum effective rate of tax to be imposed on income below which a country would be considered to be engaging in harmful tax competition." See Organisation for Economic Co-operation and Development, *Harmful Tax Competition*, para. 6. The EU similarly recognizes the right of member states

to determine their own tax rates. European Commission, *European Commission Directive on Tax Savings*, 40.

116. See Council of the Organisation for Economic Co-operation and Development, "Recommendation on Tax Avoidance and Evasion," para. 12.

117. See U.S. Department of the Treasury, Internal Revenue Service, *Tax Havens and Their Use*, 15; discussion under "Infringement of National Tax Sovereignty," above.

118. See Council of the Organisation for Economic Co-operation and Development, *Recommendation on Tax Avoidance and Evasion*, para. 12; Organisation for Economic Co-operation and Development, *Harmful Tax Competition*, para. 52. Most OECD member countries also have considered low or no taxation of income to be an indicator of "tax haven" status. See Council of the Organisation for Economic Co-operation and Development, "Recommendation on Tax Avoidance and Evasion," para. 8.

119. See Council of the Organisation for Economic Co-operation and Development, "Recommendation on Tax Avoidance and Evasion," para. 10

120. See ibid. The OECD's definition is followed up by the accusation that "the aim of legislation of a classical tax haven is to attract income from activities which are to be carried on outside the territory of the tax haven." This, of course, is the aim of legislation in any country that seeks to insert itself into the global economy.

121. An example is the U.S. approach to its domestic drug abuse problem. The United States is the largest cocaine consumer in the world. Rather than undertake meaningful efforts to provide treatment for addiction, however, over the last twenty years the United States has spent as much as $1 billion per year in Colombia, Bolivia, and other Andean countries to burn, pull out, and otherwise eradicate coca plants grown there. See Juan Forero, "Bolivia's Knot: No to Cocaine, But Yes to Coca," *New York Times*, February 12, 2006, 1. The United States has spent more than $780 million annually to eradicate poppy fields in Afghanistan, which supply 90 percent of the world's illegal heroin. See Maia Szalavitz, "Let a Thousand Licensed Poppies Bloom," *New York Times*, July 13, 2005, A1.

122. As this chapter goes to press, U.S. congressional tax writers have introduced legislation that would impose a 30 percent withholding tax on payments to foreign banks that do not identify to the Internal Revenue Service accounts held by U.S. persons and provide information on ownership, account balances, and fund transfers. See H.R. 3933 and S. 934 (2009).

123. "Exchange" is a not entirely apt description of the typical information transaction contemplated by these commitments, as OFC requests for information from onshore jurisdictions are likely to be extremely rare.

124. See Council of the Organisation for Economic Co-operation and Development, "Recommendation on Tax Avoidance and Evasion," 24.

125. See "Convention on the OECD," art. 5 and 6.

126. See C. Scott, "U.S. Treasury Secretary Says OECD Tax Haven Crackdown Is Out of Line," *Tax Notes International* 22 (May 21, 2001): 2539.

168 NOTES TO PAGES 72–79

127. See EC treaty, art. 249: "A directive shall be binding, as to the result to be achieved, upon each Member State to which it is addressed, but shall leave to the national authorities the choice of form and methods."

Chapter 4: The International Monetary Fund and the Regulation of Offshore Centers

1. Onshore jurisdictions have raised a number of other, more minor complaints against OFCs—for example, that they protect assets from judicial attachment or seizure in noncriminal cases, such as civil judgments.

2. Richard Gordon, "The International Monetary Fund: A Mandate to Fight Money Laundering and the Financing of Terrorism," in Michael P. Scharf, *The Law of International Organizations* (Chapel Hill: University of North Carolina Press, 2008), 1096–98.

3. According to discussions between the author and certain management and staff, this conclusion, reached informally in the mid-1990s, appeared to have been generally accepted.

4. All but five offshore centers (Andorra, Monaco, Liechtenstein, Tuvalu, and Nauru) are members of the IMF, either directly or as overseas territories, dependencies, special administrative areas, and so on, of a member.

5. Organisation for Economic Co-operation and Development, *Improving Access to Bank Information for Tax Purposes* (Paris: OECD, 2000), 25; Basel Committee on Banking Supervision, *Report on the Supervision of Bank's Foreign Establishments—Concordat* (Basel: Bank for International Settlements, 1975); Basel Committee on Banking Supervision, *Consolidated Supervision of Banks' International Activities* (Basel: Bank for International Settlements, 1979); Basel Committee on Banking Supervision, *Banking Secrecy and International Cooperation in Banking Supervision* (Basel: Bank for International Settlements, 1981).

6. Basel Committee on Banking Supervision, *Flows between Banking Supervisory Authorities* (Basel: Bank for International Settlements, 1990).

7. Basel Committee on Banking Supervision, *Minimum Standards for the Supervision of International Banking Groups and Their Cross-Border Establishments* (Basel: Bank for International Settlements, 1992).

8. U.S. Senate, Committee on Foreign Relations, *The BCCI Affair: A Report to the Committee on Foreign Relations, United States Senate, by Senator John Kerry and Senator Hank Brown*, 102d Cong., 2d sess. Senate Print 102-140, December 1992, http://www.fas.org/irp/congress/1992_rpt/bcci/ (accessed September 8, 2009).

9. David Folkerts-Landau and Carl-Johan Lindgren, *Toward a Framework for Financial Stability*, World Economic and Financial Surveys (Washington, D.C.: International Monetary Fund, 1998), 47.

10. Liliana Rojas-Suárez and Steven Riess Weisbrod, *Financial Market Fragilities in Latin America: From Banking Crisis Resolution to Current Policy Challenges* (Washington, D.C.: International Monetary Fund, 1994).

11. Brenda González-Hermosillo, Ceyla Pazarbasioglu, and Robert Billings, *Banking System Fragility: Likelihood versus Timing of Failure—An Application to the Mexican Financial Crisis* (Washington, D.C.: International Monetary Fund, 1996).

12. These issues became of significant interest to the IMF, which had generally been more concerned with macro rather than micro policy. Morris Goldstein and Philip Turner, "Banking Crises in Emerging Economies: Origins and Policy Options," Bank for International Settlements Economic Paper 46, October 1996, http://www.bis.org/publ/econ46.pdf?noframes=1 (accessed November 30, 2009); Carl-Johan Lindgren, Gillian Garcia, and Matthew I. Saal, *Bank Soundness and Macroeconomic Policy* (Washington, D.C.: International Monetary Fund, 1996).

13. Group of Seven, "G-7 Halifax Summit Communiqué," press release, June 16, 1995. In addition to Argentina, France, Germany, Hong Kong, Japan, Mexico, the Netherlands, Poland, Singapore, Sweden, the United Kingdom, and the United States, the working group included Thailand, Korea, and Indonesia.

14. Basel Committee on Banking Supervision, *The Supervision of Cross Border Banking* (Basel: Bank for International Settlements, 1996). Key issues addressed were preserving confidentiality of information obtained by bank supervisors from foreign supervisors and creating standard procedures for the conduct of cross-border inspections by home-country supervisors.

15. Basel Committee on Banking Supervision, *The Basel Core Principles for Effective Banking Supervision* (Basel: Bank for International Settlements, 1997), 7. The work on developing the core principles was conducted in close cooperation with both the IMF and World Bank, but particularly with the former.

16. Ibid., 2.

17. Working Group on Financial Stability in Emerging Market Economies, *Financial Stability in Emerging Market Economies* (Basel: Bank for International Settlements, 1997), 1–2 (emphasis added).

18. Taimer Baig and Ilan Goldfajn, *Financial Market Contagion in the Asian Crisis* (Washington, D.C.: International Monetary Fund, 1998); Haizhou Huang and Chenggang Xu, *Financial Institutions, Financial Contagion, and Financial Crises* (Washington, D.C.: International Monetary Fund, 2000). For a brief discussion of the IMF's bank reform conditionality for Korea, see Andreas F. Lowenfeld, "The International Monetary System and the Erosion of Sovereignty: Essay in Honor of Cynthia Lichtenstein," *Boston College International and Comparative Law Review* 25 (2002): 268–69.

19. This conclusion was obvious, even at the time. Lawrence L. C. Lee, "The Basel Accords as Soft Law: Strengthening International Banking Supervision," *Virginia Journal of International Law* 39 (1998): 1.

20. International Monetary Fund, *World Economic and Financial Surveys* (Washington, D.C.: International Monetary Fund, 1998): 2 (emphasis added).

21. Group of Twenty-Two, *Report of the Working Group on Strengthening Financial Systems* (Washington, D.C.: International Monetary Fund, 1998), 3–4, 46–50. The report was later endorsed by the G-7, although this was a foregone conclusion.

22. Luca Errico and Alberto Musalem, *Offshore Banking: An Analysis of Micro- and Macro-Prudential Issues* (Washington, D.C.: International Monetary Fund, 1999). The paper notes that offshore facilities may have contributed to problems in Thailand and Malaysia, but in those cases the offshore "centers" were within Thailand and Malaysia themselves. Ibid., 33–34.

23. Ibid., 6–7, 10.
24. Ibid., 10.
25. Ibid., 4.
26. Ibid., 29 and 29, note 41.
27. Financial Stability Forum, *Report of the Working Group on Offshore Centers* (Washington, D.C.: International Monetary Fund, 2000).
28. Ibid., 14.
29. Ibid., 2.
30. Ibid.
31. Basel Core Principle 15 stated that "banking supervisors must determine that banks have adequate policies, practices and procedures in place, including strict 'know-your-customer' rules that promote high ethical and professional standards in the financial sector and prevent the bank being used, intentionally or unintentionally, by criminal elements." Basel Committee on Banking Supervision, *Basel Core Principles*, 7. Assessments of this principle tended to be cursory.
32. "Overall compliance with the Basel Core Principles was generally appropriate to the nature of the business conducted, especially in important jurisdictions where compliance was found to be broadly in line with that in advanced economies." International Monetary Fund, *Offshore Financial Center Program: A Progress Report* (Washington, D.C.: International Monetary Fund, 2002), 4.
33. International Monetary Fund, *Offshore Financial Center Program: A Progress Report* (Washington, D.C.: International Monetary Fund, 2003); International Monetary Fund, *Offshore Financial Centers, The Assessment Program, A Progress Report and the Future of the Program* (Washington, D.C.: International Monetary Fund, 2003), 7–8.
34. International Monetary Fund, *Offshore Financial Centers, The Assessment Program, A Progress Report* (Washington, D.C.: International Monetary Fund, 2006), 11, table 2 (emphasis added).
35. Financial Action Task Force, "FATF Meets in Emergency Session," press release, October 12, 2001.
36. Financial Action Task Force, *Financial Action Task Force Money Laundering Report 1992/1993* (Paris: FATF, 1993); Financial Action Task Force, *Annual Report* (Paris: FATF, 1992), 5, 20. The "uncommitted" commitment to implement the FATF 40 was discussed at a number of CFTAT meetings and later at APF and PC-R-EV.
37. Financial Action Task Force, *The 40 Recommendations* (Paris: FATF, 1996).
38. Ibid., Recommendation 21.
39. Richard Gordon, "Anti-Money-Laundering Policies, Selected Legal, Political, and Economic Issues," *Current Developments in Monetary and Financial Law* 1 (1999):

108; Richard Gordon, "Trysts or Terrorists? Financial Institutions and the Search for the Bad Guys," *Wake Forest Law Review* 43 (2008): 699, 721–25, 728–29.

40. FATF members were invited to mention those jurisdictions where, in the recent past, there had been difficulties, with an explanation of the nature of the difficulties encountered. Financial Action Task Force, *Report on Non-Cooperative Countries and Territories* (Paris: FATF, 2000), 6–7.

41. Ibid., 6.

42. Ibid., 4.

43. Ibid., 7.

44. "No specific criteria can be considered a litmus test of a particular jurisdiction's level of co-operation in the international fight against money laundering. Rather, each jurisdiction must be judged by the overall, total effect of its laws and programmes in preventing abuse of the financial sector or impeding efforts of foreign judicial and administrative authorities." Ibid.

45. Financial Action Task Force, *FATF Review to Identify Non-Cooperating Countries or Territories: Increasing the Worldwide Effectiveness of Anti-Money Laundering Measures* (Paris: FATF, 2000).

46. See, for example, Benjamin R. Hartman, "Coercing Cooperation from Offshore Financial Centers: Identity and Coincidence of International Obligations against Money Laundering and Harmful Tax Competition," *Boston College International and Comparative Law Review* 24 (2002): 253; Jason Sharman, *Havens in a Storm: The Struggle for Global Tax Regulation* (Ithaca: Cornell University Press, 2006): 71, 101–48.

47. Peter Quirk, *Macroeconomic Implications of Money Laundering* (Washington, D.C.: International Monetary Fund, 1996).

48. Gordon, "Anti-Money-Laundering Policies," 410–13. Although not published as an IMF opinion, it was written by a senior lawyer in the legal department with the encouragement of the IMF's then general counsel.

49. Ibid., 414–17.

50. International Monetary Fund, "Treasury Secretary Lawrence H. Summers Statement to the Development Committee of the World Bank and the IMFC," press release, April 17, 2000.

51. International Monetary Fund, *Financial System Abuse, Financial Crime, and Money Laundering* (Washington, D.C.: International Monetary Fund, 2001); International Monetary Fund, *Enhancing Contributions to Combating Money Laundering: Policy Paper* (Washington, D.C.: International Monetary Fund, 2001); International Monetary Fund, "IMF Executive Board Discusses Money Laundering," press release, April 19, 2001.

52. Financial Action Task Force, *Review to Identify Non-Cooperating Countries and Territories* (Paris: FATF, 2001), 3, 4. Both Indonesia (which chose an alternate executive director for one of the Southeast Asian constituencies) and Nigeria had significant oil wealth, which added to their influence at the IMF board, and Egypt (which chose the executive director for the non-Saudi Arab constituency) was highly influential in the Arab world, which also had significant influence on the board.

53. International Monetary Fund, *Intensified Fund Involvement in Anti-Money Laundering Work and Combating the Financing of Terrorism* (Washington, D.C.: International Monetary Fund, 2001), 5–6, 10–14, 29 (emphasis added). The author of this chapter was a member of the task force and a principal author of the report.

54. International Monetary Fund, "IMF Board Discusses the Fund's Intensified Involvement in Anti-Money Laundering and Combating the Financing of Terrorism," press release, November 16, 2001.

55. International Monetary Fund, "Communiqué of the International Monetary and Financial Committee of the Board of Governors of the International Monetary Fund," press release, April 20, 2002. The author of this chapter was a principal author of the methodology.

56. Financial Action Task Force, *Review to Identify Non-Cooperating Countries and Territories* (Paris: FATF, 2002).

57. International Monetary Fund and World Bank, *Anti-Money Laundering and Combating Financing of Terrorism (AML/CFT) Materials Concerning Staff Progress towards the Development of a Comprehensive AML/CFT Methodology and Assessment Process: Joint Progress Report on the Work of the IMF and World Bank* (Washington, D.C.: International Monetary Fund, 2002), 10, note 5 (emphasis in original).

58. International Monetary Fund, "IMF Advances Efforts to Combat Money Laundering and Terrorist Finance," press release, August 8, 2002.

59. Ibid.

60. Ibid.

61. International Monetary Fund, *Cook Islands: Assessment of the Supervision and Regulation of the Financial Sector Volume I—Review of Financial Sector Regulation and Supervision* (Washington, D.C.: International Monetary Fund, 2004), 12, 31.

62. Financial Action Task Force, *Annual and Overall Review of Non-Cooperative Countries and Territories* (Paris: FATF, 2005), 1.

63. International Monetary Fund and World Bank, *Anti-Money Laundering and Combating the Financing of Terrorism: Review of the Quality and Consistency of Assessment Reports and the Effectiveness of Coordination* (Washington, D.C.: International Monetary Fund, 2006), 3.

64. Ibid.

65. International Monetary Fund, *Offshore Financial Centers: The Assessment Program: A Progress Report and the Future of the Program* (Washington, D.C.: International Monetary Fund, 2006), 12–15.

66. International Monetary Fund, *Offshore Financial Centers: The Assessment Program—An Update, Appendix II* (Washington, D.C.: International Monetary Fund, 2004), 7.

67. International Monetary Fund, *Offshore Financial Centers: The Assessment Program—A Progress Report* (Washington, D.C.: International Monetary Fund, 2005), 1, 6–8. See generally International Monetary Fund, *Offshore Financial Centers: The Assessment Program—A Progress Report* (Washington, D.C.: International Monetary Fund, 2006).

68. International Monetary Fund, "IMF Executive Board Integrates the Offshore Financial Center Assessment Program with the FSAP," press release, July 9, 2008.
69. *Global Financial Integrity,* "New Legislation Would Combat Tax Haven Abuse, Increase Transparency, Accountability," March 2, 2009.
70. Vanessa Houlder, "Harbours of Resentment," *Financial Times,* November 30, 2008.
71. *BBC News,* "Brown Urges Tax Haven Regulation," March 6, 2009.
72. Avinash Persaud, "Look for Onshore, Not Offshore Scapegoats," *Financial Times,* March 4, 2009.

Chapter 5: The Role of Offshore Financial Centers in Regulatory Competition

1. Bob Blunden, *The Money Launderers* (Gloucestershire, U.K.: Management Books 2000, 2001) summarizes the issues involved in money laundering. See also Raymond Baker, *Capitalism's Achilles Heel* (Hoboken, N.J.: John Wiley and Sons, 2005), 48–161 (detailing examples of corruption and money laundering); Martin Meredith, *The Fate of Africa: From the Hopes of Freedom to the Heart of Despair* (New York: PublicAffairs, 2005), 298 (noting that Zairian dictator Mobutu Sese Seko "funneled huge sums" into his private bank accounts outside Zaire via Swiss banks).
2. This literature is summarized by Boise in this volume.
3. Oxfam, *Tax Havens: Releasing the Hidden Billions for Poverty Eradication* (London: Oxfam Publication, 2000), 1.
4. Baker, *Capitalism's Achilles Heel*, 194.
5. Erin A. O'Hara and Larry E. Ribstein, *The Law Market* (New York: Oxford University Press 2009), 66.
6. Meredith, *Fate of Africa*, 175. Meredith's comprehensive study of African autocracies describes the nature of the constraints facing autocrats.
7. For example, "Most political scientists and trade economists agree that governments treat foreign market opening and associated increases in export opportunities as a domestic political benefit and domestic market opening as a cost." John H. Barton, Judith L. Goldstein, Timothy E. Josling, and Richard Steinberg, *The Evolution of the Trade Regime* (Princeton, N.J.: Princeton University Press, 2006), 10.
8. Politicians may sincerely believe that their preferences advance the public good, or they may simply enjoy having the world arranged to suit their own preferences. In both cases, the politicians benefit by satisfying their policy preferences.
9. See, for example, Baker, *Capitalism's Achilles Heel*, 27 (describing use of "a Caribbean tax haven" to hide "dirty money").
10. Ibid. (noting that some of the "dirty money" ends up in New York bank accounts).
11. The most important general consideration of competition for law is O'Hara and Ribstein, *Law Market*.

12. This is a vast question beyond the scope of this chapter to address comprehensively. See Dan Chirot, *Modern Tyrants* (Princeton, N.J.: Princeton University Press, 1994), 28.

13. O'Hara and Ribstein, *Law Market*, 73–77 (describing how internal interest groups benefit from increased economic activity made possible by regulatory competition).

14. In virtually every interview my colleague Craig Boise and I have conducted in jurisdictions ranging from "startup" to "mature" offshore jurisdictions, individuals in both the public and private sectors have stressed to us the importance to OFCs of "moving up the food chain" to higher value-added activities.

15. Craig Boise and Andrew P. Morriss, "Change, Dependency, and Regime Plasticity in Offshore Financial Intermediation: The Saga of the Netherlands Antilles," *Texas International Law Journal* 45: 377–456.

16. Ibid.

17. See notes 135–138.

18. O'Hara and Ribstein, *Law Market*, 6–7.

19. See, for example, Marshall J. Langer, *How to Use Foreign Tax Havens* (New York: Practising Law Institute, 1975) (J1-1403194–95) (noting that Latin American governments complained in the 1960s that the U.S.–Netherlands Antilles treaty was "encouraging capital flight" to the United States); Boise, this volume.

20. O'Hara and Ribstein, *Law Market*, 79–80.

21. Meredith, *Fate of Africa*, 185.

22. Martin Meredith, *Mugabe: Power and Plunder in Zimbabwe* (New York: PublicAffairs, 2002), 17 (quoting Phillip Chiyangwa, a millionaire businessman).

23. Transparency International, *Global Corruption Report* (Berlin: Transparency International, 2004), 13, table 1.1.

24. Meredith notes that in Africa, governments "maintained overvalued exchange rates to reduce both the cost of food imports, like wheat, corn and rice favoured by the urban elite, and the cost of other goods they cherished—like cars, household appliances and fashionable attire. The effect was to penalize farmers at every turn. Farm exporters lost income; food producers found it difficult to compete against subsidized imports. Many farmers obtained less than half the real value of their crops." Meredith, *Fate of Africa*, 279–80.

25. George B. N. Ayittey, *Africa in Chaos* (New York: St. Martin's Press, 1998), 200.

26. The notion that jurisdictions with few options are likely to compete for polluting industries has generated a substantial "race to the bottom" literature in environmental law, arguing that international standards are needed to prevent polluting industries from moving their operations to poor countries where they will be allowed to pollute. See, for example, Jonathan H. Adler, "When Is Two a Crowd? The Impact of Federal Action on State Environmental Regulation," *Harvard Environmental Law Review* 31 (2007): 67, 79–80 (describing and critiquing "race to the bottom" literature). High-tax jurisdictions have tried to make an analogous argument with respect

to low-tax jurisdictions, although the analogy between pollution and lower taxes is, at best, a tenuous one. See Boise, this volume. On the "race to the bottom" issue in international financial regulation, see Stavros Gadinis, "The Politics of Competition in International Financial Regulation," *Harvard International Law Journal* 49 (2008): 447; Dionne and Macey, this volume.

27. For example, the Petroleum Trust Fund set up in Nigeria by the dictator Ibrahim Babangida "lost" $600 million under his rule, suggesting the scope of some of the rents obtainable in natural resource–rich economies. Ayittey, *Africa in Chaos*, 35.

28. Independence coincided with a commodities boom for many countries in Africa, bringing annual growth rates of 4–6 percent annually between 1945 and 1960. Meredith, *Fate of Africa*, 141. This fueled opportunities for corruption and limited the ability of market forces to discipline the leaders of the newly independent countries. For example, $300 million of the $400 million from coffee grown in Zaire in 1978 was fraudulently diverted to regime backers. David J. Gould, *Bureaucratic Corruption and Underdevelopment in the Third World: The Case of Zaire* (New York: Pergamon Press, 1980), xiv.

29. Ayittey refers to these states as "vampire states," which operate "by extracting resources from the productive sections of the population (peasant majority)," which are then spent "in the urban areas and on the elites—a non-productive, parasitic class." Ayittey, *Africa in Chaos*, 343.

30. Ibid., 201.

31. Ibid., 48–49. Ayittey defined "statism" as "state hegemony in the economy and the direction of economic activity or development by the state through price controls, legislative acts, regulations, state ownership of the means of production, and operation of state enterprises. The statist behemoth, with wide-ranging powers, is backed by a coercive military and judicial force." Ibid., 49.

32. Ibid., 151.

33. O'Hara and Ribstein, *Law Market*, 4.

34. Saskia Sassen, *The Global City*, 2d ed. (Princeton: Princeton University Press, 2001), 76.

35. See Larry E. Ribstein, "The Evolving Partnership," *Journal of Corporation Law* 26 (2001): 819; O'Hara and Ribstein, *Law Market*, 32–33, 119–20; Susan Pace Hamill, "The Origins behind the Limited Liability Company," *Ohio State Law Journal* 59 (1998): 1459. Professor Hamill notes the origin of the LLC in the desire of the Hamilton Brothers Oil Company for a domestic vehicle similar to the Panamanian *limitada* entity. The American LLC was created because "the Hamilton Brothers Oil Company soon found that Panamanian limitadas posed administrative difficulties. . . . Because no similar entity existed in the U.S., these limitadas also created uncertainty concerning the degree that U.S. courts would respect the limited liability characteristic." After a failed effort to persuade Alaska to adopt the LLC bill the company's lawyer prepared, the company persuaded Wyoming to pass the bill. Ibid., 1463–66. The company then requested and received a favorable private-letter ruling from the IRS

approving its LLC. This request involved intervention with the IRS by the Wyoming secretary of state, governor, and senators, and took over three years. Ibid., 1466–67. After a lengthy struggle, the IRS finally issued a public revenue ruling allowing Wyoming LLCs to be taxed as partnerships. Ibid., 1469. Additional negotiation and refining of the LLC statutes were required before widespread adoption of LLC statutes.

36. O'Hara and Ribstein, *Law Market*, 4.

37. See Raoul Lemprière, *History of the Channel Islands* (London: R. Hale, 1974), 156, 215–16.

38. Andrew P. Morriss and Craig M. Boise, "Creating Cayman," working paper LE08-006, University of Illinois College of Law, 2009.

39. See Federation of Tax Administrators, "State Individual Income Taxes," compiled by the FTA from various sources, http://www.taxadmin.org/FTA/rate/ind_inc.html (accessed September 2, 2009). New Hampshire has an income tax on dividends and interest income only. The routine nature of such competition within jurisdictions such as the United States is inconsistent with those same jurisdictions' characterization of conceptually identical competition across jurisdictions internationally as "unfair."

40. Barry Eichengreen, *The European Economy since 1945: Coordinated Capitalism and Beyond* (Princeton, N.J.: Princeton University Press, 2007), 90.

41. O'Hara and Ribstein, *Law Market*, 15.

42. Ibid., 117–19.

43. See, for example, ibid., 180–83 (discussing evolution of asset protection structures).

44. Bermuda developed the captive market in the 1970s, and by 1986 had "close to 1300 insurance companies" registered. The Insurance Act of 1978, as amended in 1981, 1983, and 1985, was the primary legislation in the area in the 1980s. See David Ezekiel, *Bermuda: A Leading Domicile for Captives, Techniques of Self-Insurance*, Commercial Law and Practice Course Handbook Series, PLI Order No. A4-4170 (New York: Practising Law Institute, October 1986), 131.

45. Boise and Morriss, "Change, Dependency, and Regime Plasticity."

46. Charles M. Yablon, "The Historical Race Competition for Corporate Charters and the Rise and Decline of New Jersey: 1880–1910," *Journal of Corporation Law* 32 (2007): 323, 361, quoting Josiah Marvel, Esq. (president of Delaware Charter Guarantee and Trust Co. of Wilmington, Delaware), *Address before the Students of the Department of Finance and Economy of the University of Pennsylvania, May 14, 1902* (Wilmington, Del.: Delaware Charter Guarantee and Trust Company, 1902).

47. Yablon, "Historical Race Competition," 356–57; O'Hara and Ribstein, *Law Market*, 110–13.

48. Morriss and Boise, "Creating Cayman."

49. Viet D. Dinh, "Codetermination and Corporate Governance in a Multinational Business Enterprise," *Journal of Corporation Law* 24 (1999): 975; Eichengreen, *European Economy*.

50. See Andrew P. Morriss, "Implications of Second-Best Theory for Administrative and Regulatory Law: A Case Study of Public Utility Regulation," *Chicago-Kent Law Review* 73 (1998): 136 (discussing cross-subsidization and the impact of deregulation on such schemes).

51. Bruce Yandle and Andrew P. Morriss, "The Technologies of Property Rights: Choice among Alternative Solutions to Tragedies of the Commons," *Ecological Law Quarterly* 28 (2001): 123 (discussing law as a technology).

52. See A.W. B. Simpson, *A History of the Land Law*, 2d ed. (New York: Oxford University Press, 1986), 256–60 (discussing impact of landmark case of *Tulk v. Moxhay* [1848] 41 Eng. Rep. 1143, which created equitable servitudes).

53. Douglas A. Irwin, *Free Trade Under Fire*, 2d ed. (Princeton, N.J.: Princeton University Press, 2005), 70–71, 82. The U.S. Government Accountability Office estimates that the U.S. sugar program provided approximately $1 billion in benefits to U.S. sugar producers at a cost to U.S. consumers of approximately $1.9 billion in 1998. U.S. Government Accountability Office, *Supporting Sugar Prices Has Increased Users' Costs While Benefiting Producers*, GAO RCED-00-126, June 2000, http://www.gao.gov/archive/2000/rc00126.pdf (accessed November 30, 2009). For a general historical analysis of sugar programs, see Katherine E. Monahan, Note, "U.S. Sugar Policy: Domestic and International Repercussions of Sour Law," *Hastings International and Comparative Law Review* 15 (1992): 325.

54. Irwin, *Free Trade under Fire*, 82.

55. For example, under the dictator Sekou Touré, trading without government permission became a crime in Guinea. "Police roadblocks were set up around the country to control internal trade. The state set up a monopoly on foreign trade and smuggling became punishable by death. Currency trafficking was punishable by 15 to 20 years in prison." Many autocratic regimes have used price controls and other methods of economic control to transfer wealth to the regime. Ibid., 139 (explaining how "price controls . . . became tools for the systematic exploitation of the peasants" in African autocracies).

56. Scott E. Harrington, "Insurance Deregulation and the Public Interest," AEI–Brookings Joint Center for Regulatory Studies, 2000, 43, http://aei-brookings.org/admin/authorpdfs/redirect-safely.php?fname=../pdffiles/harrington.pdf (accessed September 2, 2009).

57. O'Hara and Ribstein, *Law Market*, 80–81.

58. Where governments do not use the least distortionary form of taxation available, regulatory competition creates an even greater incentive to engage in arbitrage.

59. O'Hara and Ribstein, *Law Market*, 20–23.

60. Ibid., 16 ("There is no way to determine objectively which regulations are reasonable and which not.")

61. J. R. Hicks, "Annual Survey of Economic Theory: The Theory of Monopoly," *Econometrica* 3 (1935): 1, 8.

62. Meredith, *Fate of Africa*, 257.

63. Ayittey, *Africa in Chaos*, 160.
64. Anne O. Krueger, *Trade Policies and Developing Nations* (Washington, D.C.: Brookings Institution Press, 1995), 63.
65. It is not impossible, just more expensive, to engage in such transactions. Hernando De Soto, *The Mystery of Capital* (New York: Basic Books, 2003).
66. Irwin, *Free Trade under Fire*, 15.
67. Sassen, *Global City,* 46.
68. O'Hara and Ribstein, *Law Market,* 27–29 (discussing limits to exit strategy).
69. Jenny Anderson, "U.S. Financial Sector Is Losing Its Edge, Report Says," *New York Times*, January 22, 2007, 3 (discussing report by McKinsey & Co., commissioned by New York City's mayor, on city's competitiveness in financial business).
70. Daniel W. Drezner, *All Politics Is Global: Explaining International Regulatory Regimes* (Princeton, N.J.: Princeton University Press, 2007), 119.
71. Michael D. Bordo, Barry Eichengreen, and Douglas A. Irwin, "Is Globalization Today Really Different from Globalization a Hundred Years Ago?" in *Brookings Trade Forum: 1999*, ed. Robert Z. Lawrence and Susan M. Collins (Washington, D.C.: Brookings Institution Press, 1999).
72. Irwin, *Free Trade under Fire*, 20.
73. Sassen, *Global City,* 31.
74. Ibid., 37.
75. Barton et al., *Evolution of the Trade Regime,* 204.
76. Krueger, *Trade Policies and Developing Nations*, 72.
77. Ibid., 1. The original General Agreement on Tariffs and Trade (GATT) allowed such policies, allowing developing countries the benefit of tariff reductions in developed countries while simultaneously permitting them to erect substantial barriers to imports. Ibid., 38.
78. Ibid.
79. Barton et al., *Evolution of the Trade Regime,* 3.
80. Francis Cairncross, *The Death of Distance* (Boston: Harvard Business School Press, 1997), 1.
81. Morriss and Boise, "Creating Cayman."
82. See, for example, Reuters, "Bermuda Battles Caymans for Offshore Funds," December 11, 2007, http://www.reuters.com/article/bankingfinancial-SP-A/idUSN1152015120071213 (accessed September 2, 2009).
83. Morriss and Boise, "Creating Cayman."
84. Ayittey, *Africa in Chaos*, 32.
85. Craig M. Boise and Andrew P. Morriss, "What It Means to be 'Offshore,'" working paper LE08-007, University of Illinois College of Law, 2009.
86. The United States does not generally tax interest on bank deposits or Treasury securities held by nonresidents and exempts such income from withholding tax as well. See Boise, this volume.

87. Barry Eichengreen, *Global Imbalances and the Lessons of Bretton Woods* (Cambridge, Mass.: MIT Press, 2007), 128.

88. Rawi Abdelal, *Capital Rules: The Construction of Global Finance* (Cambridge, Mass: Harvard University Press, 2007), 16.

89. Houman B. Shadab, "Innovation and Corporate Governance: The Impact of Sarbanes Oxley," *University of Pennsylvania Journal of Business and Employment Law* 10 (forthcoming); Joseph D. Piotroski and Suraj Srinivasan, "Regulation and Bonding: The Sarbanes-Oxley Act and the Flow of International Listings" (working paper no. 11, Rock Center for Corporate Governance, Stanford University, 2008), http://ssrn.com/abstract=956987 (accessed September 2, 2009); O'Hara and Ribstein, *Law Market*, 29–31.

90. See, generally, O'Hara and Ribstein, *Law Market* (discussing competition in real property law and family law, among others).

91. See Barton et al., *Evolution of the Trade Regime*, 210 (explaining expansion of the liberal trade regime as "in the interest of powerful participants. The United States and the European Union have benefited greatly from the international trading regime created by the WTO. It is not only a source of their economic strength; it is also a mechanism to help them achieve their national policy goals.")

92. Thomas Friedman, *The Lexus and the Olive Tree: Understanding Globalization* (New York: Farrar, Straus, and Giroux, 1999), 86. The evolution of the GATT into the WTO increased this by requiring countries to sign onto the entire package rather than allowing opt-outs of particular aspects of liberalization, as the GATT had done. Barton et al., *Evolution of the Trade Regime*, 208.

93. Boise and Morriss, "Offshore."

94. As Daniel Drezner argues, despite the appearance of multilateral institutions, the "great powers," those "governments that oversee large internal markets," are "the primary actors writing the rules that regulate the global economy." Drezner, *All Politics Is Global*, 5.

95. Ibid., 143.

96. Gordon, this volume.

97. Meredith, *Fate of Africa*, 273.

98. See Jeremy Jennings, "France and the 'Anglo-Saxon' Model: Contemporary and Historical Perspectives," *European Review* 14 (2006): 537.

99. It has long been recognized that industrialization is "hard to accomplish" in such small jurisdictions. See, for example, Morely Ayearst, *The British West Indies: The Search for Self-Government* (London: Allen and Unwin, 1960), 45. Tourism, the other mainstay of many of these jurisdictions, is often closely tied to the financial center business. One Caymanian expert estimated that almost half of Cayman's tourist industry is due to its financial center business. Morriss and Boise, "Creating Cayman."

100. Ibid.

101. Boise and Morriss, "Change, Dependency, and Regime Plasticity."

102. O'Hara and Ribstein, *Law Market*, 111–13 (discussing bonding in the context of Delaware).
103. Antoine, this volume.
104. Morriss and Boise, "Creating Cayman."
105. Andrew P. Morriss, "Regulatory Intensity and Offshore Financial Centers," working paper, University of Illinois College of Law, 2009).
106. Ibid.
107. Vassel Johnson, *As I See It: How Cayman Became a Leading Financial Sector* (East Sussex, U.K.: The Book Guild, Ltd., 2001), 159–60. Note that the banker, Jean Doucet, eventually did end up behind bars on an unrelated matter. Ibid., 163–64.
108. Morriss, "Regulatory Intensity."
109. Ibid.
110. Barry Eichengreen, *Globalizing Capital: A History of the International Monetary System* (Princeton, N.J.: Princeton University Press, 1998), 4, 73.
111. Ibid., 4.
112. Ibid., 4–5.
113. Ibid., 194.
114. Mark Hampton and Jason Abbott, introduction to *Offshore Financial Centers and Tax Havens,* ed. Mark Hampton and Jason Abbott (West Lafayette, Ind.: Purdue University Press, 1999), 1, 13.
115. Morriss and Boise, "Creating Cayman."
116. Ibid.
117. This section is based on a more extensive (and heavily documented) discussion of the topic in Boise and Morriss, *Change, Dependency, and Regime Plasticity*.
118. Oscar L. Altman, "Euro-Dollars," in *Readings in the Euro-Dollar,* ed. Eric B. Chalmers (London: Griffith, 1969), 1, 2 3.
119. Stuart W. Robinson Jr., *Multinational Banking* (Leiden, Netherlands: Sijthoff, 1972), 167, 188–89.
120. Ibid., 277–78.
121. Ibid.
122. U.S. House of Representatives, Committee on Government Operations, Subcommittee on Commerce, Consumer, and Monetary Affairs, *Tax Evasion through the Netherlands Antilles and Other Tax Haven Countries: Hearings before a Subcommittee of the Committee on Government Operations*, 98th Cong., sess. 1, April 12–13, 1983, statement of Roscoe L. Egger Jr., commissioner, Internal Revenue Service, 205.
123. Langer, *Foreign Tax Havens*, 193.
124. U.S. House of Representatives, *Tax Evasion*, 236.
125. One estimate put Eurobond volume at 40–50 percent of all U.S. corporate bonds in the early 1980s. *Business Week*, "A Treaty That May Sink Havens," February 14, 1983, cited in House of Representatives, *Tax Evasion*, 782.
126. Ibid.

127. The treaty negotiations are described in detail in Boise and Morriss, *Change, Dependency, and Regime Plasticity*.
128. See Victor E. Schwartz and Fred S. Souk, "Recent Developments in Self-Insurance: Is It Time to Stop Worrying and Love Risk Retention?" *Forum* 18 (1983): 636, 642.
129. Scott A. Taylor, "Taxing Captive Insurance: A New Solution for an Old Problem," *Tax Lawyer* 42 (1989): 859–60 (citing industry estimates).
130. Linda Haddleton, "Continuing Growth," in *Global Reinsurance: Special Cayman Report 2004*, 2004, 13, available at http://www.globalreinsurance.com/Contacts.asp?navcode=208.
131. Laura Jereski, "Vermont: Land of Green Mountains and Self-Insurance," *Business Week*, August 21, 1989.
132. Ibid.
133. Ibid.
134. Ibid.
135. Professor Maureen Sanders describes the initial passage of the PLRRA. Maureen A. Sanders, "Risk Retention Groups: Who's Sorry Now?" *Southern Illinois University Law Journal* 17 (1992–93): 531, 532.
136. 15 U.S.C. §3901(2)(a)(4)(A-E) (1981). See Sanders, "Risk Retention Groups," 533 ("The overriding function of the 1981 Act was to preempt many state laws that prohibited or hindered the formation of interstate risk retention or purchasing groups.")
137. H.R. Rep. 97-190 (97th Cong., 1st sess., 1981), 1440.
138. U.S. General Accounting Office, *Insurance: Activity under the Product Liability Risk Retention Act of 1981*, GAO HRD-86-120BR, July 1986, http://archive.gao.gov/d4t4/130549.pdf (accessed November 30, 2009).
139. 15 U.S.C. 3901 et seq.
140. Leon Jacobsen, *Self-Insurance Using Captives and Risk Retention Groups and Purchasing Groups, Current Problems and Issues in Liability Insurance*, PLI A4-4184 (New York: Practising Law Institute, 1987), 207, 213–14.
141. Ibid., 216.
142. Onshore and offshore captive statutes differ in a number of particulars. For example, many onshore jurisdictions include considerable detail concerning the captive's structure, including investment options and the number of officers. Offshore captives, by contrast, generally have greater flexibility in these areas.
143. The term in Guernsey is "protected cell company" and in Cayman, "segregated portfolio company." Bermuda also has cell captives, which are known as "segregated account companies," and Vermont has "sponsored captives."
144. By 1999, a total of fifteen states had adopted statutes permitting captive insurance firms (Colorado, Delaware, Florida, Georgia, Hawaii, Illinois, Kansas, Maine, New York, Rhode Island, South Dakota, Tennessee, Vermont, Virginia, and Washington). Mary Cannon Veed, "The Re-Engineering of the U.S. Commercial Insurance Market: Open Doors or Open Season?" in *Insurance Market 1999: Capitalizing on*

Change, Commercial Law and Practice Course Handbook Series 152 (New York: Practising Law Institute, 1999).

145. See Thorsten Rinman and Rigmore Brodefors, *The History of Commercial Shipping* (Gothenburg, Sweden: Rinman and Linden, 1983); Rodney Carlisle, *Sovereignty for Sale* (Annapolis, Md.: Naval Institute Press, 1981).

146. O'Hara and Ribstein, *Law Market*, 73–77 (describing "seller side" incentives in the market for law).

147. Rene De La Pedraja, *The Rise and Decline of U.S. Merchant Shipping in the Twentieth Century* (New York: Maxwell Macmillan International, 1992), 134.

148. Rinman and Brodefors, *History of Commercial Shipping*, 134–35.

149. Note that it is not necessary that autocrats have a different set of preferences for there to be different outcomes. Development economist Arthur Lewis's study of African one-party states concluded that "much of what is going on in some of these countries is fully explained in terms of the normal lust of human beings for power and wealth. The stakes are high. Office carries power, prestige and money. The power is incredible." W. Arthur Lewis, *Politics in West Africa* (London: Allen & Unwin, 1965), 31–32.

150. Chirot, *Modern Tyrants*, 244.

151. Meredith, *Fate of Africa*, 165.

152. Ibid., 169.

153. Hampton Smith, Tim Merrill, and Sandra W. Meditz, "The Economy," in *Zaire: A Country Study*, ed. Sandra W. Meditz and Tim Merrill (Washington, D.C.: Division, 1993), 160. The black market rate was already five times the official rate in 1983. Ibid., 159.

154. Ibid., 159 ("The overvaluation of the zaire led to consistent shortages of hard currency at the official rate, making it difficult for local industries to import necessary inputs and spare parts.")

155. Ibid., 160.

156. Ibid.

157. A second cause of the looting is, of course, the outside funding of autocrats by the West, China, Russia, and the Soviet bloc, despite the blatant corruption.

158. Drezner identifies as a political cost of liberalizing capital flows for "governments with repressed capital markets" the "lost political patronage power over the allocation of scarce finance," since "one of the most potent levers in less developed countries is access to government-owned or government-influenced financial institutions." Drezner, *All Politics Is Global*, 128.

159. Smith et al., "The Economy," 154 ("Because no one could be sure of remaining in office for very long, the incentive was to profit as quickly and as much as possible.")

160. David J. Gould, *Bureaucratic Corruption*, xiii.

161. Meredith, *Fate of Africa*, 280.

162. Ayittey, *Africa in Chaos*, 176–77.

163. Ibid., 176–77, quoting *The Economist*, August 21, 1993.

164. Baker, *Capitalism's Achilles Heel*, 194.
165. Meredith, *Fate of Africa*, 688.
166. Chirot, *Modern Tyrants*, 163.
167. Ayittey, *Africa in Chaos*, 262.

Index

Abacus, In re, 42
Administration of tax laws, cost of, 61
Africa, corruption of governments in, 111, 125, 145, 175n28, 182n149
See also individual nations
Alternative financial markets, OFCs as, 12, 16
AML/Combating the Cost of Terrorism (CFT) ROSCs, 95
Antideferral regime, 160n18, 20
Anti-money laundering (AML) policies
    assessment of OFC cooperation level, 171n44
    focus on primary criminal activity instead, 110
    IMF's role in, 76–77, 88–99
    and legitimacy of OFCs, 25
    U.S. pressure for, 93–94, 149n14
Anti-terrorism financing programs, 95, 149n14
Antoine, Rose-Marie Belle, 16
Aron, Ravi, 23–24
Articles of Agreement, IMF, 75
Aruba, 2
Asian financial crisis, 80
Asset protection, OFCs as instruments for, 1, 43–44, 53
    See also Tax havens
Asset protection trust, 43
Autocratic governments
    natural resources regime problem, 175n28
    open market effects on, 125, 182n158
    and power of personal interest, 182n149
    regulatory competition effects on, 104–5, 111, 117, 128–29, 141–44, 145–46
Avi-Yonah, Reuven, 60
Ayittey, George, 111, 145, 175n29, 31

Bahamas, 32, 115, 133
Baker, Raymond, 102, 145
Banda, Hastings, 142
Bank of Credit and Commerce International (BCCI), 77
Bank of Nova Scotia v. Tremblay (Barbados), 34
Banks
    confidentiality issue, 36, 57, 63–64, 69, 77, 83
    prudent supervision issue, 76–88, 170n31
Barbados, 1, 113
Basel Committee on Banking Supervision, 77–78, 79–80
Basel Core Principles (PCP), 81, 82, 170n31
BCCI (Bank of Credit and Commerce International), 77

Beneficiary in offshore trust, legal
   principles, 40, 41, 42–43, 44–45
Benefits of regulatory competition
   conclusion, 27–29
   controversy review, 17–18
   and criminal activity risk, 13, 24–26
   critics vs. supporters, 10–13
   efficiency, 13, 19–22, 64–65
   for governmental incentives to serve
      people, 119–21
   innovation, 22–24, 140
   introduction, 8–10
   and offshore trusts' contributions,
      39–45
   and onshore jurisdictions' attempt to
      limit OFCs, 13–16
   overview, 1–2
   public choice and opposition to
      OFCs, 26–27
Bermuda, 115, 137–38
"Blacklisting" of OFCs, 14, 15, 25,
   32–33, 164n69
   See also NCCT
Boise, Craig, 125
Bourguiba, Habib, 142
Brandeis, Louis D., 17
British Virgin Islands, 16
Brown, Gordon, 99–100
Bush, George W., 66

Cairncross, Francis, 124
Canada, 35, 43, 46, 93, 140
Capacity, identifying settlor's, 46
Capital
   diversion of by OFCs, 50, 58–59, 64
   geographically vs. nongeographically
      mobile, 55–56, 58–59, 65
Captive insurance, 1, 115, 136–38,
   181n142
Caribbean area, 14
   See also individual nations
Casani v. Mattei (Italy), 46–47

Cayman Islands
   and BCCI failure, 77
   captive insurance market, 1, 137–38
   commonalities with onshore financial
      centers, 126
   confidentiality credibility of, 63, 131
   duties on imports as revenue,
      164n72
   finance services strategy, 130, 133
   hedge fund business, 115
   innovation in, 131–32
   and NCCT status, 93
   shift of banking from Bahamas to,
      115
Central America, 14
Channel Islands, 113
Chartering, corporate, 17, 27, 87, 115,
   130–31
Chirot, Dan, 145
Combating the Cost of Terrorism (CFT)
   ROSCs, 95
Comity and confidentiality, 38–39
Commodities and rent seeking, 111
Common-law vs. offshore trust, legal
   distinctions, 39–45
Communication costs, historical reduction in, 124–25
Company chartering, 17, 27, 87, 115,
   130–31
Competition in laxity, 17, 18–19
Confidentiality
   banking, 36, 57, 63–64, 69, 77, 83
   as basis for OFCs internal regulation
      system, 63
   as benefit of OFCs for clients, 10–11,
      131, 132
   and criminal activity risk, 2, 11, 14,
      35, 110
   as foundational principle of common
      law, 36, 63
   human rights law on privacy, 37–38
   and legal perspective on OFCs, 35–39

limits to, 36–37
OFCs resistance to erosion of, 63–64
onshore jurisdictions' attempts to
regulate, 14, 50, 57, 69
onshore jurisdictions' inconsistency
about, 35–36
and privacy for corruption, 106
and protecting trusts from beneficiaries, 43–44
scope of acceptance, 36
striking balance with, 15
Conflict of laws rules, 45–47
Constitutional protections for confidentiality/privacy, 37–38
Contagion in financial collapses due to banking supervision problems, 80–81, 84
Cook Islands, 98
Copycatting of OFC structures by onshore jurisdictions, 47–48
Corporations
benefits of OFCs for, 10–11
chartering of, regulatory competition for, 17, 27, 87, 115, 130–31
governance scandals and OFCs, 11
IBCs, 112, 113
tax use of OFCs, 52–53
Corruption
African problems with, 111, 125, 145, 175n28, 182n149
as motive for jurisdictional competition, 106, 109–10
regulatory competition's limitation incentive, 120
Creditors for trusts, identifying legitimate, 44–45
Criminal activity risk
benefits of regulatory competition as worth, 13, 24–26
and confidentiality issue, 2, 11, 14, 35, 110
and OFCs, 2, 13, 21, 88–89, 149n15

onshore jurisdictions' pressure on OFCs, 11, 14, 76–77, 88, 93–94, 95
onshore location of majority of, 32
terrorism financing issue, 2, 11, 88–99, 95
See also Money laundering
Cross-border banking supervisory challenges, 77–78

Delaware's favorable chartering law, 17, 27, 115, 130–31
Democratically constrained governments, 104, 117, 118, 128–29, 139–41, 145
Direct implicit costs of regulation, 116
Direct vs. indirect methods for economic goals without regulatory competition, 118–19
Diversion of capital by OFCs, 50, 58–59, 64
Drezner, Daniel W., 123
Drug trade, OFCs as havens for, 11
Duress and flight clauses in offshore trusts, 45, 157n46
Duties vs. income taxes as OFC revenue source, 62–63, 65, 159n12, 164n72

Easterbrook, Frank, 20
Ecuadorian financial crisis, 80
Efficiency benefit of regulatory competition, 13, 19–22, 64–65
Egger, Roscoe Jr., 135
Eichengreen, Barry, 133
Emerging market crises, banking supervision failure in, 78–79
Enforcer, purpose trust, 43
Environmental and resource use competition, 174–75n26
Erosion of tax base by OFCs, assumption of, 11, 54, 59–60, 64, 148n8

EU (European Union)
 definition, 159n6
 private behavior regulatory incentives, 114
 regulatory attempts on OFCs, 3, 72–73
 savings tax directive, 57, 69, 72–73, 166n114
 as successful competitor in global markets, 126
 tax competition regulation, 56–57, 68–69, 72–73, 166–67n115
 value of market beyond cost of participation, 108
Eurobonds, 134–36
Eurodollar markets, 107, 134–36
European enclave states, 14

FATF (Financial Action Task Force), 14, 21, 85–99, 127–28
FATF 40 standards, 89–92
FATF-style regional bodies (FSRBs), 90, 97
Finance subsidiaries, 1, 134–36
Financial Action Task Force (FATF), 14, 21, 85–99, 127–28
Financial Clearing Corporation, In re, 37
Financial Sector Assessment Program (FSAP), 82, 88, 99
Financial services trade, increase in, 123–24
 See also Offshore financial centers (OFCs)
Financial Stability Forum (FSF), 81, 83, 84
Fiscal policy, effect of tax revenue loss on, 59–60
Flight and duress clauses in offshore trusts, 45, 157n46
Foreign direct investment shift to technology, 123
Form-over-substance approach in tax arrangements, 33

France, 89, 93, 96, 100
Fraudulent conveyances, 2, 44–45
Free rider problem, assumption of, 60
FSAP (Financial Sector Assessment Program), 82, 88, 99
FSF (Financial Stability Forum), 81, 83, 84
FSRBs (FATF-style regional bodies), 90, 97

G-7 (Group of Seven industrialized nations), 54, 79, 83
G-22 (Group of Twenty-Two), 82
GATT (General Agreement on Tariffs and Trade), 117, 124
Geographically vs. nongeographically mobile capital, 55–56, 58–59, 65
Germany, 97, 100, 116, 161n26
Global financial system
 bank supervision failures, 77–82
 historical reduction in stability of, 133
 OFCs' important role in, 3, 9–10, 13
 and offshore economies' health, 15, 17, 22–23
 onshore blaming of OFCs for meltdown of, 84, 100
Globalization and increase in regulatory competition, 123
Global welfare assumption and tax competition inefficiency, 57–58
Governments
 democratically constrained, 104, 117, 118, 128–29, 139–41, 145
 fiscal policy, effect of tax revenue loss on, 59–60
 monopolistic activity, costs of, 120–21
 See also Autocratic governments
Green v. Jernigan (Canada), 46
Group of Seven industrialized nations (G-7), 79
Group of Twenty-Two (G-22), 82

Guernsey, 1
Gulf area, 14

Hague Convention on Trusts, 41, 46, 47
"Harmful preferential tax regimes," OECD's, 54, 55, 65, 67, 93, 161–62nn39–41
Harmful tax practices and IMF's regulatory role, 74–76
  See also Tax havens
Hedge funds, 1, 16, 21, 115
Hicks, J. R., 119
Higginbotham's Petition, In re, 45
Hong Kong, 1–2, 14
Human rights law and privacy/confidentiality, 37–38
Hybrid trust, 40

IAIS (International Association of Insurance Supervisors), 80
IBCs (international business corporations), 112, 113
IMF (International Monetary Fund)
  conclusions, 100–101
  and harmful tax practices, 74–76
  and money laundering/terrorism financing, 76–77, 88–99
  OFCs as members of, 168n4
  overview, 74
  and prudent supervision, 76–88, 170n31
  recent developments, 99–100
Implicit costs of regulation on economic activity, 116
Income taxation
  vs. duties as OFC revenue source, 62–63, 65, 159n12, 164n72
  interest income, taxation of in EU, 57, 68–69
  OFCs as break from onshore taxation, 50, 52–53
  offshore/onshore discrepancies in, 50
  progressivity, OFCs' impact on, 60–61
  and sovereignty issue, 51–52
  state competition in U.S., 114
Indirect implicit costs of regulation, 116
Indirect vs. direct methods for economic goals without regulatory competition, 118–19
Individuals' use of OFCs, 10, 52, 60–61
Inefficiency
  assumption of for regulatory competition, 57–58
  of excessive regulation in onshore jurisdictions, 12, 19, 21–22, 28
Information exchange agreements, OFCs/OECD, 67–68, 71–72
Information flow among bank supervisors, 77
Information on offshore trusts, accessibility to beneficiaries, 43–44
Initial public offerings (IPOs), global shift in, 22, 28
Innovations
  benefit to onshore jurisdictions, 22–24, 140
  and limitations on autocrats, 143–44
  OFCs' impetus to innovate, 13, 131–32
  and offshore trusts, 39–45
  transactions cost-reducing legal, 112, 115
Insurance markets
  captive insurance, 1, 115, 136–38, 181n142
  international best practices/standards for, 80
  OFC participation in, 1, 16, 107, 115, 137–38
  segregated cell insurance entities, 112
Interest groups, 10, 26–27, 117–18
Interest income, taxation of in EU, 57, 68–69

190 OFFSHORE FINANCIAL CENTERS

Interjurisdictional competition, *See* Legal principles; Onshore jurisdictions; Regulatory competition; Tax competition
International Association of Insurance Supervisors (IAIS), 80
International Monetary Fund (IMF), *See* IMF
International Money Laundering Abatement and Anti-Terrorist Financing Act (2001) (U.S. Patriot Act), 149n14
International Organization of Securities Commissions (IOSCO), 80
International organizations, *See* IMF; OECD
Inversion transactions, 160n19
Investment Advisers Act (1940) (U.S.), 21
IOSCO (International Organization of Securities Commissions), 80
IPOs (initial public offerings), global shift in, 22, 28

Jernigan, Green v. (Canada), 46
Johns, R. A., 14
Jurisdictional competition, *See* Legal principles; Onshore jurisdictions; Regulatory competition; Tax competition

Krueger, Anne O., 120

Langer, Marshall, 11
Law enforcement as outside IMF's jurisdiction, 94
Legal principles
 conclusion, 48–49
 confidentiality issue, 35–39
 conflict of laws rules, 45–47
 and context for regulatory competition, 31–33, 113–14
 copycatting of OFC structures by onshore jurisdictions, 47–48
 introduction, 30
 offshore trusts, 39–45
 tax issues, 33–35
Level-playing field argument for tax competition, 65–66
Liberal trade regime, 124
Liberty for common people, market forces as impetus for, 106
Liechtenstein, 93, 126, 161n26
Limited liability company (LLC), 31–32, 112, 175–76n35
Looting in developing and post-Communist regimes, 106, 143, 145

Malawi, 141–42
Mattei, Casani v. (Italy), 46–47
McCann, Hilton, 9
Meridien Bank International, 78
Mexican Peso Crisis, 79
MLATs (mutual legal assistance treaties), 64
Mobutu Sese Seko, 110–11, 142, 143
Money laundering
 and confidentiality issue for OFCs, 14
 onshore complaints of OFCs allowance for, 11, 21, 109–10
 onshore locations for majority of, 32, 91
 See also Anti-money laundering (AML) policies
Monopolistic activity by governments, costs of, 120–21
Mugabe, Robert, 109
Mutual legal assistance treaties (MLATs), 64

Natural resources regimes, corruptibility of, 110–11
NCCT (noncooperating countries and territories), 85, 91–95, 96–98

INDEX 191

Netherlands Antilles, 130, 135–36
Nevis, 46
Nigeria, 110
Noncooperating countries and territories (NCCT), 85, 91–95, 96–98
Nonenforcement of foreign fiscal law, 33
Nongeographically vs. geographically mobile capital, 55–56, 58–59, 65

Obama, Barack, 99
OECD (Organisation for Economic Co-operation and Development)
  composition of, 158n5
  and confidentiality issue, 36
  desire to restrict OFCs, 3, 32
  and FATF's assessment of OFCs, 91–92, 93
  vs. IMF in approach to OFCs, 81, 85, 86
  and onshore preferential tax regimes, 54, 55, 65, 67, 93, 161–62nn39–41
  report of cooperation from offshore jurisdictions, 15
  results of regulatory attempts on OFCs, 71–72
  sovereignty challenge to, 62, 150–51n40, 166n115
  and tax competition, 14, 54–56, 66–68
  tax haven designation, 54–56, 62–63, 66–67, 70, 167n120
"Offshore Banking: An Analysis of Micro- and Macro-Prudential Issues" (IMF), 83
Offshore Financial Center Assessment Program, 87, 88, 99
Offshore financial centers (OFCs)
  as alternative financial markets, 12, 16
  as asset protection instruments, 1, 43–44, 53
  and banking supervision, 83–84, 86–87
  "blacklisting" of, 14, 15, 25, 32–33, 164n69
  changes in bases for competition, 16
  and corruption risk, 106, 109–10
  definitional issue, 158n1
  distinctive features of, 62, 129–34
  diversion of capital by, 50, 58–59, 64
  downward pressure on costs and fees, 108
  duties vs. income taxes, 62–63, 65, 159n12, 164n72
  employment limits in, 52, 159n13
  erosion of tax base assumption, 11, 54, 59–60, 64, 148n8
  global financial system role of, 3, 9–10, 13
  growth of, 11, 13–14, 50
  as IMF members, 168n4
  IMF's assessment of, 75–76, 86–87, 99, 100
  improving integrity of, 14–15
  innovation impetus for, 13, 131–32
  insurance market participation, 1, 16, 107, 115, 137–38
  level-playing field argument, 65–66
  and OECD, 3, 32, 67–68, 71–72, 81, 85, 86, 91–92, 93
  onshore jurisdictions' attempts to control, 71, 75, 99–100, 127–28
  politics of, 132–33
  scope of effects, 121
  sovereignty issue, 37, 46, 51, 62–63, 150–51n40, 166–67n115
  as tax avoidance resources, 51–52
  See also Confidentiality; Criminal activity risk; Legal principles; Regulatory competition; Tax competition
Offshore financial law, defined, 31
  See also Legal principles
Offshore Group of Banking Supervisors (OGBS), 77, 87–88

Offshore trusts, 39–45
O'Hara, Erin, 103, 108–9, 112, 114
Onshore jurisdictions
    attempts to control OFCs, 71, 75, 99–100, 127–28
    banking supervision record of, 88
    blaming of OFCs for financial melt down, 84, 100
    capital losses to OFCs, 50, 58–59, 64
    commonalities with OFCs, 47–48, 104
    confidentiality issue, 14, 35–36, 50, 57, 69
    copycatting of OFC structures by, 47–48
    excessive regulation inefficiency, 12, 19, 21–22, 28
    financial services competition among, 126
    as money-laundering havens, 32, 91
    on NCCT list, 97
    vs. offshore contexts, 129–34
    perceived threats from OFCs, 2–3, 99–100, 102
    practical support for regulatory competition, 125–27
    preferential tax regimes in, 54, 55, 65, 67, 93, 161–62nn39–41
    special-interest group influence, 10, 26–27, 117–18
    tax issues, poor legal position on, 33–34
    trust structures vs. offshore, 39–45
    value of markets beyond cost of participation, 108
    See also Benefits of regulatory competition; Criminal activity risk; Governments; *individual nations*
Open economies, historical vindication of, 125
Ownership of trust fund in OFCs, 40

Personal interest as motive for jurisdictional competition, 106, 109–10
    See also Corruption
PGs (purchasing groups), 138
Pharmaceutical companies, use of OFCs by, 53, 160n23
PLRRA (Product Liability Risk Retention Act), 137–38
Politics
    interest group influence, 10, 26–27, 117–18
    and motivations for competition, 105–12
    of OFCs, 132–33
    See also Governments
Privacy, individual right to, and confidentiality, 37–38
Private behavior incentives and regulatory laws, 114, 139–40
Private international law, impact on offshore financial law, 31
Product Liability Risk Retention Act (PLRRA), 137–38
Progressivity of income tax, OFCs' effect on, 60–61
Property rights, offshore trust's protection of, 41
Protector role in offshore trust, 41
Provincial Bank, Tournier v. (UK), 36, 63
Prudent supervision and IMF's regulatory role, 76–88, 170n31
Public finance laws, regulatory competition impact on, 139
Public goods provision
    and free rider problem, 60
    and legal context for regulatory competition, 114
    as motive for jurisdictional competition, 106, 107–9
    regulatory competition effects on, 139
    and Tiebout hypothesis, 64–65

Public interest motive for jurisdictional competition, 106–7, 113–14
Purchasing groups (PGs), 138
Purpose trust, 42–43

"Race to the bottom" view of regulatory competition, 17, 18–19, 20
Rahman on sham doctrine, 42
Regulation
　balanced approach to, 19–21
　confidentiality as basis for OFCs', 63
　costs of, 12, 19, 21–22, 28, 116
　as necessary to robust capital markets, 19, 25–26
　and onshore special-interest groups, 10, 26–27, 117–18
Regulatory competition
　book overview, 1–7
　chartering of corporations, 17, 27, 87, 115, 130–31
　conclusion, 144–46
　effects on jurisdictions, 117–23
　environments for, 122
　historical development of, 123–38
　increase in, 123
　introduction to analysis, 102–5
　legal context for, 113–14
　motivations for competition, 105–12
　necessary conditions for, 127–28
　onshore jurisdictions' practical support for, 125–27
　policy effects of, 129
　scope of, 104, 112–13, 121–22
　workings of competition, 112–17
　See also Benefits of regulatory competition; Governments; Tax competition
Rent-seeking and regulatory competition, 110–11, 117–18
Residence-based taxation, 51, 53, 159n10, 160nn17–18
Ribstein, Larry, 103, 108–9, 112, 114

Ridley, Timothy, 15
"Ring-fencing" regimes, 55, 162n40
Risk Retention Act (1986) (U.S.), 138
Risk retention groups (RRGs), 138
ROSCs ("Reports on the Observance of Standards and Codes"), 82, 95–98
Rosewood Trust Ltd., Schmidt v., 44
RRGs (risk retention groups), 138
Rule of law and OFCs as business havens, 2
Russian financial crisis, 80

Sarbanes-Oxley Act (2002), 22, 27, 28
Sassen, Saskia, 112, 121, 123
Saunders v. Vautier, 42
Savings tax directive, EU, 57, 69, 72–73, 166n114
Schmidt v. Rosewood Trust Ltd., 44
Secrecy, *See* Confidentiality
Securities and Exchange Commission (SEC), 21–22
Securities markets, best practices/standards for, 80
Segregated cell insurance entities, 112
Settlors, duties and rights of, 34, 41, 42, 46
Sham doctrine, 42
SIFCs (Small International Financial Services Centers), *See* Offshore financial centers (OFCs)
Singapore, 14
Source-based taxation, 51, 53, 159n11
Sovereignty issue
　and income taxation policies, 51
　infringement of national tax sovereignty, 62–63
　protection of OFCs' sovereignty, 37, 46, 150–51n40
　tax competition regulation, 166–67n115
Special-interest groups, 10, 26–27, 117–18

Stanford, R. Allen, 2
Stanford International Bank, 2
States in U.S.
  captive insurance, 137, 138
  corporate charter competition, 17, 27, 115, 130–31
  emulation of offshore jurisdictions, 47
  income tax competition among, 114
"Statism" definition, 111, 175n31
Sterling, Claire, 2
Stop Tax Haven Abuse Bill (U.S.), 3, 99
Strasbourg Convention, 89
Summers, Lawrence, 94
Surveillance, IMF right to, 75

Tanzania, 120
Taxation
  erosion of tax base by OFCs, assumption of, 11, 54, 59–60, 64, 148n8
  IMF's role in, 74–76
  increased economic activity as substitute for, 107
  and legal principles of OFCs, 33–35
  residence-based, 51, 53, 159n10, 160nn17–18
  savings tax directive, EU, 57, 69, 72–73, 166n114
  source-based, 51, 53, 159n11
  and sovereignty issue, 62, 150–51n40, 166n115
  withholding tax on interest payments, U.S., 134–36, 167n122
  "worldwide," 52, 159n15
  See also Income taxation
Tax avoidance
  and freedom to invest, 33
  OECD's characterization as harmful, 56
  OFCs as resources for, 51–52
  support for corporate use of, 52–53
  vs. tax evasion, 11, 33
Tax competition
  and ambiguity of OFC net impact, 108–9
  argument against regulating, 61–66
  argument in favor of regulating, 57–61
  defining, 53–57
  EU control measures, 56–57, 68–69, 72–73, 166–67nn114-115
  and EU internal competition, 56
  future prospects, 69–73
  IMF's role in controlling, 74–76
  introduction, 50–51
  as limitation on government excesses, 111
  OECD control measures, 14, 54–56, 66–68
  onshore jurisdictions' focus on, 121
  onshore preferential tax regimes, 54, 55, 65, 67, 93, 161–62nn39–41
  sovereignty issue, 51, 62–63, 166–67n115
Tax evasion, 11, 33, 52, 56
Tax havens
  definitional issue, 158n1
  as early function of OFCs, 74–75
  lost revenue for onshore jurisdictions, 148n8
  OECD's designation of, 54–56, 62–63, 66–67, 70, 167n120
  onshore jurisdictions as, 12–13
Tax information exchange agreements (TIEAs), 64
Territorial tax systems, 52, 159–60n16
Terrorism financing issue, 2, 11, 88–99, 95
TIEAs (tax information exchange agreements), 64
Tiebout, Charles, 64–65
Tournier v. National Provincial Bank (UK), 36, 63

Toward a Framework for Financial Stability (IMF), 82
Trade barriers, historical lowering of, 123–24
Trade secrets and confidentiality's scope, 35
Transactions cost-reducing legal innovations, 112, 115
Transnational organizations, *See* IMF; OECD
Transparency issue, *See* Confidentiality
Transportation costs, historical reduction in, 124–25
Tremblay, Bank of Nova Scotia v. (Barbados), 34
Trustees, duties of, 34, 36
Trusts, 34–35, 36, 39–45, 87
Tunisia, 142

Ukrainian financial crisis, 80
United Kingdom (UK)
  on attempts by U.S. to obtain disclosure from OFCs, 38
  avoidance of NCCT status for territories, 93
  complicity in bank supervision failures, 78
  confidentiality support in legal system, 36, 63
  financial services competition with U.S., 126
  recent increase in anti-OFC activity, 99–100
United States (U.S.)
  complicity in bank supervision failures, 78
  and confidentiality issue, 35, 38
  criminal activity concerns about OFCs, 11, 93–94, 95, 149n14
  erosion of tax base by OFCs, 59
  financial services competition with UK, 126
  LLC development in, 112
  overregulation in, 21–22
  recent increase in anti-OFC activity, 99
  self-settle, protective trusts in, 48
  and sham doctrine, 42
  Stop Tax Haven Abuse Bill, 3, 99
  as successful competitor in global markets, 126
  as tax haven, 12–13
  withholding tax on interest payments, 134–36, 167n122
  "worldwide" taxation policy, 52, 159n15
  See also States in U.S.

"Vampire states," 175n29
Vautier, Saunders v., 42
Vienna Convention (1988), 89
VISTA trust, 39

Wealth increase as motive for jurisdictional competition, 106–7
Wealthy individuals, use OFCs, 10, 52, 60–61
Westminster rule, 33
Withholding tax on interest payments, U.S., 134–36, 167n122
Working Party on Financial Stability, 80
World Bank, banking supervision role of, 79, 81, 82
"Worldwide" taxation, U.S. employment of, 52, 159n15
WTO (World Trade Organization), 117, 124

Zaire, 110–11, 142, 143
Zimbabwe, 109

About the Authors

Rose-Marie Belle Antoine is a partner in the law firm Anthony & Antoine, St. Lucia, and professor of labor law and offshore financial law, and deputy dean of outreach on the Faculty of Law, University of West Indies, Cave Hill Campus, Barbados. Professor Antoine has degrees from Oxford (DPhil), Cambridge (LLM), and the University of West Indies (LLB). She has consulted for governments and international organizations, including the government of Canada, the International Development Bank, the World Bank, the Caribbean Community (CARICOM), the United Nations Children's Fund, the International Labor Organization, the United Nations Development Fund for Women, the United Nations Drug Control Program, and the Pan-Caribbean Partnership Against HIV/AIDS, and she drafted the Labour Code of Saint Lucia and the CARICOM Harmonization of Labour Law Report, the blueprint for CARICOM labor reform. She is the author of many articles, books, and book chapters, including *Confidentiality in Offshore Financial Law* (Oxford University Press, 2002) and *Trusts and Tax in Offshore Financial Law* (Oxford University Press, 2005).

Craig M. Boise is professor of law, director of tax programs, and director of the Institute for Offshore Financial Center Studies at DePaul University College of Law. Professor Boise has degrees from New York University (LLM, Taxation), the University of Chicago (JD), and the University of Missouri–Kansas City (BA). Prior to becoming a professor, Boise practiced for several years at law firms including Cleary Gottlieb and Akin Gump in New York. Before entering private practice, Boise clerked for the Honorable Pasco M. Bowman II, U.S. Court of Appeals for the Eighth Circuit. Boise's research focuses on the policies underlying domestic and foreign taxation of international transactions, with particular emphasis on the role of offshore financial centers. His articles include "Playing with Monopoly Money: Phony Profits, Fraud Penalties and Equity," *Minnesota Law Review* (2005); "Breaking Open Offshore Piggybanks: Deferral and the Utility of Amnesty," *George Mason Law Review* (2007); and "Change, Dependency, and Regime Plasticity in Offshore Financial Intermediation: The Saga of the Netherlands Antilles," *Texas International Law Journal* (with Andrew P. Morriss, 2009).

Anna Manasco Dionne is an associate at Bradley Arant Boult Cummings LLP (of course, the views in this book are those of the author, not her firm). Before Dr. Dionne joined Bradley, she clerked for the Honorable William H. Pryor Jr., U.S. Court of Appeals for the Eleventh Circuit. Dr. Dionne has degrees from Yale (JD), the University of Oxford (DPhil, MSc), and Emory University (BA). She is the author of "Living on the Edge: Fiduciary Duties, Business Judgment and Expensive Uncertainty in the Zone of Insolvency," *Stanford Journal of Law, Business and Finance* (2007), and "Note, 'In Time of Whenever the Secretary Says': The Constitutional Case against Court-Martial Jurisdiction over Accompanying Civilians during Contingency Operations," *Yale Law and Policy Review* (2009). Her book, *Men, Women and Women's Representation in the British Parliaments: Magic Numbers?* is forthcoming (Manchester University Press, 2010).

Richard K. Gordon is associate professor of law at Case Western Reserve University School of Law, and was a visiting associate professor of international studies, Brown University, academic year 2008–9. Professor Gordon has degrees from Harvard (JD) and Yale (AB). Prior to coming to CWRU, Mr. Gordon practiced law at Dewey Ballantine (now Dewey and LeBoeuf) in Washington and taught at the School of Oriental and African Studies of the University of London, where he was a visiting lecturer on the law faculty, and the Harvard Law School, where he was deputy director of the International Tax Program. After leaving Harvard, Mr. Gordon joined the staff of the International Monetary Fund, where he worked on a wide variety of issues, including public international law, governance, sovereign debt restructuring, and taxation. Following the attacks of September 11, 2001, he was appointed to the select IMF Task Force on Terrorism Finance and was a principal author of the report on the role of the IMF and the World Bank in countering terrorism finance and money laundering. He is a principal author of the book *Tax Law Design and Drafting* (Aspen, 2001) and the author of numerous scholarly articles and book chapters, including "On the Use and Abuse of Standards for Law: Global Governance and Offshore Centers," *North Carolina Law Review* (2009).

Jonathan R. Macey is deputy dean and Sam Harris Professor of Corporate Law, Corporate Finance, and Securities Law, Yale Law School, and professor in the Yale School of Management. Professor Macey has degrees from Yale (JD), Harvard (BA), and the Stockholm School of Economics (PhD *honoris causa*). He is the author of *Macey on Corporation Laws* and coauthor of *Corporations: Including Partnerships and Limited Liability Companies* and *Banking Law and Regulation*, as well as numerous articles and book chapters. In 1995, Professor Macey was awarded the Paul M. Bator prize for excellence in teaching, scholarship, and public service by the Federalist Society for Law and Public Policy.

Andrew P. Morriss is H. Ross and Helen Workman Professor of Law and Business and professor at the Institute of Government and Public Affairs, University of Illinois, Urbana-Champaign. He has degrees from the Massachusetts Institute of Technology (PhD, economics), the University of Texas at Austin (JD, M.Pub.Aff.) and Princeton (AB). Prior to entering teaching, he clerked for U.S. District Judge H. Barefoot Sanders in Dallas, Texas, and then worked for Texas Rural Legal Aid in Hereford and Plainview, Texas. He is also a senior scholar at the Mercatus Center at George Mason University. He is the author and coauthor of numerous books, book chapters, and articles, including *Regulation by Litigation* (with Bruce Yandle and Andrew Dorchak, Yale University Press, 2008) and "Change, Dependency, and Regime Plasticity in Offshore Financial Intermediation: The Saga of the Netherlands Antilles," *Texas International Law Journal* (with Craig M. Boise, 2009).

Board of Trustees

Kevin B. Rollins, *Chairman*
Senior Adviser
TPG Capital

Tully M. Friedman, *Treasurer*
Chairman and CEO
Friedman Fleischer & Lowe, LLC

Gordon M. Binder
Managing Director
Coastview Capital, LLC

Arthur C. Brooks
President
American Enterprise Institute

The Honorable
Richard B. Cheney

Harlan Crow
Chairman and CEO
Crow Holdings

Daniel A. D'Aniello
Cofounder and Managing Director
The Carlyle Group

John V. Faraci
Chairman and CEO
International Paper

Christopher B. Galvin
Chairman
Harrison Street Capital, LLC

Raymond V. Gilmartin
Harvard Business School

Harvey Golub
Chairman and CEO, Retired
American Express Company

Robert F. Greenhill
Founder and Chairman
Greenhill & Co., Inc.

Roger Hertog

Bruce Kovner
Chairman
Caxton Associates, LP

Marc S. Lipschultz
Partner
Kohlberg Kravis Roberts & Co.

John A. Luke Jr.
Chairman and CEO
MeadWestvaco Corporation

Robert A. Pritzker
President and CEO
Colson Associates, Inc.

J. Peter Ricketts
President and Director
Platte Institute for Economic
  Research, Inc.

Edward B. Rust Jr.
Chairman and CEO
State Farm Insurance Companies

D. Gideon Searle
Managing Partner
The Serafin Group, LLC

Mel Sembler
Founder and Chairman
The Sembler Company

Wilson H. Taylor
Chairman Emeritus
CIGNA Corporation

William H. Walton
Managing Member
Rockpoint Group, LLC

William L. Walton
Chairman
Allied Capital Corporation

The Honorable
Marilyn Ware

James Q. Wilson
Boston College and
  Pepperdine University

Emeritus Trustees

Willard C. Butcher
Richard B. Madden
Robert H. Malott
Paul W. McCracken
Paul F. Oreffice
Henry Wendt

Officers

Arthur C. Brooks
President

David Gerson
Executive Vice President

Jason Bertsch
Vice President, Marketing

Henry Olsen
Vice President, Director,
National Research Initiative

Danielle Pletka
Vice President, Foreign and Defense
  Policy Studies

The American Enterprise Institute for Public Policy Research

Founded in 1943, AEI is a nonpartisan, nonprofit research and educational organization based in Washington, D.C. The Institute sponsors research, conducts seminars and conferences, and publishes books and periodicals.

AEI's research is carried out under three major programs: Economic Policy Studies, Foreign Policy and Defense Studies, and Social and Political Studies. The resident scholars and fellows listed in these pages are part of a network that also includes ninety adjunct scholars at leading universities throughout the United States and in several foreign countries.

The views expressed in AEI publications are those of the authors and do not necessarily reflect the views of the staff, advisory panels, officers, or trustees.

Council of Academic Advisers

James Q. Wilson, *Chairman*
Boston College and
  Pepperdine University

Alan J. Auerbach
Robert D. Burch Professor of
  Economics and Law
University of California, Berkeley

Eliot A. Cohen
Paul H. Nitze School of Advanced
  International Studies
Johns Hopkins University

Martin Feldstein
George F. Baker Professor
  of Economics
Harvard University

Robert P. George
McCormick Professor of Jurisprudence
Director, James Madison Program
  in American Ideals and Institutions
Princeton University

Gertrude Himmelfarb
Distinguished Professor of History
  Emeritus
City University of New York

R. Glenn Hubbard
Dean and Russell L. Carson Professor
  of Finance and Economics
Columbia Business School

John L. Palmer
University Professor and Dean
  Emeritus
Maxwell School of Citizenship and
  Public Affairs
Syracuse University

Sam Peltzman
Ralph and Dorothy Keller
  Distinguished Service Professor
  of Economics
Booth School of Business
University of Chicago

George L. Priest
John M. Olin Professor of Law
  and Economics
Yale Law School

Jeremy A. Rabkin
Professor of Law
George Mason University
  School of Law

Richard J. Zeckhauser
Frank Plumpton Ramsey Professor
  of Political Economy
Kennedy School of Government
Harvard University

Research Staff

Ali Alfoneh
Visiting Research Fellow

Joseph Antos
Wilson H. Taylor Scholar in Health
  Care and Retirement Policy

Leon Aron
Resident Scholar; Director,
  Russian Studies

Paul S. Atkins
Visiting Scholar

Michael Auslin
Resident Scholar

Claude Barfield
Resident Scholar

Michael Barone
Resident Fellow

Roger Bate
Legatum Fellow in Global Prosperity

Walter Berns
Resident Scholar

Andrew G. Biggs
Resident Scholar

Edward Blum
Visiting Fellow

Dan Blumenthal
Resident Fellow

John R. Bolton
Senior Fellow

Karlyn Bowman
Senior Fellow

Alex Brill
Research Fellow

John E. Calfee
Resident Scholar

Charles W. Calomiris
Visiting Scholar

Lynne V. Cheney
Senior Fellow

Steven J. Davis
Visiting Scholar

Mauro De Lorenzo
Visiting Fellow

Christopher DeMuth
D. C. Searle Senior Fellow

Thomas Donnelly
Resident Fellow

Nicholas Eberstadt
Henry Wendt Scholar in Political
  Economy

Jon Entine
Visiting Fellow

John C. Fortier
Research Fellow

David Frum
Resident Fellow

Newt Gingrich
Senior Fellow

Scott Gottlieb, M.D.
Resident Fellow

Kenneth P. Green
Resident Scholar

Michael S. Greve
John G. Searle Scholar

Kevin A. Hassett
Senior Fellow; Director,
  Economic Policy Studies

Steven F. Hayward
F. K. Weyerhaeuser Fellow

Robert B. Helms
Resident Scholar

Frederick M. Hess
Resident Scholar; Director,
  Education Policy Studies

Ayaan Hirsi Ali
Resident Fellow

R. Glenn Hubbard
Visiting Scholar

Frederick W. Kagan
Resident Scholar; Director,
  AEI Critical Threats Project

Leon R. Kass, M.D.
Madden-Jewett Chair

Andrew P. Kelly
Research Fellow

Desmond Lachman
Resident Fellow

Lee Lane
Resident Fellow; Codirector,
  AEI Geoengineering Project

Adam Lerrick
Visiting Scholar

Philip I. Levy
Resident Scholar

Lawrence B. Lindsey
Visiting Scholar

John H. Makin
Visiting Scholar

Aparna Mathur
Resident Fellow

Lawrence M. Mead
Visiting Scholar

Allan H. Meltzer
Visiting Scholar

Thomas P. Miller
Resident Fellow

Charles Murray
W. H. Brady Scholar

Roger F. Noriega
Visiting Fellow

Michael Novak
George Frederick Jewett Scholar
  in Religion, Philosophy, and
  Public Policy

Norman J. Ornstein
Resident Scholar

Richard Perle
Resident Fellow

Ioana Petrescu
NRI Fellow

Tomas J. Philipson
Visiting Scholar

Alex J. Pollock
Resident Fellow

Vincent R. Reinhart
Resident Scholar

Michael Rubin
Resident Scholar

Sally Satel, M.D.
Resident Scholar

Gary J. Schmitt
Resident Scholar; Director,
  Advanced Strategic Studies

Mark Schneider
Visiting Scholar

David Schoenbrod
Visiting Scholar

Nick Schulz
DeWitt Wallace Fellow; Editor-in-Chief,
  American.com

Roger Scruton
Resident Scholar

Kent Smetters
Visiting Scholar

Christina Hoff Sommers
Resident Scholar; Director,
  W. H. Brady Program

Tim Sullivan
Research Fellow

Phillip Swagel
Visiting Scholar

Samuel Thernstrom
Resident Fellow; Codirector,
  AEI Geoengineering Project

Bill Thomas
Visiting Fellow

Alan D. Viard
Resident Scholar

Peter J. Wallison
Arthur F. Burns Fellow in
  Financial Policy Studies

David A. Weisbach
Visiting Scholar

Paul Wolfowitz
Visiting Scholar

John Yoo
Visiting Scholar

Benjamin Zycher
NRI Visiting Fellow